[redacted]

ATTENTION DEFICIT HYPERACTIVITY DISORDER

Volume 5 of the York Spectrum Monographs
A series based on the Spectrum of Developmental Disabilities Course
sponsored by the Kennedy Fellows Association

ATTENTION DEFICIT HYPERACTIVITY DISORDER

THE CLINICAL SPECTRUM

Edited by Brian T. Rogers, M.D.,
Thomas R. Montgomery, M.D.,
Thomas M. Lock, M.D., and
Pascal J. Accardo, M.D.

YORK PRESS Baltimore

This book was manufactured in the United States of America.

Typography by Type Shoppe II Productions, Ltd.
Printing and binding by McNaughton & Gunn, Inc.
Cover design by Joseph Dieter, Jr.

Library of Congress Cataloging-In-Publication Data

Attention deficit hyperactivity disorder : the clinical spectrum / edited by Brian T. Rogers ... [et al.].

p. ; cm. -- (York spectrum monograms ; v. 5)

Includes bibliographical references and index.

ISBN 0-912752-62-9

1. Attention-deficit hyperactivity disorder. I. Rogers, Brian T. II. Series.

[DNLM: 1. Attention Deficit Disorder with Hyperactivity--diagnosis. 2. Attention Deficit Disorder with Hyperactivity--therapy. WS 350.8.A8 A8833 2001]

RJ506.H9 A934 2001

618.92'8589--dc21

2001045568

Contents

Contributors

Pasquale Accardo, M.D.
New York Medical College and Westchester Institute for Human Development
Valhalla, New York 10595
pasquale_accardo@nymc.edu

L. Eugene Arnold, M.Ed., M.D.
Professor Emeritus of Psychiatry, Ohio State U.
479 South Galena Road
Sunbury, Ohio 43074

David E. Bender, Ph.D.
Department of Physiology and Biophysics
School of Medicine and Biomedical Sciences
State University of New York at Buffalo
329 Cary Hall
Buffalo, New York 14214
david@bender.med.buffalo.edu

Roger A. Brumback, M.D.
Professor and Chairman
Department of Pathology
Creighton University School of Medicine
Saint Joseph Hospital
Omaha, Nebraska

Anil Chacko
University of Buffalo, ADHD Program
Diefendorf Hall, Room 318
3435 Main Street, Building 20
Buffalo, New York 14217-3093
achacko@acsu.buffalo.edu

Gregory A. Fabiano
University of Buffalo, ADHD Program
Diefendorf Hall, Room 318
3435 Main Street, Building 20
Buffalo, New York 14217-3093

Robert L. Findling, M.D.
Department of Psychiatry
University Hospitals of Cleveland
Case Western Reserve University
11100 Euclid Avenue
Cleveland, Ohio 44106-5080

Marianne M. Glanzmann, M.D.
Children's Seashore House of The Children's Hospital of Philadelphia
34th Street and Civic Center Boulevard
Philadelphia, Pennsylvania 19104
glanzman@email.chop.edu

Barbara L. Gracious, M.D.
Department of Psychiatry
University Hospitals of Cleveland
Case Western Reserve University
11100 Euclid Avenue
Cleveland, Ohio 44106-5080

Caryn R. Harper, M.S.
Department of Neurology
University of Texas Southwestern Medical Center at Dallas
Dallas, Texas

Lily Hechtman, M.D., F.R.C.P. (C)
Division of Child Psychiatry
McGill University, Montreal Children's Hospital
4018 St. Catherine Street, West
Montreal, Quebec H3Z 1P2
Canada
lhechtman@hotmail.com

Thomas M. Lock, M.D.
Department of Pediatrics
School of Medicine and Biomedical Sciences
State University of New York at Buffalo
Robert Warner Rehabilitation Center
936 Delaware Avenue
Buffalo, New York 14209-1887
tlock@upa.chob.edu

Frank E. Musiek, Ph.D.
Dartmouth Hitchcock Medical Center
One Medical Center Drive
Lebanon, New Hampshire 03756
Frank.E.Musiek@Hitchcock.org

Chrystyna Nebesh-Jatsyshyn, M.D.
Associates in Adult, Adolescent, and Child Psychotherapy, Inc.
Brecksville Commons, Building 2, Lower Level
8223 Brecksville Road
Brecksville, Ohio 44141

William E. Pelham Jr. Ph.D
University of Buffalo, ADHD Program
Diefendorf Hall, Room 318
3435 Main Street, Building 20
Buffalo, New York 14217-3093

Eliane Schochat, Ph.D.
Dartmouth Hitchcock Medical Center
One Medical Center Drive
Lebanon, New Hampshire 03756
And Sao Paulo University
School of Medicine
Sao Paulo, Brazil
Eliane.Schochat@Hitchcock.org

Bruce K. Shapiro, M.D.
The Johns Hopkins University School of Medicine and
Kennedy Krieger Institute
707 North Broadway
Baltimore, Maryland 21205
shapiro@kennedykrieger.org

Jennifer Shinn, M.S.
Dartmouth Hitchcock Medical Center
One Medical Center Drive
Lebanon, New Hampshire 03756
Jennifer.B.Shinn@Hitchcock.org

Larry B. Silver, M.D.
Georgetown University Medical Center
Washington, D.C.

Mark A. Stein, Ph.D.
Children's National Medical Center and George Washington University School of Medicine
Neuroscience and Behavioral Medicine Research
111 Michigan Avenue, N.W.
Washington, DC 20010-2970

Warren A. Weinberg, M.D.
Departments of Neurology and Pediatrics
University of Texas Southwestern Medical Center at Dallas and
Pediatric Behavioral Neurology Program
Division of Pediatric Neurology
Children's Medical Center
6303 Forest Park, Suite 13.350
Dallas, Texas 75390-9119

Andy Williams
University of Buffalo, ADHD Program
Diefendorf Hall, Room 318
3435 Main Street, Building 20
Buffalo, New York 14217-3093

Preface

This is the fifth volume in the series of York Spectrum Monographs based upon the annual Spectrum of Developmental Disabilities course at John Hopkins in Baltimore, Maryland in the spring of each year. The first Spectrum course was held in 1979: the papers in the present volume are selected from the 22nd course in that series sponsored by the Kennedy Fellows Association. The Spectrum course, the Kennedy fellows association, and, indeed, the new sub-specialty of Neuro-developmental Disabilities in Pediatrics and Child Neurology, are all brain-children of Arnold J. Capute, M.D., M.P.H., the first and current holder of the Arnold J. Capute Chair in Developmental Pediatrics. The particular theme of the current offering is especially dear to him under its older rubric, minimal brain dysfunction (MBD).

In the mid 1970s, the training program in Developmental Pediatrics that Dr. Capute directed at the John Kennedy Institute at Hopkins blossomed under his leadership into an academic program with a significant research component. Since the trainees and junior faculty involved in the program numbered the mystical seven, they quickly assumed alternate identities:

Sneezy, Pasquale Accardo, M.D.
Doc, Sisan E. Farrell,M.D.
Bashful, Frederick B. Palmer,M.D.
Grumpy, James E. Rubenstein, M.D.
Sleepy, Bruce K. Shapiro, M.D.
Happy, Eileen P. G. Vining, M.D.
Dopey, Renee Wachtel, M.D.
With of course their fearless leader, Snow White, Arnold Capute, M.D.

Appropriate cartoon logos from the Disney Store long adorned the traditional long blue coats that identified the Kennedy pediatric fellows/faculty. After completing training, most of this class stayed on to form the Clinical Research Unit (CRU) and participate in a large scale Maternal and Child Health funded research project.

The formation of a new academic discipline requires both an expansive teaching function and a defined research base. Not only must sub-specialties master the clinical and research aspects of their field, but their field must have something to communicate to generalists and other practitioners in the community; they must demonstrate that they can communicate it. This mandate is especially important in the area of Developmental Pediatrics because of the multi-specialty and multidisciplinary nature of the diagnostic and management processes with children with developmental disabilities. Thus the annual Spectrum presentations were understood as another step aimed at defining the field from an interdisciplinary teaching perspective. They opened a forum that went beyond the approach of the formal textbooks that were being written. Later this educational mandate would be further expanded and refined by the formation of a new section on Children with Disabilities within the American Academy of Pediatrics and by the inauguration of a new journal, Mental Retardation and Developmental Disabilities Research Reviews by Mark l. Batshaw, M.D.

Late in 2001, the standardization of the Capute Scales, a screening and assessment instrument for the pediatrician and others involved with the birth-to-three population, will be completed. The components of this instrument, the Clinical Adaptive Test (CAT), and the Clinical Linguistic and Auditory Milestones Scale (CLAMS), sometimes known together as CAT-CLAMS, have frequently been presented at various Spectrum programs over the past two decades.

Meanwhile, the long road toward the achievement of sub-specialty recognition was about to be formalized. The more than two decade campaign, with all its marshaling of resources, activities, and goals, all its strategy and tactics, had been carried out with only a single general—Dr. Capute.

Finally, on April 3, 2001, the American Board of Pediatrics and the American Board of Psychiatry and Neurology, offered the first certifying examination for sub-specialization in Neuro-developmental Disabilities in Pediatrics and Child Neurology—what had for the previous half-century been referred to around Hopkins as "Arnold's Board."

During his past 35 years at Hopkins, Dr. Capute has trained well over 100 sub-specialty pediatric fellows at the Kennedy Institute and thousands of Harriet Lane house staff. If the influence of any single human being on those around him or her is always difficult to track and estimate, then the influence of Arnold Capute on this area of pediatric medicine and several generations of specialists and non-specialists is truly incalculable. But it is not without a showing of gratitude from those who were touched. The Program Committee for the Spectrum Course (and the editors of this volume) would like to dedicate the present conference proceedings, the four previous volumes in this series, and for that matter, all the volumes to come, to their teacher and friend, il maestro di color che sanno (Inf. Iv, 131), Arnold Capute.

PJA

Section • I

Pathophysiology

Chapter • 1

An Update on the Pathophysiology of ADHD

Marianne M. Glanzman

Scientists and clinicians are actively researching the neurobiologic underpinnings of Attention-Deficit/Hyperactivity Disorder (ADHD), in hopes of developing a better understanding of this complex disorder and more effective interventions. Researchers appreciate that the list of behavioral features that characterize and are used to diagnose ADHD, must arise from underlying differences in information processing. Taking advantage of decades of research in the neuropsychological characteristics of attention, working memory, and behavior regulation carried out by cognitive scientists has allowed ADHD researchers to develop sound neuropsychological hypotheses that are testable with rapidly evolving technology. It is suspected that differences in frontal cortical-basal ganglia transmission are central in ADHD. Scientists continue to "close in" on the mechanisms that can lead to altered transmission via studies of epidemiology and molecular genetics, neuropsychology, electrophysiology, neurochemistry, and structural and functional neuroimaging.

Neuropsychological studies have been critical in focusing research on frontal cortical-basal ganglia dysregulation in ADHD. Long before the current explosion of interest in the neurobiology of ADHD, it was recognized that individuals who sustained isolated frontal lobe damage developed a clinical profile much like that of ADHD, characterized by deficiencies in sustained mental effort, inhibition, and motivation, without the loss of cognitive skills. Even more specifically, damage to the frontal poles tended to result in decrements in motor and mental drive or motivation such that the subject was at the mercy of immediate environmental stimuli in order to act, while damage to the orbitofrontal region resulted in impairments in judgement including "moral judgement." Although children with ADHD are not the same as adults with acquired isolated frontal lobe damage, these centuries-old observations point us unmistakably toward the prefrontal cortex in our search to understand the vexing mix of symptoms seen in individuals with ADHD and associated comorbidities.

The frontal lobes of the brain can be divided into prefrontal cortex, premotor cortex, and supplementary motor cortex. Premotor and supplementary motor cortex play important roles in the execution of movement, but unlike the motor cortex which lies just behind them, rather than being responsible for the execution of motor movements in the strictest sense, they are related to the higher cognitive aspects of motor regulation including preparation for motor execution, motor planning, and affective and motivational contributions to movement. The frontal eye fields overlap the premotor and prefrontal areas and (analogous to the premotor/supplementary motor areas) are responsible for the higher level coordination of extraocular movement. The prefrontal cortex is often subdivided into the dorsolateral, orbital, and cingulate portions. The prefrontal cortex receives input from the thalamus, and a variety of cortical regions, particularly the temporal and parietal association cortices. The orbital portion receives a predominance of information from the mesencephalic reticular formation (the portion of the brainstem most closely related to alertness functions), and limbic structures (amygdala, piriform and inferior temporal cortices). Output from the prefrontal cortex goes to the supplementary and premotor cortices and the basal ganglia (particularly caudate nucleus). The orbital portion also innervates the hypothalamus and subthalamus, septum, mesencephalon, and pons (reviewed in Niedermeyer 1998).

Information from the entire cortex projects in a series of neuron connections to the basal ganglia, thalamus, and back to the frontal cortex in a loop that can be considered the major "information processing" highway in the brain (reviewed in Afifi 1994a and b). Within this "highway" are several parallel loops subserving cognitive, sensorimotor, oculomotor, and affective functions. These loops are topographically organized in the basal ganglia and thalamus, but there is also "crosstalk" between loops at each of these levels, as well as input from other brain regions. The entire cortex projects topographically to the striatum, the central structure of the basal ganglia. In primates and humans the striatum is divided into the caudate (cognitive portion), the putamen (sensorimotor portion) and the nucleus accumbens (affective portion). The striatum is a compact region where cortical functions are "funneled" into the "information processing" highway; it is particularly vulnerable to insults during development (Toft 1999), and it is the target (along with specific layers of the prefrontal cortex) of the densest dopaminergic innervation of the brain, a key neurotransmitter in ADHD.

Studies of the neurochemical underpinnings of ADHD were fueled by the observation that medications that were effective in ameliorating the symptoms of ADHD uniformly increased the availability of the transmitters dopamine and norepinephrine while medications that were not effective, did not. In addition, the innervation patterns of these transmitters are consistent with implicated regions in anatomical studies of ADHD. For example, norepinephrine neurons project from a small nucleus in the pontine tegmentum (the locus ceruleus) throughout the cortex, with differential innervation of different regions and layers. Studies of locus ceruleus (norepinephrine) neurons indicate that this system is important in alerting to stimuli and distinguishing novel stimuli, which can be summarized as regulating what is considered "signal" and what is considered "noise" among incoming stimuli. Dopamine neurons project primarily to the striaum and prefrontal cortex from (primarily) two contiguous midbrain nuclei, the substantia nigra and ventral tegmental area. This system is important in all aspects of prefrontal-striatal regulation including motor, sensorimotor, oculomotor, cognitive, and affective. Rather than basic alerting, modulation of these regions by the dopamine system fine tunes exploratory, strategic, and motivational behavior. The dopamine system is important in linking cognitive, sensory, and affective behavior to motor output (reviewed in Afifi 1994a and b; Castellanos 1997; Mercugliano 1995 and 2000; Solanto 1998).

Cognitive scientists were studying the neuropsychological construct of attention well before the current level of interest developed in the neurobiology of ADHD. Most neuropsychological models of attention go well beyond the concept of "paying attention" or receiving incoming information. They include, in addition to stimulus detection, encoding or processing detected information, sustaining attention to relevant stimuli while filtering out others, shifting attention when appropriate, inhibiting the involuntary shifting of attention (distractibility), and organizing or preparing a response to incoming information (including inhibiting responses until all relevant information has been considered). Each of these levels of "attention" has been associated, in animal and human experiments, with subregions of the prefrontal cortex and its descending connections. Tests have been developed in attempts to separate the different stages of attentional processing, and investigators are beginning to determine what stage or stages of the attentional construct are disrupted by different disorders or other factors. Applying these more complex attention constructs to ADHD is in its infancy, but this approach has already refocused the long-held hypothesis about ADHD as a disorder of signal detection to a disorder of information processing and response organization (inhibition) (reviewed in Mirsky 1996).

Tests that have been linked specifically to frontal lobe dysfunction in adults or primates with isolated frontal lobe injuries (some more strongly or specifically than others) are the kinds of tests most likely to be abnormal in individuals with ADHD. These tests are generally presumed to measure sustained or selective attention, mental flexibility and strategy development, or response preparation/inhibition. Frontal lobe functions as a group are often referred to as "executive" functions, including self-regulation, sequencing, flexibility, planning, and response organization and inhibition. One requirement for executive function, verbal working memory, is very interesting in terms of the common association of auditory processing and comprehension issues in ADHD. Verbal working memory refers to the ability to keep information in mind while manipulating or working with it, and seems to be a particular weakness in children with ADHD. At this time, neuropsychological results can enhance, but not replace, the remainder of the clinical evaluation. Nonetheless, improving our recognition and understanding of ADHD as a disorder of information processing (cognitive, emotional, sensorimotor) rather than a list of operationalized behaviors is a critical step in the development of more effective long-term interventions (reviewed in Barkley 2000; Denkla 1996; Lazar and Frank 1998; Mercugliano 1999).

Electrophysiologic techniques that have been used to study ADHD in humans include evoked potential and quantitative EEG recordings. Evoked potentials, also called event-related potentials, or ERPs, are electrical changes in the brain that occur in response to specific sensory, motor, and cognitive events. Scalp recordings result in a reproducible pattern of positive and negative wave forms that occur in a characteristic temporal pattern after the stimulus. The latency to onset and amplitude of ERPs during attention or frontal lobe-related cognitive tasks can tell us something about cortical processing in individuals with ADHD compared with controls. The anatomic resolution of this technique is a weakness, but it is non-invasive and can thus be easily repeated under a variety of conditions.

The ERP waves that have been most frequently studied in ADHD include the early N1/N2 wave and the P3 or P300 wave. P3 is a large positive wave that peaks from 300 to 500 msec after the stimulus, with maximal amplitudes recorded over parietal and midline regions, and it is believed to reflect post-detection processing (probably cortical-to-subcortical activation) of incoming signals. P3 latency is thought to reflect processing time, and increases as more memory is required to process the signal. P3 amplitude is thought to reflect capacity allocation because it decreases as more complex competing tasks are added. These are general statements—there is still controversy about precisely what is represented by the P3 wave, and where and how it is generated. Developmental changes in ERPs are commonly found in controls and must be considered in studies of ADHD.

Though not all studies are comparable or consistent, children with ADHD have generally been shown to have decreased amplitude in their P3 waves compared with controls, and increased latency to its onset (reviewed in Tannock 1998). Some, but not most, studies have also found abnormalities in the earlier, signal-detection components of the ERP (Brandeis et al. 1998; Kilpelainen et al. 1999; van Leeuwen et al. 1998). It appears that the earlier (signal detection) abnormalities are found in studies of younger children and in studies in which signal detection is made more complicated by distracting features. Several studies suggest that auditory tasks show more prominent ERP abnormalities than visual tasks, especially at the signal detection stage, but abnormalities in visual processing have been found as well (Jonkman et al. 1997; Satterfield, Schell, and Nicholas 1994). A few studies have looked at ERP components that are even later than P3, presumed to be involved in response preparation or selection, and these components also show abnormalities. Overall, ERP findings are consistent with the emerging view of ADHD as a disorder, not only, or even primarily, of "paying attention" or signal detection, but perhaps even more prominently, of signal processing and response generation (reviewed in Mercugliano 1999).

P3 abnormalities, along with clinical performance, improve in response to stimulant medications (Lazzaro et al. 1997). ERP abnormalities are not specific to ADHD, having also been found in individuals with learning disabilities, depression, schizophrenia, and dementia. Current research is focused on the developmental profile of ERP changes in ADHD, the specificity of findings in regard to diagnosis and the cognitive task used in the experiment, and the use of ERP technology as a treatment response predictor (Frank, Seiden, and Napolitano 1998; Loo, Teale, and Reite 1999; Sunohara et al. 1997).

Quantitative EEG studies use computerized EEG techniques, including spectral analysis, in order to quantify the power and map the location of the conventional EEG rhythms (alpha, beta, delta, and theta). There are fewer studies using this technique than ERP measurements, and a variety of technical problems (spatial resolution, electrical artifacts, and different techniques for data manipulation) make it difficult to compare studies. Because there has been very little developmental study of the technique, it is presently unclear whether the observed differences in ADHD represent a developmental delay or a stable deviance (Ucles and Lorente 1996). Though not uniformly consistent, several studies report increased theta, or slow wave, activity in frontal regions (electrical "hypoactivity"), although others report decreased delta or increased beta activity (both reflective of electrical "hyperactivity") over the left hemisphere. These results appear to suggest that some groups of subjects with ADHD may be under-aroused while others are over-aroused, clearly suggesting a role for this technique in differentiating potential biological subtypes of the disorder (reviewed in Tannock 1998).

Structural neuroimaging studies have provided important clues to the brain regions involved in ADHD, though there are several differences in findings between the different labs engaged in this line of investigation. Structural imaging using computed axial tomography (CAT) or magnetic resonance imaging (MRI) as they are used clinically has not provided substantial insight into differences between the brain structure of individuals with ADHD and controls. However, careful regional volumetric analysis of MRI scans shows promise as a tool for detecting subtle difference in brain structure. First, it should be noted that there is relatively little data about subtle differences in normal subjects during the course of development, and in relation to gender, handedness, or hemisphere, though there is enough to indicate that all of these factors may be relevant. Some of the inconsistencies in volumetric MRI studies across labs may reflect relatively small numbers of subjects, differences in technique, and differences in the composition of control and subject populations in regards to the factors noted above.

The most consistent findings across labs are smaller prefrontal, caudate, and corpus callosum volumes in subjects. There is less agreement about abnormalities of caudate asymmetry or which subregion of the corpus callosum accounts for the decreased volume (reviewed in Tannock 1998). Decreases in prefrontal cortex, caudate, and globus pallidus (but not putamen) volume correlate with the degree of response inhibition deficit on neuropsychological testing in children with ADHD. Significant correlations occurred predominantly for right hemisphere structures (Casey et al. 1997; Semrud-Clikeman et al. 2000). Recent studies also indicate that the posterior inferior lobe of the cerebellar vermis is also smaller in individuals with ADHD compared with age- and IQ-matched controls (Berquin et al. 1998, Mostofsky et al. 1998). This finding is of significant interest, given the increasing recognition of the role of the cerebellum in cognitive function.

Functional neuroimaging provides a way to study the general metabolic activity, glucose utilization, or more specific transmitter markers in specific brain regions. Techniques include positron emission tomography (PET), single photon emission computerized tomography (SPECT) and functional MRI (fMRI). There are a small number of studies with a small number of subjects, so these results need confirmation. Positron emission tomography studies suggest mild decreases in metabolic activity or glucose utilization in several of the areas already implicated in ADHD. Age and gender differences again seem to be important and will require further study. In PET studies using a labeled dopa analogue (which is converted to dopamine in nerve terminals by the enzyme dopa decarboxylase), children with ADHD were found to have higher dopa accumulation in the right midbrain suggestive of an abnormality at the level of the dopamine neuron cell bodies. A similar study in adults showed lower prefrontal dopa accumulation, particularly on the left. The authors hypothesize that the prefrontal abnormalities may be secondary to the midbrain abnormalities, and that they may develop over time (Ernst et al. 1998; Ernst et al. 1999).

Several earlier PET studies (reviewed in Tannock 1998; Hale, Hariri, and McCracken 2000) revealed decreased metabolic activity in the brains of individuals with ADHD compared with controls, particularly in the frontal and striatal regions. Recent SPECT studies show (1) decreased prefrontal activation in response to a cognitive challenge (Amen and Carmichael 1997) and (2) decreased activity in the left frontal and parietal regions (Sieg et al. 1994). Two reports of fMRI studies, both with small numbers, suggest abnormalities in ADHD. The first showed decreased activation of right hemisphere anterior and posterior attention-related structures during a visual-motor response inhibition task (Rubia et al. 1999), and the second showed differences in how methylphenidate affects striatal activation in children with ADHD compared with controls during a visual continuous performance paradigm (Vaidya et al. 1998). Most recently, PET studies done in adults using a ligand for the dopamine transporter suggest a higher density in ADHD than in controls (Dougherty et al. 1999). Treatment with methylphenidate reduced the level of binding, as would be expected given its transporter binding properties (Krause et al. 2000).

The epidemiologic studies of ADHD or ADHD symptoms in families, twins, and adoptees indicate that it is highly heritable. Twin studies indicate that there is also a role for non-shared environmental factors (biologic or environmental factors that can be unique to one twin). Family genetic studies initially suggested that ADHD might be caused by a single dominant gene with reduced penetrance, but other models of multiple gene interaction must be considered, and it is presently thought to be more likely that several susceptibility and protective genes may contribute to an individual's overall risk. Family studies also suggest that the association of different common coexisting diagnoses may have different mechanisms for their coexistence, with some being likely to be genetically co-inherited while others are not (learning disability) (reviewed in Faraone and Biederman 1994, 1998). Clearly, the family genetic studies can provide important clues as to the types of genetic and non-genetic factors that may contribute to ADHD. A better clinical understanding of the genetic relationship of common comorbidities to ADHD is critical in order to interpret molecular genetic data accurately. For the most part, molecular genetic studies of this disorder to date have required that the clinical diagnosis be "present" or "absent" and in order to do this, one needs to know if the subject with ADHD and oppositional defiant disorder is the same kind of "present" as the subject with ADHD alone.

In addition to the unclear genetic relationship of coexisting disorders to ADHD, molecular genetic studies of ADHD are complicated by the complexity of diagnosing ADHD in adults, the not uncommon phenomenon of bilineal transmission in ADHD and related disorders, and the need for large sample sizes to provide adequate power. There are several different ways in which the genes contributing to a multigenic disorder may relate to each other, and the nature of this relationship determines the best way to analyze genetic information statistically. Yet, in the early stages of molecular study of a disorder, the nature of the association is not known, so there is an increased risk of errant conclusions because of the necessity of choosing assumptions during the analysis of data. Advances in both genetic and statistical techniques are creating more promising ways to study complex disorders, and information about the genetics of ADHD can be expected to accumulate rapidly over the next few decades. Most studies thus far have used linkage disequilibrium to identify the association between the presence of ADHD and certain candidate genes. Linkage disequilibrium studies can result in mistaken conclusions when subjects and controls are drawn from even slightly genetically different populations because there may be a population difference in the frequency of different alleles for a specific gene. Linkage disequilibrium studies within families are considered more accurate for this reason (reviewed in Ryan 1999). Association in family-based studies has been identified and replicated for specific alleles of the dopamine transporter and dopamine receptor type 4 genes. The dopamine transporter gene includes a region that codes for mRNA (but not the final protein) that contains a variable number of repeats of a specific 40 base pair sequence. There does not appear to be a mutation in the protein coding portion of the gene, but heterozygous parents more often transmit the 10 copy repeat allele (the most common one) to offspring with ADHD compared to others. Similarly, the 7-repeat allele of the dopamine-4 receptor gene is preferentially transmitted from parents to children with ADHD and is preferentially present in children affected by ADHD among sibling pairs (Cook 1999, 2000). Because of the level of their relative predominance in individuals with ADHD, these are considered to be genes with relatively weak effects, so it is likely that the "really important" genes are still waiting to be discovered. These genes are called "candidate" genes. They were targeted for study because other kinds of neurobiological information lead us to believe that the neurotransmitter dopamine is intimately involved in the symptoms of ADHD. As yet, there has been no reported genome-wide screening for ADHD-associated genes, but this type of study is in progress. Genome-wide screening, comparing affected and unaffected individuals within families may turn up important genes that could not have been predicted clinically, as has happened in a number of other genetic disorders.

In summary, ADHD most likely involves several pathways, regions, and neurochemicals, because sustained attention and self-regulation are among our most complex human functions. It is likely that a variety of genetic and environmental factors can result in sub-optimal efficiency of the entire system because of their influence on one or more component. Prefrontal-striatal regions and the neurotransmitters dopamine and norepinephrine seem most saliently involved, and a variety of neurochemical, anatomical, and genetic evidence supports this, but there are likely to be many more (and some surprising) pieces to discover before completion of the puzzle that is ADHD.

REFERENCES

Afifi, A. K. 1994a. Basal ganglia: Functional anatomy and physiology. Part I. *Journal of Child Neurology* 9:249–60.

Afifi, A. K. 1994b. Basal ganglia: Functional anatomy and physiology. Part II. *Journal of Child Neurology* 9:352–61.

Amen, D. G., and Carmichael, B. D. 1997. High resolution SPECT imaging in ADHD. *Annals of Clinical Psychiatry* 9:81–86.

Barkley, R. A. 2000. Genetics of childhood disorders: XVII. ADHD, Part I: The executive functions and ADHD. *Journal of the American Academy of Child and Adolescent Psychiatry* 39:1064–8.

Berquin, P. C., Giedd, J. N., Jacobsen, L. K., Hamburger, S. D., Krain, A. L., Rapoport, J. L., and Castellanos, F. X. 1998. Cerebellum in attention-deficit hyperactivity disorder: A morphometric MRI study. *Neurology* 50:1087–93.

Brandeis, D., van Leeuwen, T. H., Rubia, K., Vitacco, D., Steger, J., Pascual-Marqui, R. D., and Steinhausen, H.-Ch. 1998. Neuroelectric mapping reveals precursor of stop failures in children with attention deficits. *Behavioral Brain Research* 94:111–25.

Casey, B. J., Castellanos, F. X., Giedd, J. N., Marsh, W. L., Hamburger, S. D., Schubert, A. B., Vauss, Y. C., Vaituzis, A. C., Dickstein, D. P., Sarfatti, S. E., and Rapoport, J. L. 1997. Implication of right frontostriatal circuitry in response inhibition and attention-deficit/hyperactivity disorder. *Journal of the American Academy of Child and Adolescent Psychiatry* 36:374–83.

Castellanos, F. X. 1997. Toward a pathophysiology of attention-deficit/hyperactivity disorder. *Clinical Pediatrics*. July:381–93.

Cook, E. H. 1999. Genetics of ADHD. *MRDD Research Reviews* 5:191–98.

Cook, E. H. 2000. Molecular genetic sudies of ADHD. In *Attention Deficits and Hyperactivity in Children and Adults*, eds. P. J. Accardo, T. A. Blondis, B. Y. Whitman, and M. A. Stein. New York: Marcel Dekker.

Denkla, M. B.1996. Biological correlates of learning and attention: What is relevant to learning disability and attention-deficit hyperactivity disorder? *Developmental and Behavioral Pediatrics* 17:114–19.

Dougherty, D. D., Bonab, A. A., Spencer, T. J., Rauch, S. L., Madras, B. K., and Fischman, A. J. 1999. Dopamine transporter density in patients with attention deficit hyperactivity disorder. *Lancet* 354:2132–3.

Ernst, M., Zametkin, A. J., Matochik, J. A., Jons, P. H., and Cohen, R. M. 1998. DOPA decarboxylase activity in attention deficit hyperactivity disorder adults. A [fluorine-18]fluorodopa positron emission tomographic study. *Journal of Neuroscience* 18:5901–7.

Ernst, M., Zametkin, A. J., Matochik, J. A., Pascualvaca, D., Jons, P. H., and Cohen, R. M. 1999. High midbrain [18F] DOPA accumulation in children with attention deficit hyperactivity disorder. *American Journal of Psychiatry* 156:1209–15.

Faraone, S. V.and Biederman, J. 1994. Genetics of attention-deficit hyperactivity disorder. *Child and Adolescent Psychiatric Clinics of North America* 3:285–301.

Faraone, S. V. and Biederman, J. 1998. Neurobiology of attention-deficit/hyperactivity disorder. *Biological Psychiatry* 44:951–58.

Frank, Y., Seiden, J. A., and Napolitano, B. 1998. Electrophysiological changes in children with learning and attentional abnormalities as a function of age: Event-related potentials to an "oddball" paradigm. *Clinical Electroencephalography* 29:188–93.

Hale, T. S., Hariri, A. R., and McCracken, J. T. 2000. Attention deficit hyperactivity disorder: Perspectives from neuroimaging. *MRDD Research Reviews* 6:214–19.

Jonkman, L. M., Kemner, C., Verbaten, M., Koelega, H. S., Camfferman, G., van den Gaag, R.-J., Buitelaar, J., and van England, H. 1997. Event-related potentials and performance of attention-deficit hyperactivity disorder children and normal controls in auditory and visual selective attention tasks. *Biological Psychiatry* 41:595–611.

Kilpelainen, R., Luoma, L., Herrgard, E., Sipila, P., Ypparila, H., Partanen, J., and Karhu, J. 1999. Distractible children show abnormal orienting to nonattended auditory stimuli. *Neuroreport* 10:1869–74.

Krause, K. H., Dresel, S. H., Krause, J., Kung, H. F., and Tatsch, K. 2000. Increased striatal dopamine transporter in adult patients with attention deficit hyperactivity disorder: Effects of methylphenidate as measured by single photon emission computed tomography. *Neuroscience Letters* 285:107–10.

Lazar, W. J., and Frank, Y. 1998. Frontal systems dysfunction in children with attention-deficit/ hyperactivity disorder and learning disabilities. *Journal of Neuropsychiatry and Clinical Neuroscience* 10:160.

Lazzaro, I., Anderson, J., Gordon, E., Clarke, S., Leong, J., and Meares, R. 1997. Single trial variability within the P300 (250–500 ms) processing window in adolescents with attention deficit hyperactivity disorder. *Psychiatry Research* 73:91–101.

van Leeuwen, T. H., Steinhausen, H. C., Overtoom, C. C., Pascual-Marqui, R. D., van't Klooster, B., Rothenberger, A., Sergeant, J. A., and Brandeis, D. 1998. The continuous performance test revisited with neuroelectric mapping: Impaired orienting in children with attention deficits. *Behavioral Brain Research* 94:97–110.

Loo, S. K., Teale, P. D., Reite, M. L. 1999. EEG correlates of methylphenidate response among children with ADHD: A preliminary report. *Biological Psychiatry* 45:1657–60.

Mercugliano, M. 1995. Neurotransmitter alterations in ADHD. *MRDD Research Reviews* 1:220–26.

Mercugliano, M. 1999. What is attention-deficit/hyperactivity disorder? *Pediatric Clinics of North America* 46:831–43.

Mercugliano, M. 2000. Neurochemistry of ADHD. In *Attention Deficits and Hyperactivity in Children and Adults*, eds. P. J. Accardo, T. A. Blondis, B. Y. Whitman, and M. A. Stein. New York: Marcel Dekker.

Mirsky, A. F. 1996. Disorders of attention. In *Attention, Memory, and Executive Function*, eds. G. R. Lyon and N. A. Krasnegor. Baltimore: Paul H. Brookes.

Mostofsky, S. H., Reiss, A. L., Lockhart, P., and Denkla, M. B. 1998. Evaluation of cerebellar size in attention-deficit hyperactivity disorder. *Journal of Child Neurology* 13:434–39.

Niedermeyer, E. 1998. Frontal lobe functions and dysfunctions. *Clinical Electroencephalography* 29:79–90.

Rubia, K., Overmeyer, S., Taylor, E., Brammer, M., Williams, S. C. R., Simmons, A., and Bullmore E. T. 1999. Hypofrontality in attention deficit hyperactivity disorder during higher-order motor control: A study with functional MRI. *American Journal of Psychiatry* 156:891–96.

Ryan, S. G. 1999. Genetic susceptibility to neurodevelopmental disorders. *Journal of Child Neurology* 14:187–95.

Satterfield, J. H., Schell, A. M., and Nicholas, T. 1994. Preferential neural processing of attention-deficit hyperactivity disorder and normal boys. *Psychophysiology* 31:1–10.

Semrud-Clikeman, M., Steingard, R. J., Filipek, P., Biederman, J., Bekken, K., and Renshaw, P. F. 2000. Using MRI to examine brain-behavior relationships in males with attention deficit disorder with hyperactivity. *Journal of the American Academy of Child and Adolescent Psychiatry* 39:477–84.

Sieg, K. G., Gaffney, G. R., Preston, D. F., and Hellings, J. A. 1995. SPECT brain imaging abnormalities in attention deficit hyperactivity disorder. *Clinical Nuclear Medicine* 20:55–60.

Solanto, M. V. 1998. Neuropsychopharmacological mechanisms of stimulant drug action in ADHD: A review and integration. *Behavioral Brain Research* 94:127–52.

Strandburg, R. J., Marsh, T. J., Brown, W. S., Asarnow, R. F., Higa, J., Harper, R., and Guthrie, D. 1996. Continuous processing-related event-related potentials in children with attention deficit hyperactivity disorder. *Biological Psychiatry* 40:964–80.

Sunohara, G. A., Voros, J. G., Malone, M. A., and Taylor, M. J. 1997. Effects of methylphenidate in children with attention deficit hyperactivity disorder: A comparison of event-related potentials between medication responders and non-responders. *International Journal of Psychophysiology* 27:9–14.

Tannock, R. 1998. Attention deficit hyperactivity disorder: Advances in cognitive, neurobiological, and genetic research. *Journal of Child Psychology and Psychiatry* 39:65–99.

Toft, P. B. 1999. Prenatal and perinatal striatal injury: A hypothetical cause of attention-deficit—hyperactivity disorder? *Pediatric Neurology* 21:602–10.

Ucles, P., and Lorente, S. 1996. Electrophysiologic measures of delayed maturation in attention-deficit hyperactivity disorder. *Journal of Child Neurology* 11:155–56.

Vaidya, C. J., Austin, G., Kirkorian, G., Ridlehuber, H. W., Desmond, J. E., Glover, G. H., and Gabrieli, J. D. E. 1998. Selective effects of methylphenidate in attention deficit hyperactivity disorder: A functional magnetic resonance study. *Proceedings of the National Academy of Science*. USA 95:14494–9.

Chapter • 2

A Neurophysiologic Perspective on Attention

Thomas M. Lock and David B. Bender

> Everyone knows what attention is. It is the taking possession of the mind, in clear and vivid form, of one out of what seem several simultaneous possible objects or trains of thought. Focalization, concentration of consciousness are of its essence. It implies withdrawal from some things in order to deal effectively with others . . .
>
> William James 1890

> Because everyone knows that attention and set exist, we had better get the skeleton out of the closet and see what can be done with it.
>
> D. O. Hebb 1949

Although the concept of attention has been discussed by philosophers and psychologists for many years, the systematic scientific study of attention has occurred only over the past 30 to 40 years. In this chapter we will review some of the lessons that have been learned about how attention is manifest in the brain and suggest some of the fundamental cell membrane properties that may be involved. This discussion will be limited to studies of attention in the visual system because most of the work has been done in this system. The discussion will be selective, illustrating major examples, rather than a review of the attention literature. We also assume that attention in modalities other than vision involves similar mechanisms, so that an understanding of how attention works in vision may provide insight no matter what sensory modality may be involved in any specific case of ADHD.

Sensory stimuli are represented in the nervous system by the discharge of neurons. In the visual system, any one neuron will respond to stimuli only over a restricted part of the retina, the neuron's "receptive field" (RF), which means, of course, only in a restricted part of the visual field, depending on where the eye happens to be directed at the moment. Typically, a neuron will generate different numbers of action potentials in response to a stimulus depending on properties of the stimulus such as its color, shape, or movement. Neurons also respond with more or fewer action potentials to the very same stimulus depending on the mental or behavioral state of the animal. Here is where attention comes in. By systematically changing the instructions given to an animal, an experimenter can influence how a neuron will respond to a given stimulus. This change in excitability with a change in behavioral condition is the neurophysiological manifestation of attention.

From such studies we have learned much about how attention is reflected in the discharge of neurons and a number of lessons may be drawn:

- Attention affects excitability at the later, but not at the earliest stages of visual processing.
- If attention to a stimulus is habitually associated with a particular behavior (e.g. looking), neuronal responses related to that behavior can easily be misinterpreted as related to attention.
- Attention is reflected in relatively small quantitative changes in neuronal excitability, not in large all-or-none effects.
- Attention may either increase or decrease excitability in a given neuron, perhaps a reflection of James's words "withdrawal from some things to deal more effectively with others."
- Attention-dependent changes in excitability are widespread over multiple cortical and subcortical areas.

What neural systems and cellular mechanisms might produce such changes in responsiveness? Answers to this question are speculative. In the final sections of this chapter we will introduce some systems that are likely to be involved.

EFFECTS OF ATTENTION AT THE EARLY AND LATE STAGES OF VISUAL PROCESSING.

When light enters the eye and strikes the retina, information is processed by retinal neurons and the signal is relayed to the brain by the axons of retinal ganglion cells. Most axons from retinal ganglion cells project to the lateral geniculate nucleus (LGN) and synapse with cells there; a few project to the superior colliculus and synapse with cells there. LGN cells then send their axons to the primary visual cortex (striate cortex or V1). These structures, retina, LGN, and striate cortex comprise the "early" stages of visual processing (figure 1a). Neurons in these areas have small receptive fields, usually responding to stimuli in an area less than one degree of visual angle. Each point in the visual field is analyzed by a large number of neurons, each responding to some elementary aspect of the stimulus such as the color, the tilt of an edge, the direction of movement of the stimulus, etc. Attention has little or no effect on neuronal discharge in these areas (although recent work has shown that in V1 attention may affect responsiveness under specific circumstances).

Much of the cerebral cortex in the occipital, parietal, and temporal lobes anterior to striate cortex is also visually responsive and is divided into a mosaic of visual areas. These "prestriate" areas may be thought of as the "later stages" of visual processing and are arranged in a hierarchically interconnected system. Only a few areas receive direct input from striate cortex and they, in turn, project to other areas, and so forth (Felleman and Van Essen 1991). This network of areas segregates into two major "streams" of processing (Ungerleider and Mishkin 1982). There is a "dorsal pathway" leading into the parietal lobe that is concerned with localizing objects and directing movements in space. The second or "ventral pathway" leads into the temporal lobe and is more concerned with object recognition and visual memory (figure 1b). In these later stages of processing several trends are apparent: receptive fields become larger (up to 30 degrees of visual angle), neurons respond to more abstract aspects of the stimulus, and most important for this discussion, the behavioral state of the animal affects the responses of increasing proportions of neurons.

The later stages of visual processing are not limited to the prestriate cortex, but also include thalamic nuclei. The pulvinar and the thalamic reticular nucleus receive input from primary visual cortex and are reciprocally connected to many prestriate areas. Also, in addition to receiving direct retinal input, the superior colliculus receives inputs from cortical areas later in the visual hierarchy, as well as cortical areas in the frontal lobe associated with oculomotor planning. This interrelationship between predominantly sensory areas and areas with oculomotor functions is a reminder of the habitual linkage between gaze and attention in primates.

NEURONAL RESPONSES RELATED TO MOTOR BEHAVIORS CAN EASILY BE MISINTERPRETED AS RELATED TO ATTENTION

The early studies of Robert Wurtz and his colleagues at the National Institutes of Health serve as examples of the techniques used to study

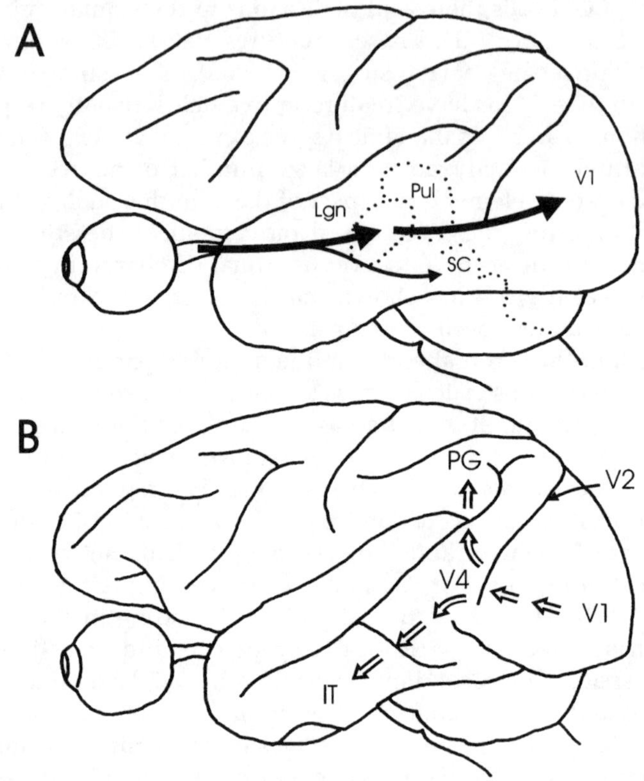

Figure 1. A: Schematic representation of pathways (heavy arrows) connecting early stages of visual processing. Lateral view of monkey brain; structures deep to temporal cortex shown as dotted lines. Lgn: lateral geniculate nucleus; V1: primary visual cortex; Pul: pulvinar; SC: superior colliculus. B: Later stages of visual processing. Double arrows indicate dorsal and ventral processing streams. Visual area V2 is buried in sulcus (thin arrow). PG: parietal cortex Area 7; IT: inferior temporal cortex.

Table I. Comparison of visual responsiveness of cells early and late in the hierarchy of visual processing.

	Early Processing	Late Processing
Receptive Fields	Small	Large
Respond To	Simple "Primitives" color angle movement binocular disparity	Abstract aspects objects concentric motion
Attentional Effects	Small or Absent	Prominent

attention in experimental animals, and of the careful control of experimental situations required to prevent one from being misled by the results.

Wurtz and his colleagues were studying the receptive field properties of cells in the superior colliculus when they noticed that a neuron would typically respond more strongly if the animal "paid attention" to a stimulus that was flashed in the neuron's receptive field (Goldberg and Wurtz 1972). In their experiment, monkeys were trained to gaze at a small spot of light (a "fixation point") using a simple procedure. The monkey pressed a bar to turn on the spot; the spot stayed on for a variable period of time and then dimmed briefly. If the monkey released the bar during the dimming, it was rewarded. While the monkey's eyes were fixated on the spot, a light was flashed in the receptive field of a neuron in the colliculus (figure 2a). In this condition, when the stimulus meant nothing to the animal, the colliculus neuron responded with a brief, irregular burst of action potentials (figure 2b). However, if the task was modified slightly so that the animal had to pay attention to the RF stimulus, the response increased. In this modified task, the fixation point turned off when the RF stimulus came on, and the monkey had to wait for the RF stimulus to dim before releasing the lever. Now the stimulus evoked more action potentials from the neuron. It was clear the RF stimulus was meaningful to the monkey because the animal habitually looked at the RF stimulus shortly after it turned on (figure 2c). Only the neural activity preceding the eye movement was measured, since the eye movement removed the stimulus from the neuron's receptive field. Thus, the same physical stimulus, in the receptive field of the same neuron, evoked a larger discharge when the monkey "paid attention" to it. This phenomenon was called "enhancement." About half of all colliculus neurons show such an enhanced discharge, and the increase is typically about 50% more action potentials.

But was this really "attention"? Attention is independent of response modality; we "pay attention" to a stimulus whether for the purpose of looking at it, thinking about it, touching it, or detecting its dimming. What if the monkey were not allowed to look at the receptive field stimulus, yet still had to detect its dimming? To answer this question, the task was changed again: the monkey still had to respond to, and thus pay attention to, the stimulus, but now the fixation point was left on and the monkey was trained not to look at the RF stimulus when it came on (the trial simply terminated if gaze shifted away from the fixation point). In this situation (figure 2d), the "enhancement" vanished (Wurtz and Mohler 1974). Thus what appeared to be attentional modulation might more properly be called a correlate of "motor set," because the enhancement occurred only during the preparation for an eye

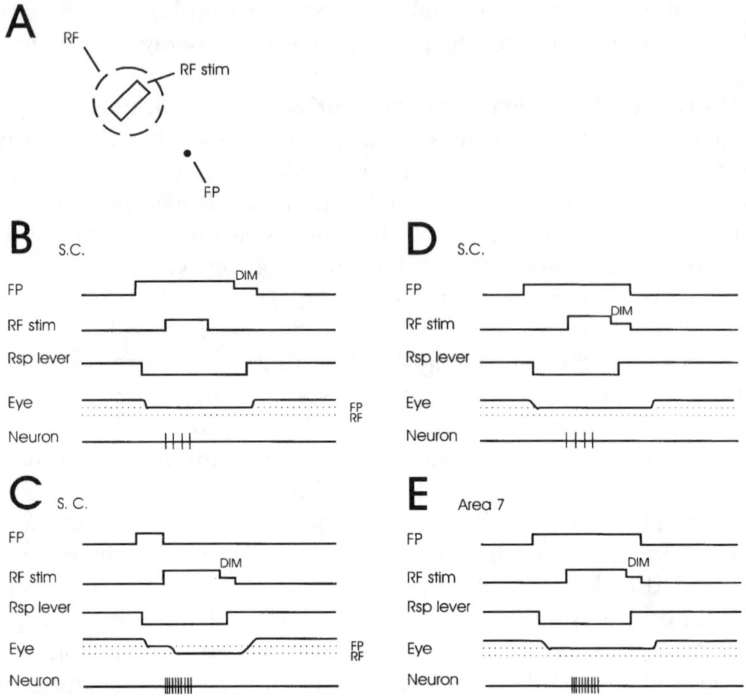

Figure 2. Sequence of events and neuronal response during the "enhancement" paradigm (see text). A: Stimuli as seen by monkey. FP: fixation point; RF: outline of receptive field; RF stim: receptive field stimulus. B: Response of colliculus neuron to RF stim when it is irrelevant. Stimuli on- and off-sets shown by upward and downward deflections of event markers. DIM: dimming of FP; Eye: eye position trace indicating steady gaze at FP when FP is on; Rsp lever: response lever pushed down after FP onset, released during FP dimming. C: Enhanced response from same neuron when RF stim is relevant (dims). Eye looks from FP to RF stim when FP turns off and RF stim turns on. D: No enhanced response from colliculus neuron when animal pays attention to RF stim but does not look at it. E: Area 7 neuron gives enhanced response during same paradigm as in D.

movement. And indeed, subsequent experiments established that the superior colliculus, through its input from the basal ganglia, has an important role in preparing voluntary movement of the eyes (Wurtz and Hikosaka 1986). The "no saccade" attention task does, however, result in enhanced responses from neurons in other areas of the brain, at later stages of visual processing. For example, enhancement of responses in parietal cortex (area 7) was not eliminated when eye movements were prohibited (Bushnell, Goldberg, and Robinson 1981; Goldberg and Bruce 1985) (figure 2e). Enhanced responses in area 7 are also found if the animal is rewarded not for looking, but rather for reaching towards the RF stimulus, thus establishing that the response to the stimulus is enhanced independent of the motor act for which the stimulus was relevant and thereby worthy of the animal's attention. Such changes in excitability varied from cell to cell but typically were on the order of 50 to 100 percent, and were present in about 40 percent of the visually responsive cells. Other cells, about 20 percent of visual cells, responded differently; instead of giving enhanced responses to the attended stimulus, their responses became weaker. We will come back to that point in a later section.

This series of experiments illustrates both the methods that can be used to control attentional states and the exquisite control of the subject's response to the stimulus that may be required to separate discharge that is related to attention from that related to other behavior. This lesson may well apply to studies of ADHD in children. One wonders, for example, if uncontrolled differences in direction of gaze, or other motor activity, rather than some neuropathologic difference, may have produced some of the differences in cerebral activity that have been observed in functional imaging studies of children with ADHD, particularly in view of the hyperactivity of the children.

THE MAGNITUDE OF ATTENTIONAL RESPONSES.

In the preceding examples, neurons encoded a stimulus with a larger or smaller response when the animal did or did not attend to that stimulus. This is not the only manifestation of attention. Particularly in brain areas concerned with visual recognition and memory, the neuronal mechanics of attention seem to solve a problem that arises directly from the nature of receptive fields. As discussed earlier, receptive fields get larger the farther we go along the visual hierarchy. Eventually, cells with receptive fields in which it is easy to fit more than just a single stimulus become common. This creates a problem: Suppose two apples, one red and one green, happen to be imaged within the receptive field of a single neuron. If that neuron is tuned to red, say, so that its discharge indicates to other neurons that something red is in the receptive field, how will the other neurons "know" which apple the discharge refers to? The large receptive field has created a fundamental ambiguity which, it turns out, is resolved by attention. If the animal is attending to the apple on the left (which happens to be red) the neuron will give a vigorous response, but if attending to the apple on the right (which is green) a weaker response. It is as though attending to one of the apples in effect shrinks the receptive field around the attended object, removing the ambiguity. Desimone and his colleagues have demonstrated this phenomenon in V2, V4, and inferior temporal cortex (Desimone et al.

1990; Moran and Desimone 1985; Luck et al. 1997). While the animal gazed at a small fixation point (to keep the eyes steady—see figure 3a), two small stimuli were simultaneously flashed at neighboring sites within the receptive field of a neuron. The stimuli had been chosen so that one matched the cell's trigger feature, and the other did not; in the case of a neuron tuned to red for example, a red rectangle and a green rectangle. The stimuli could also vary in another stimulus dimension that did not affect the neuron's responsiveness, for example, orientation. The animal performed a task that required it to attend to the stimuli flashed at one site and ignore those flashed at the other, and that allowed the experimenter to switch the locus of attention back and forth between the two sites in blocks of trials. A "delayed match-to-sample" task was used to direct attention at one site or the other. In this paradigm, sequences of two stimuli, separated by a short delay, are presented. The animal is rewarded for making one response if the two stimuli in a sequence are the same (for example vertical followed by vertical), and for making another response if they are different (for example, vertical followed by horizontal). By rewarding responses based on the sequence at one of the two sites, the experimenter can force the animal to attend to that site. One can even verify that the animal did indeed attend there simply by having the simultaneously presented sequence at the other site call for the opposite response, and then checking that that performance was correct.

Under these conditions, a cell tuned to red, for example, responded well to red rectangles at the attended site, but poorly to red rectangles at the ignored site (figure 3a). This suppression at the unattended site averaged about 60% to 70%, and it was found in half to 3/4 of all the cells tested in these later stages of the ventral pathway, V4 and inferior temporal cortex. Interestingly, if only one of the two sites was in the receptive field, i.e., when there was no ambiguity about which stimulus the cell's discharge would have referred to, there was no suppression (figure 3b). Thus when attention is needed to "filter out" distracting stimuli in order to perform a short-term memory job like the delayed match-to-sample task, the underlying physiology seems to involve a "shrinking" of receptive fields around the attended location, but only for those neurons that might provide ambiguous signals. One can imagine how poor a child's performance would be if this "shrinking" did not happen.

In both this and the previous example, attending or not to a place or a stimulus made the difference between stronger or weaker responses, not between a response or no response. This seems to be the general case, that attention does not work like an "on-off" switch but rather operates through relatively small quantitative changes in neuronal responsivity.

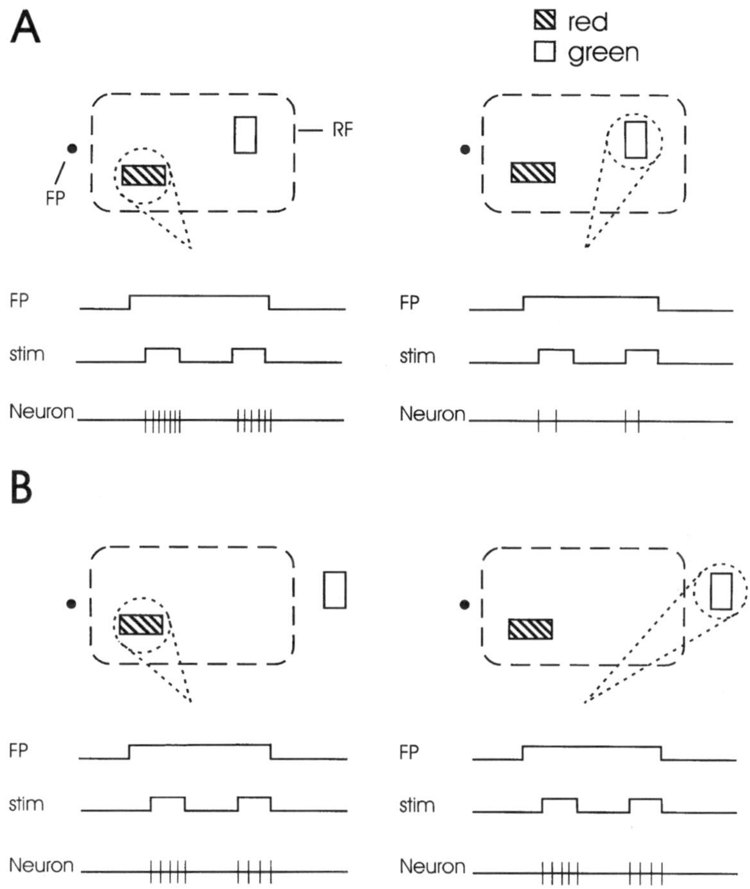

Figure 3. Effect of directing attention at the location of an effective (left column) or ineffective (right column) stimulus; dashed cone indicates locus of attention. See text for details. Event markers indicate sequence of stimuli during delayed match-to-sample trial; 1st stimulus is sample, 2nd is match. A: Both attentional locations within RF. B: One attentional locus inside, the other outside RF.

ATTENTION MAY EITHER INCREASE OR DECREASE EXCITABILITY IN A GIVEN NEURON, PERHAPS A REFLECTION OF JAMES'S WORDS "WITHDRAWAL FROM SOME THINGS TO DEAL MORE EFFECTIVELY WITH OTHERS."

We saw in the example of Wurtz' enhancement paradigm that attention to a particular stimulus could either increase or decrease a neuron's response to that stimulus. Changes in more global aspects of behavioral state can also change neuronal responsiveness, even to irrelevant stimuli. A good example of this occurs in the "attentive fixation" paradigm developed by Mountcastle and his colleagues at Johns Hopkins (Mountcastle, Andersen, and Motter 1981; Mountcastle et al. 1987). In these experiments, the animal is again required to look at a fixation point, and wait for it to dim, before it can respond and obtain a reward. The fixation point comes on automatically and irregularly so the animal is always in one of two states, vigilantly awaiting the fixation point or attentively fixating it. This time, however, the RF stimulus may be flashed during either phase of the task, when the animal is looking at the fixation point or when it is not, and is always irrelevant to the behavior of the animal. This paradigm was first used while recording from neurons in area 7 of the parietal lobe. About 70% of visually responsive neurons in this area were found to respond more strongly during fixation than while the monkey was just waiting for the fixation point to come on; about 10% responded less strongly. This was contrasted with prestriate area V4 where neurons responded strongly during both phases of the task.

More recently, this task was used not only to reinvestigate the attentional modulation seen in area 7, but also with the idea of comparing these effects across many different visual areas (Bender and Youakim 2001). Thus, recordings were made in the visual thalamus (LGN and pulvinar) as well as at different levels of the visual cortical hierarchy (V2, V4, and area 7). All aspects of the behavioral situation were fixed so that a careful quantitative comparison of attentional effects could be made across all these areas. With conditions and computations carefully controlled, now it was clear that in all these areas, except the LGN, as many cells showed decreased responsiveness during the attentive fixation phase as showed increased responsiveness. In the LGN, there was no attentional modulation, which made a useful control showing that the modulation seen more centrally could not have been an artifact of some peripheral change (e.g., pupil size) associated with the behavioral states. Prevalence of attentional modulation was generally modest, but nonetheless doubled as one proceeded up the hierarchical stages of processing; from about 20% in V2, to more than 40% in area 7, with an intermediate prevalence in the pulvinar. In similar fashion, the magnitude of the change in responsiveness with attentional state also got larger at higher levels, though still was rather modest. The attention-dependent change in discharge, expressed as a percent of the maximum possible, increased from about 20% in the pulvinar and V2 to about 40% in area 7.

The quantitative approach of this study also revealed something about the magnitude of these attention-dependent changes in neuronal responsiveness that had not been noticed previously. It has been known for many years that neurons are, in general, variable in their responsiveness. When an animal performs a behavioral task, and the identical stimulus is flashed in the receptive of a cell in the same state, trial after trial, the responses evoked by the stimulus will vary from trial to trial, even though all experimental conditions are held rigidly constant. Typically, this variability is about 25% to 30% of response size at the earliest stages of vision, e.g., in the LGN, but increases to be quite significant at higher levels, reaching 60% to 70% of response size in area 7. What this study showed was that when the magnitude of attentional modulation was compared to this variability of response, making a kind of "signal to noise" ratio of attention, that ratio was the same in every area, and rather small: The change in discharge due to attention, relative to the variability or noise, was just 1.3 + 10%. So when the intrinsic noisiness of neurons is taken into account, together with the fact that it differs across brain areas, attention is seen to have the same effect in all areas, and an effect only 30% larger than the noise.

THESE EFFECTS ARE WIDESPREAD OVER MANY CORTICAL AND SUBCORTICAL AREAS.

We have now seen attentional modulation of neuronal responses in a number of cortical and subcortical areas: V2, V4, inferior temporal cortex, parietal area 7, pulvinar. This is only a partial listing, but it should be clear that attentional processes are widely distributed over many brain areas and are important for most aspects of visual processing.

There is even evidence that attention is operating as early in visual processing as primary visual cortex. Motter (1993) trained monkeys to discriminate the tilt of one bar in an array of oriented bars; the critical bar, which had to be attended to in order to solve the problem, was cued in advance at the start of each trial. About a third of V1 neurons were affected by attention in this paradigm. Typically the response to the attended bar changed 20% to 40%, up or down, provided the bar tilt was close to the preferred orientation of the cell.

Given the widespread nature of the neuronal changes that can be found in attention, it appears likely that attention is not the responsibility of some single "attention control" area or structure, but rather a property of broadly distributed systems. What sort of systems are distributed throughout the brain that might contribute to this control? Does it make sense to look for local areas of increased or decreased neuronal activity in functional studies, and attribute causes of attentional dysfunction to these areas, when we have seen that normal attentional function is both widely distributed and push-pull in nature?

SUBCORTICAL SYSTEMS INVOLVED IN ATTENTION-DEPENDENT EXCITABILITY

There are two major subcortical systems that must be considered in understanding the changes in neuronal excitability that we have described. The first is the thalamocortical circuit, the second is the long ascending brainstem system. Both systems are composed of a number of similar subsystems. In general the thalamocortical circuits are involved in fast, point-to-point neuronal transmission whereas the long ascending systems involve fewer neurons with much less topological order and slow, modulatory neurotransmission.

The thalamocortical system involves both ascending projections from the thalamus to cortex and descending projections from cortex to the thalamus. There is a high degree of topological order in this system, with groups of neurons in different areas talking to each other only when both groups process information from the same portion of the visual field. Synaptic transmission here is related to high speed visual processing with neurons responding or pausing almost simultaneously with changes in visual stimuli. This system typically uses glutamate for excitation and γ-aminobutyric acid (GABA) for inhibition. These neurons, thalamic and cortical, are the ones in which single neuron attentional effects have been found.

The thalamocortical circuit can be contrasted with the long ascending brainstem circuit. This circuit consists of groups of neurons whose cell bodies lie within the brainstem and project widely throughout the cerebral cortex, with little point-to-point correspondence. In part, they constitute what was originally called the "reticular activating system." With the advent of modern histochemical staining techniques, it became clear that these groups of neurons could be divided into transmitter specific systems, for example those using the biogenic amines and acetylcholine rather than glutamate or GABA. These subsystems include the locus ceruleus and its norepinephrine containing cells, the dorsal raphe and its serotonin containing cells, the tuberomamillary nucleus and its histamine containing cells, the substantia nigra and mesocortical dopamine systems, and the nucleus basalis of Meynert and its acetylcholine-containing cells. This circuit, though not directly engaged in attentional processing, influences the general excitability of cells in the thalamocortical circuit, modulating the rates, durations, and even the fine temporal structure of neuronal firing within that circuit, and this can affect attentional processing. The medications with known effects on attention, impulsivity, hyperactivity, perseveration, obsessions and mood are all known to affect transmitter metabolism or release in the long ascending brainstem circuits.

MEMBRANE CURRENTS UNDERLYING ATTENTION-DEPENDENT EXCITABILITY

If attention is manifest in relative responsiveness, how do transmitters, fast or slow, affect responsiveness? For the answer to this we have to look at the cellular basis for response, the membrane potential. Most of us will recall, if vaguely, that mammalian neurons have a resting potential of about –70 to –50 mV. When the membrane potential is depolarized above about –50 mV, voltage-dependent sodium channels open and an action potential is produced. The moment to moment variation of resting potential is controlled by myriad other channels specific to each neuron (figure 4). Some channels are associated with receptors, producing small hyperpolarizing (inhibitory), depolarizing (excitatory), or stabilizing currents (e.g. inhibitory chloride currents that tend to keep membrane potential near resting potential, resisting depolarization). Other channels may be voltage-dependent or have small, constant currents leading to rhythmic discharge.

If the membrane potential is determined by membrane permeability to ions from moment to moment, then which axons connect to a given neuron, and which channels are present in the membrane will determine its responsivity. Connectivity differences among neurons are presumably important in brain damage syndromes and major disabilities. The strength of connections is presumably affected by conditioning and experience. In syndromes in which there is a major hereditary factor, it seems likely that differences in some of the many ion channels or transmitter transporters will be found.

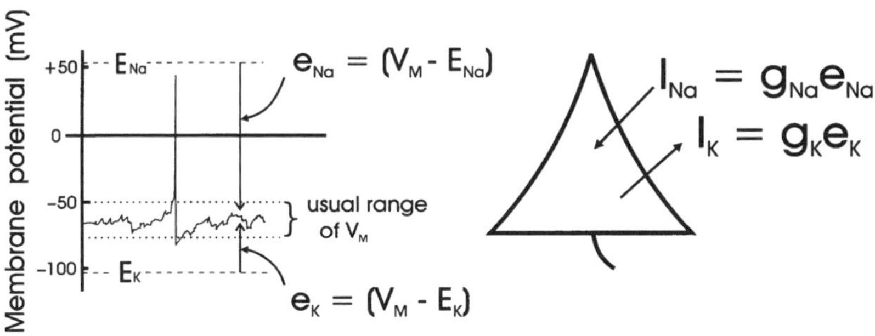

Figure 4. Left:Typical fluctuations of membrane potential, V_M, over time; except during an action potential, V_M is usually within the dotted lines. Vertical arrows: driving force on sodium, e_{Na}, and on potassium, e_K. Dashed lines: equilibrium potentials for sodium, E_{Na}, and for potassium, E_K. Right: Schematic neuron showing the two major cationic currents that determine the level of V_M. Note that small changes in sodium conductance, g_{Na}, can have large effects on V_M because of the large e_{Na}.

We will discuss two examples from one family of channels—potassium channels. To date, over 40 different K+ channels have been identified. One of these, I_{AHP} is the current associated with a calcium-dependent K^+ channel. This channel is not voltage dependent, but is dependent on the intracellular concentration of calcium ions ($[Ca^{++}]$). $[Ca^{++}]$ increases with each action potential. As $[Ca^{++}]$ increases I_{AHP} increases. This moves the membrane potential towards the potassium equilibrium potential, hyperpolarizing the cell and decreasing responsivity. This produces the phenomenon of "spike-frequency adaptation." When the driving input to the cell is constant, this channel opens and reduces responsivity. A number of neuromodulators can turn off I_{AHP} through second messenger systems (NE, ACh, histamine, 5-HT). It is easy to see how polymorphisms in this channel or individual differences in neuromodulator systems could produce changes in vigilance or adaptation to repeated stimulation in children.

An example of a human disorder that has been linked to a polymorphism in an ion channel is benign familial neonatal epilepsy. In humans, a gene on chromosome 20q13.3 codes for a transiently expressed K+ channel. When there is a deletion for this gene the result is a nonconducting channel, neuronal hyperexcitability, and seizures (Biervert et al. 1998). Presumably the polymorphisms responsible for ADHD will be more subtle than this.

CONCLUSIONS

We all have the subjective experience of attention and a belief that a lack of or dysfunction in attention is important in ADHD. There are many aspects of attention; the increased potency of an important stimulus, the selection of one stimulus from among a number of distractions, and the increased mental effort to solve difficult problems. The underlying physiology of attention can be, and has been, studied in experimental animals at the single neuron level. At that level, attention is observed as altered neuronal excitability. This altered excitability results in relatively small changes in discharge rates, not large all-or-none effects. The size of these changes appears to be related to the intrinsic trial-to-trial variability of neuronal response in any given brain area. In any one neuron, the change can be an increase or decrease. These effects are widely distributed throughout the brain, occurring simultaneously in many areas. Two major circuits must be considered in understanding the modulation of neuronal activity that is attention: The thalamocortical pathways that use fast synaptic transmission and in which this modulation occurs, and the long ascending brainstem pathways that use biogenic amines and acetylcholine to shape general levels of activity in the thalamocortical circuits(our currently available medications affect the latter system). The specific connectivity of a neuron, and the presence or absence of many different ion channels in its membrane which, in turn, are coded by large gene families, control membrane excitability. Therefore, there is a diversity of cell mechanisms contributing to attention and a diversity of treatments that may be effective regardless of the specific cause of attentional dysfunction in a given individual. The widespread nature and diversity of attentional modulation at the neuronal level suggests that there are intrinsic limitations to brain imaging methods that average over many neurons. Progress in molecular neuroscience should produce new treatments for ADHD in the near future.

Note: A more complete treatment of this subject may be found in:

Lock, T. M., and Bender, D. B. 2000. Single neuron studies of attention. In *Attention Deficits and Hyperactivity in Children and Adults*, eds. P. A. Accardo, T. A. Blondis, B. Y. Whitman, and M. A. Stein. New York, NY: Marcel Dekker.

REFERENCES

Bender, D. B. and Youakim, M. 2001. Effect of attentive fixation in macaque thalamus and cortex. *Journal of Neurophysiology* 85:219–34.

Biervert, C., Schroeder, B. C., Kubisch, C., Berkovic, S. F., Propping, P., Jentsch, T. J., and Steinlein, O. K. 1998. A potassium channel mutation in neonatal human epilepsy. *Science* 279:403–406.

Bushnell, M. D., Goldberg, M. E., and Robinson, D. L. 1982. Behavioral enhancement of visual responses in monkey cerebral cortex. I. Modulation in posterior parietal cortex related to selective visual attention. *Journal of Neurophysiology* 46:755–72.

Desimone, R., Wessinger, M., Thomas, L., and Schneider, W. 1990. Attentional control of visual perception: Cortical and subcortical mechanisms. Cold Spring Harbor Symposia on Quantitative Biology 55:963–71.

Felleman, D. J., and Van Essen, D. C. 1991. Distributed hierarchical processing in the primate cerebral cortex. *Cerebral Cortex* 1:1–47.

Goldberg, M. E., and Bruce, C. J. 1985. Cerebral cortical activity associated with the orientation of visual attention in the rhesus monkey. *Visual Research* 25:471–81.

Goldberg, M. E., and Wurtz, R. H. 1972. Activity of superior colliculus in behaving monkey. II. Effect of attention on neuronal responses. *Journal of Neurophysiology* 35:560–74.

Hebb, D. O. 1949. *The Organization of Behavior: A Neuropsychological Theory.* 1961 ed. New York, NY: Science Editions.

James, W. 1890. *The Principles of Psychology.* Authorized Edition ed. v. 1. New York, NY: Dover Publications, Inc.

Luck, S. J., Chelazzi, L., Hillyard, S. A., and Desimone, R. 1997. Neural mechanisms of spatial selective attention in areas V1, V2, and V4 of macaque visual cortex. *Journal of Neurophysiology* 77:24–42.

Moran, J., and Desimone, R. 1985. Selective attention gates visual processing in the extrastriate cortex. *Science* 229:782–84.

Motter, B. C. 1993. Focal attention produces spatially selective processing in visual cortical areas V1, V2, and V4 in the presence of competing stimuli. *Journal of Neurophysiology* 70:909–19.
Mountcastle, V. B., Andersen, R. A., and Motter, B. C. 1981. The influence of attentive fixation upon the excitability of the light-sensitive neurons of the posterior parietal cortex. *Journal of Neuroscience* 1:1218–35.
Mountcastle, V. B., Motter, B. C., Steinmetz, M. A., and Sestokas, A. K. 1987. Common and differential effects of attentive fixation on the excitability of parietal and prestriate (V4) cortical visual neurons in the macaque monkey. *Journal of Neuroscience* 7:2239–55.
Ungerleider, L. G., and Mishkin M. 1982. Two cortical visual systems. In: *Analysis of Visual Behavior*, eds. Ingle, D. J., Goodale, M. A., and Mansfield, R. J. W. Cambridge, MA: M.I.T. Press.
Wurtz, R. H., and Hikosaka, O. 1986. Role of the basal ganglia in the initiation of saccadic eye movements. *Progress in Brain Research* 64:175–90.
Wurtz, R. H., and Mohler, C. W. 1974. Selection of visual targets for the initiation of saccadic eye movements. *Brain Research* 71:209–14.

Section • II

Differential Diagnosis

Chapter • 3

ADHD
The Neurodevelopmentalist's Perspective

Pasquale J. Accardo

Concern about the possible over-diagnosis and over-treatment of attention deficit hyperactivity disorder (ADHD) in children recently arose with the publication of several papers documenting an increasing incidence (LeFever, Dawson, and Morrow 1999; Zito et al 2000). One of the mainstays of the cyclically recurrent criticism of ADHD as a real diagnostic entity is its "unusually high" prevalence rate. This same criticism has been applied to the earlier epidemic of learning disabilities and the current pandemic of autistic spectrum disorders. It appears to represent a not atypical phenomenon in the identification of trait disorders. If, for example, mental retardation is a trait disorder, then its occurrence in the general population can be predicted, by normal distribution (a Gaussian or bell curve), to be on the order of 2% to 3%. Why then do such disorders as ADHD, neurologically based specific learning disabilities (NBSLD), and communication disorders (CD) reach prevalence estimates between 5% and 20 %?

Two explanations can be offered. (1) Each of these functional diagnostic categories is actually composed of distinct etiological subtypes. It is quite possible that after these subtypes have been accurately classified, each of the component disorders will remain within the predicted 2% to 3% incidence. (2) Because the behaviors that make up these disorders are traits that exist on a continuum, milder degrees of impairment may be defined as disorders. When an intelligence quotient (IQ) of 85 was used as the upper limit of "borderline mental retardation," that cutoff raised the prevalence of mental retardation to more than 15% of the general population. Such individuals may no longer be classified as mentally retarded, but this cognitively limited sub-population may still be in need of specialized services or consideration.

This approach to a continuum of functional developmental diagnoses is characteristic of neurodevelopmental pediatricians. Before entering upon a discussion of the neurodevelopmentalist's perspective on attention deficit hyperactivity disorder (ADHD), two provisos need to be entered. (1) It is difficult to discuss ADHD without also covering the associated learning disabilities that are so commonly found in children with ADHD as to make them virtually part of the same syndrome. In that sense, the older construct of minimal brain dysfunction (MBD) conforms closer to the clinical reality that about a quarter of a century ago was broken up into ADHD, NBSLD, and CD (Accardo 1997). (2) It would perhaps be well to define at the beginning exactly what a "neurodevelopmentalist" is (Accardo, Painter, and Capute 2000). A neurodevelopmentalist is a medical professional who focuses upon the importance of the neurological substrate to the presentation of behavioral and developmental symptoms. Behaviors such as struggling in school, school failure, attentional deficits, impulsivity, hyperactivity, and acting out, are all open to a wide variety of interpretations. The neurodevelopmentalist is concerned with identifying the central nervous system contribution to the evolution of these problems. If that contribution is found to be clinically significant, then the relevance of classroom techniques and family interactions will not necessarily be lessened but will be placed in a very different perspective. In other words, from a neurodevelopmental perspective, behavior has its origin in one of four ways.

First, the behavior in question may originate in the child, involuntarily. Then, behavioral or developmental problems in the form of ADHD or NBSLD will be attributed to "brain damage," static encephalopathy, "brain chemistry," "poor wiring," or some other congenitally based central nervous system anomaly.

Second, the behavior in question may originate in the child, voluntarily. Then, behavioral or developmental problems will be attributed to willfulness, oppositional disorders, lack of motivation, or just plain laziness. It has been argued that oppositional defiant disorder (ODD) does not actually exist except as a symptom of the first option: children become increasingly oppositional when an underlying neurodevelopmental disorder interferes with age expected compliance with reasonable adult demands (Accardo 1994). Attentional deficits and language disorders are the most frequent culprits in this situation.

Third, the behavior in question may originate from the influence of the environment (either the school or the home) on the child. There are certainly mismanaged classrooms, inexperienced teachers, and inappropriate curriculum expectations that can contribute to such misbehavior. Chaotic family life, possibly extending into the neglectful or even abusive end of the spectrum, can also encourage, or at the least not discourage, such behavior. On the other hand, for the more common and most classic presentations of ADHD, such factors are rarely primary etiologies.

Fourth, the behavior in question may originate in some combination of the above. This fourth choice, so respectful of the complexity of real life, so nonjudgmental in its refusal to place blame where blame is due, is an easy option—indeed all too easy. It is, in reality, a cop-out. The majority of children who present with signs and symptoms of ADHD actually have—ADHD. Much of the tortured angst spilled over a multifaceted psychosocial differential diagnosis of these presenting behavioral symptoms reflects more the uncertainty of the examiner than the true complexity of the case. Family stress plays a significant role in susceptibility to strep throat; the diagnosis and treatment of strep throat do not require that such stress be explored.

Although many ADHD children have associated learning disabilities, most of their secondary emotional symptoms represent complications following the failure to diagnose and treat their primary neurological diagnosis adequately. An interactional perspective succeeds in spreading the blame and thus providing numerous escape routes to avoid censure in the event of treatment failure; it also mutes the efficacy of more carefully targeted diagnosis and multistage treatment plans. Posing a problem in terms of infinite complexity invites a fatalism that will excuse just those specific choices that promise the greatest effectiveness.

That summarizes, at a level of broad philosophical abstraction, a neurodevelopmentalist's perspective. The decision-making process in which selected variables are either emphasized or demoted in significance will now be fleshed out in a unidisciplinary fashion. The neurodevelopmentalist's perspective will be described by listing what one neurodevelopmentalist does.

NEURODEVELOPMENTAL ASSESSMENT

It is not unusual to find the outline for a neurodevelopmental evaluation presented in such extensive detail and complexity as to terrify any primary care provider from even considering its application. Time constraints alone would seem to prohibit its use in an office setting (Accardo 1999). In contrast, it needs to be emphasized that much of the basic assessment of children for disorders of attention and learning depends predominantly on a carefully elicited history. It cannot be overstated that while such a detailed neurodevelopmental history frequently can take up to an hour to conduct (not counting a review of reports of classroom behavior and academic performance, as well as of records of previous evaluations and testing), almost every aspect of the history can be obtained with a much smaller investment of time by the primary care physician in the course of routine well-child check ups over the life span. In other words, most of what a neurodevelopmental pediatrician does is to go back over what could have been much more easily and more accurately obtained prospectively by the family doctor.

If one is going to place a great deal of reliance on the history, the accuracy of the reporter must be assessed. The two most commonly used reporters are the mother and the teacher. Their descriptions can be considered most reliable when they concur. Should they disagree, then the source of the inconsistency will need to be investigated. In describing their child, parents more typically underestimate the severity of problem behaviors for the simple reason that they interact with their children on a more one-to-one basis and in generally less structured, less demanding situations than school. (The availability of age peers for comparison may also be limited.) Because there will be fewer problems relating to attention and learning in such situations, parental reports tend to be less concerned than those of the same child's teachers. In addition, the tremendous pressure on all parents to want their child to be "normal" contributes to a degree of denial that understandably causes them to minimize symptoms.

Teachers, on the other hand, are rarely neutral about describing children's behavior to outside evaluators. When completing Conners behavior rating scales, for example, they are quite aware that higher scores will possibly contribute to a child's being tried on medication, while lower scores will diminish the probability of a medication trial. This will not cause them to falsify data, but will certainly influence how any borderline or marginal behaviors are scored. The issue of medicating children is viewed by few educators in dispassionate isolation: some are philosophically opposed to such a course (indeed, equating it with child abuse), while others would prefer Ritalin or one of its congeners to be administered through the school's drinking water supply. Between these extremes runs a gamut of complex and quite often misinformed opinions, none of which can fail to have an impact on teachers' descriptions of classroom behavior. To help identify such prejudices, the request for a descriptive letter from the teacher (either instead of or in addition to a formal checklist such as the Conners rating scale) will often allow biases to reveal themselves.

As important as this step is for diagnosis, it will become increasingly important for inaugurating a treatment program in which the teacher's collaboration and understanding is vital.

The issue of professional training is related to professional bias. A child psychologist is quite competent to make the diagnosis of ADHD. The same cannot be assumed of the school psychological examiner. Standards for such professionals vary markedly from state to state, and individual experience can play a major role in each clinician's competence to assess children with such problems. Because ADHD is not a specific service category for educational intervention, many school psychological examiners are not well versed in exploring this diagnosis. The power of a single professional non-diagnosis cannot be underestimated.

Meanwhile, the first step in any neurodevelopmental history is the family history.

Family History

The first thing that a family physician must do is to know the family: this is "history" in its intergenerational aspect. It includes knowledge of both parents and siblings as well as selected information on more distant (i.e., second degree) relatives.

Parents. A physician should not only inquire about parental attentional, learning, and behavioral difficulties in school, but should also look carefully for any obvious discrepancies among parental educational level, job history, spoken language, written language, and effectiveness with regard to child rearing. For example, a parent with two doctoral degrees and an inability to hold a job may have a serious attentional problem. Another parent with excellent spoken language, excellent child care skills (superb practical intelligence), but with illegible handwriting and no high school diploma may be an adult with an undiagnosed learning disability. Such discrepancies often lack neat diagnostic labels at the same time that they virtually scream out their relevance.

Siblings. The focus on family history is a focus on genetics. It is surprising how people's understanding limits the practical implications of modern genetic findings. Everyone recognizes the heredibility of skin, hair and eye color, body habitus and facies, but under plays a similar inheritance of neurobehavioral traits.

Cousins, and other relatives. In eliciting a family medical history for a pediatric patient, conditions such as coronary artery disease, diabetes, stroke, and cancer frequently and inexplicably take predominance. This is very peculiar when dealing with young children whose risks for such conditions remain quite low. The general risk for neurodevelopmental disorders, on the other hand, is by comparison much higher. It is here that familial patterns can be especially helpful. A physician should routinely survey the family pedigree for relatives with ADHD or learning difficulties or simply school failure and academic underachievement. It is also important to identify relatives known as "black sheep," juvenile delinquents, criminals, substance abusers, those with significant psychiatric problems, late developers, and those who made sudden improvements or later deteriorations in their academic or social behavior across the life span. It is even more important (although often very difficult) to discover whether these relatives may have experienced learning and attentional difficulties before the full-blown onset of psychiatric problems in adulthood. Sometimes details about such relatives are a "family secret." Parental fears that their child might take after one of these members of the family tree may either precipitate or delay a referral or consultation.

One final point about the family history. Heredibility may relate more to the entire spectrum of neurodevelopmental disabilities rather than to a specific disorder. Thus, people inherit a tendency to develop allergies rather than an allergy to a specific food or pollen. Genetic dyslexia may run through a family pedigree, but it will be more common to encounter a family tree with mixed combinations of ADHD, NBSLD, and CD in the various members.

Perinatal History

The perinatal history needs to be placed in perspective against this backdrop of family history: the major factors to be investigated here include intrauterine exposure to toxins, fetal activity level, and asphyxia at birth:

Intrauterine exposure. Apart from other possible effects, it appears that intrauterine exposure to alcohol and cocaine are major risks for the later development of ADHD. Alcohol (but not cocaine) is also related to a spectrum of learning problems including mental retardation, learning disabilites, and communication disorders (Clarren 2000). Infants of substance abusing mothers (ISAM) have often been exposed in utero to an indeterminate potpourri of chemical substances, the final impact of which can be very difficult to predict.

Fetal activity level. Fetal hyperactivity noted in the third trimester is weakly associated with the later manifestation of ADHD with hyperactivity (Accardo et al. 1997). (Fetal hypoactivity is more strongly correlated with the later manifestation of mental retardation.) Attempting to quantitatively grade "excess" fetal activity can present difficulties. Many mothers, however, can readily make comparisons among their different pregnancies, while some singleton reports are sufficiently striking to receive note: "He kicked dad out of bed several times during the last trimester," "His gymnastics would keep me awake all night sometimes." Lest there be concern that parents who are "seeking" a label of ADHD for their child might fabricate such information, most parents of truly hyperactive children are often thoroughly surprised at the continuity of the child's excess motor behavior backwards into the prenatal period. Having been miseducated that all behavior is environmentally conditioned, these parents rarely even suspect such continuity or its implications.

Birth asphyxia. The original conceptualization of the "brain injured child" syndrome virtually equated static encephalopathy with perinatal asphyxia. More recent research suggests that this pathology is, in fact, one of the least common etiologies for later neurobehavioral problems (Accardo 1997). Nevertheless, its presence must be investigated if only to provide parents with appropriate reassurance. Apgar scores are typically irrelevant to the etiology or diagnosis of ADHD or learning disabilities. Spotting or bleeding during pregnancy, urinary tract infections (UTIs), and symptoms of placental insufficiency remain non-specific risk factors for later neurobehavioral problems and so may relate to learning and attentional problems.

Postnatal History

Postnatal medical factors that can contribute to the presence of ADHD include:

Lead exposure (clinical or subclinical lead poisoning). Needleman's work has explored the association between chronic low level lead exposure and later attentional and learning problems (Blondis and Chisolm 2000). These concerns contributed to a lowering of the recorded levels of blood lead that indicate intervention.

Serious head injury. Although serious head injury can produce cognitive or motor impairment, children much more commonly recover with some degree of attentional impairment; this may be either transient or permanent. In other words, the most common long-term sequela to serious head injury (itself uncommon) is ADHD. It needs to be pointed out, however, that milder head injuries, such as the typical falls of infancy and the toddler years, have no correlation with the onset of ADHD. Indeed, here the relationship is probably reversed in that toddlers with severe ADHD are probably more prone to accidents.

Meningitis/encephalitis. Central nervous system infections can also produce permanent cognitive, motor, and attentional impairments.

Parents will often be able to describe a change in their child's behavior first noted after recovery from such insults.

Hydrocephalus or other neurosurgical conditions. The association between neurosurgical procedures and relatively mild neurobehavioral disorders seems too obvious to mention except for the fact that it is often overlooked as contributing to the difficulties exhibited by such children receiving neurosurgical follow up in which the emphasis is restricted to disorders at the severe end of the spectrum.

Drugs. Certain drugs can have the effect of mimicking or worsening the symptoms of ADHD; chief among these are phenobarbitol and certain asthma preparations. Many children with ADHD demonstrate paradoxical reactions to a wide variety of drugs that can produce sedation or affect alertness. Thus, antihistamines and other sedatives frequently result in an ADHD child becoming "wired" and more hyperactive. (Such "paradoxical" responses often predict a positive response to treatment with stimulants.)

Infant Behavior

Behavioral difficulties frequently encountered in young children with ADHD include:

Decreased sleep duration in infancy as well as later sleep problems. On the one hand, many children with ADHD seem to truly require less sleep than same age peers; their proneness to keep alert and active into the night frequently contributes to family stress. On the other hand, one of the points in a differential diagnosis of ADHD is the impact of a possible sleep disorder: a child who snores, mouth breathes, and possibly grinds his teeth (bruxism) is likely to not be well rested in the morning. Lack of appropriate rest can certainly contribute to inattention and irritability during the day. Many ADHD children exhibit restlessness and excessive movement during sleep so that parents do not consider it possible for those children to be rested when, in fact, they are.

Colic/irritability in infancy. Classic infant colic occurs during the first three months of life at a particular time of day and for a limited duration (usually the evening hours); the irritability that can be associated with ADHD is more diffuse, occurring throughout the day and across the first year of life.

Feeding disorders. Attention deficit hyperactivity disorder is not typically associated with feeding disorders except for the infant who rushes during feeding; older ADHD children will tend not to sit for meals, but rather eat their meals on the run. Parents may find it difficult to discriminate this peculiarly mobile mode of eating from the ingestion of sufficient quantities of food. Meanwhile, the presence of true oral motor based feeding disorders in infancy remains a risk factor for later speech and language disorders and language-based learning disabilities, themselves associated with ADHD.

Advanced motor development. Some observers consider that ADHD children may be accelerated in their gross motor development. This may be true, in part because such children often lack the caution to wait for all the needed protective responses (such as the anterior parachute reflex) to evolve prior to rushing into trying their newly emerging skills. In other words, it may reflect more impulsivity rather than truly advanced motor coordination. Accident proneness is then understandably more common in these ADHD children with advanced motor milestones. For most children, the age for the onset of walking precedes that for running by several months; many hyperactive children run as soon as, if not before, they walk.

Speech and language disorders in infancy and early childhood present both diagnostic clues and diagnostic challenges. On the one hand, such problems are among the best early markers for later learning disabilities; on the other hand, a severe language delay can mimic an attentional deficit. This will almost certainly occur when the verbal-nonverbal discrepancy is on the order of 50 points. Its relevance to discrepancies of a lesser magnitude is not as clear: it is just as likely for both a communication disorder and an attentional deficit to co-occur at these lower levels.

Developmental Patterns

The timing of onset of school learning and behavioral problems can be helpful information in diagnosis (Accardo 1998). Understanding which patterns of neurobehavioral problems present at different ages can provide helpful clues to differential diagnosis.

Preschool. Learning disabilities are rarely seen in preschool. Attentional problems and speech and/or language delays are the most likely causes of difficulties in this age group. Attentional deficits with hyperactivity and impulsivity can lead to a toddler being expelled from day care or preschool. Changes in the pattern of maternal out-of-home employment have contributed to the well-documented increase in the diagnosis of ADHD among preschoolers.

KG-3rd grade. Only the most severe learning disabilities will be diagnosed in kindergarten (KG). Attentional deficits without hyperactivity will also tend to be overlooked. Attentional deficits with hyperactivity will, however, become noticed at this age level. Continuing on through the first three grades, mild learning disabilities and attentional disorders will contribute to a child's finding school work increasingly difficult and to the development of an increasingly negative attitude towards school, sometimes even with psychosomatic symptoms. Although the child may struggle, failure will be unlikely in the presence of normal cognitive ability and a supportive home environment. Indeed, the brighter child may very well excel during these early grades.

Oppositional defiant disorder is typically encountered in late preschool to early school age children. It should not be considered as an entity standing alone in the absence of a precipitating underlying neurodevelopmental disorder. Most children who become oppositional have neurobehavioral deficits in the form of attentional, communication, or cognitive deficits that limit their ability to comply (Accardo 1993). Focusing on type of discipline used is like grabbing the knife from the wrong end. Ineffective discipline needs to be reinterpreted from the ground up.

Petit mal. It is not uncommon for children with attentional problems but without hyperactivity to be referred for an EEG to rule out petit mal epilepsy. Most often these episodes represent daydreaming rather than true epileptic activity. The distinction can usually be clarified by the history rather than an electroencephalogram. Hyperventilation may also be used.

Fourth grade. This grade represents a "brick wall" for many students with milder or otherwise compensated learning and attentional problems. The first three grades emphasize rote learning of basic phonics and calculation (mathematics computation). The impact of a mild learning or attentional problem will often be compensated for by the continual repetition of the material to be learned. Fourth grade, on the other hand, demands that these previously mastered skills now be applied with facility to a large body of more complex and longer assignments (such as word problems and reading comprehension). This change in emphasis, targets the particular weaknesses of children with mild learning and attentional problems who have not mastered skills taught earlier (Accardo, Haake, and Whitman 1989). This phenomenon may occur earlier (late third grade) in private or parochial schools with accelerated curricula.

For school age children, discrepancies among academic grades, effort grades, group achievement scores, group and individualized standardized test scores, and homework can be very helpful in determining the presence of an attentional deficit or learning disability (Accardo and Lindsay 1998). Neurologically based specific learning disabilities tend to have a consistent impact on performance in given subjects or modes of learning and testing. For example, a child with a left brain deficit pattern will exhibit difficulty in reading and language-based learning but can still excell in mathematics and graphomotor areas. He or she will consistently succeed in the one and consistently struggle in the other.

In contrast, the child with ADHD will exhibit unpredictable variations in day-to-day performance across all subjects, sometimes excelling in reading and mathematics, and sometimes failing both subjects. Such diurnal fluctuation can be considered almost pathognomonic of ADHD children. The discrepancy can be noted by a parent when a child studies for a test and has mastered the work the evening before, only to perform unpredictably the next day in class, sometimes "acing" the exam and other times "drawing a blank."

When success in a cumulative subject area follows episodes of failure in the same subject, the intermittent failure can be interpreted as most probably secondary to an attentional deficit rather than to a failure to master the content. Alternately, many children with ADHD do well on group achievement tests because these are multiple choice tests with short answers as opposed to essay tests that tap attention span as well as knowledge. Similarly some children with attentional problems are struggling in class because a large part of the child's grade is based on the timely completion of in-class assignments and/or homework. Such children may be able to focus their attention sufficiently to do well on critical tests and final examinations only to have the teacher consider these "flukes" and unrepresentative of the child's classroom performance.

Such pure scenarios as described above are not very common because the majority of cases will present with a mixture of ADHD and NBSLD. On the other hand, they do occur, and the examiner should "never look a gift horse in the mouth."

The most serious "red flag" with regard to a possible disorder of learning and attention is the threat of retention. Accardo and Lindsay (1998) argued that retention is always and everywhere an unacceptable intervention; when retention is being considered, the student should be evaluated carefully for the presence of an attention or learning problem.

Middle school. The next major hurdle for children whose attentional or learning disorders push to the limit their abilitiy to compensate (and so incite what has been referred to as "high output failure") occurs with the onset of departmentalization in which the child moves from class to class and from teacher to teacher at least a half dozen times a day. This pattern removes the tremendous support provided by the structure and routine of a single teacher and classroom. Many ADHD children, and some with learning disabilities, handle change poorly; transitions place significant stress on their limited coping mechanisms.

Higher education. Some attentional and learning problems will not precipitate difficulties until a bright child is stressed by the lack of structure in college or by the high pressure of graduate or professional school (Accardo, Haake, and Whitman 1989). Such relativity in onset does not destroy the fundamental conceptualization of such high frequency, low intensity disorders. Dyslexia only became a problem when universal literacy became a requirement to function in a post-industrial society. Until societal expectations were increased, there was no such disability, despite the fact that the underlying neurocognitive profile was already present in the population.

Typically, the symptoms of ADHD ameliorate over time. Approximately half the children who are positive responders to pharmacological intervention will no longer demonstrate a sufficiently strong response to medication to warrant its continuation after age 15 years. In contrast to this general trend towards spontaneous improvement, certain specific diagnoses raise the possibility of worsening in adolescence. Fetal alcohol syndrome (FAS) appears to provide an example of such deterioration. This may relate not to the ADHD per se but to its association with more subtle cognitive and language impairments.

Long-term failure to adjust expectations and inaugurate appropriate accommodations and counseling options for ADHD and NBSLD can contribute to academic underachievement, poor self-image, and chronic sadness. This sadness can be distinguished from depression by its strong association with the school calendar: the child is much happier when academic pressures are removed, as during vacations and long holidays. With supportive counseling, such "depression" can disappear with surprising rapidity by the use of psychostimulant medication. Somatization (including stomach aches and head aches) can reflect this same emotional stress. Allowing them to continue undiagnosed and untreated can ultimately contribute to the evolution of a full blown depression that will require more prolonged therapy.

The Physical Examination

The physical examination contributes little to the final diagnosis of ADHD. Certain components of the examiner's interaction with the child can, however, provide important information in formulating a diagnostic impression.

Behavior. Most children (approximately 9 out of 10) who actually have ADHD will not exhibit any behavioral signs of the disorder during the routine office visit. For the one in ten who does, the physician should be able to discriminate the fairly inappropriate activity level and impulsivity from the more typical nervousness seen in a child in a doctor's office. For the remaining children, deficits in attention may be noted if the child's attention span is stressed by one of the tests below.

Language sample. Professionals who evaluate children need to familiarize themselves with how children talk and learn to assess a child's communicative style and abilities. There are several aspects of children's conversation that can support a diagnosis of ADHD. Some ADHD children are loud; others are described as chatterboxes ("motor mouth"), they talk very fast ("brain too fast for mouth"), they will blurt out embarrassing statements. Some of these speech patterns reflect a verbal hyperactivity, others a verbal impulsivity. Such children frequently interrupt others, many get into trouble for talking out of turn in class. For some children with severe ADHD, the free association and distractibility in their brain leads them to talk very tangentially, with little apparent connection between the fragments of their spoken language. To some observers, this pattern will seem to resemble the speech pattern of patients with schizophrenia.

Dysmorphology. The presence of more than four dysmorphic features (see table I) on physical examination strongly suggests an organic basis for any behavioral difficulties; in addition, the presence of significant dysmorphology further suggests the presence of ADHD-LD comorbidity (Accardo et al. 1991). Such dysmorphology can be useful in demonstrating to parents the presence of a non-environmental contribution to the child's developmental problems (Aase 1990).

Neurological assessment. The purpose of a neurological assessment is to rule out the presence of more serious underlying nervous system pathology. An expanded neurological assessment of "soft neurological signs" or signs of "minor neuromotor dysfunction" rarely contributes to the diagnosis but may correlate to the presence of visual motor and visual perceptual learning disability patterns.

Digit span. Digit span is a useful brief measure of attentional problems; discrepancies between digits forward and digits reversed can reflect right brain-left brain learning problems because digits forward is likely to be more impaired in left brain learning deficits while digits reversed is likely to be relatively more impaired in right brain learning deficits.

Raven's Progressive Coloured Matrices. The Raven's is an excellent brief screening test of cognition that is free of both verbal and visual motor components. Its administration can also provide a useful sample

Table I. Minor Dysmorphic Features Associated with Attentional Difficulties in Children

electric hair
hair whorl abnormality
absent hair whorl
multiple hair whorls ("cowlicks")
poorly defined hair whorl
clockwise hair whorl
frontal up sweep ("widow's peak")
head circumference more that 1.5 SD above or below the mean
epicanthal folds
hypertelorism
low-set ears
pinna abnormalities
malformed pinnae
protuberant pinnae ("jughead ears")
flattened pinnae
posteriorly rotated ears
absent ear lobules (adherent lobes)
high arched or steepled palate
geographic tongue
fifth finger clinodactyly (short fifth fingers)
fifth finger brachydactyly (curved fifth fingers)
palmar crease abnormality
simian crease (single palmar transverse fourfinger crease)
Sydney line (proximal fourfinger palmar crease)
hockeystick crease (distal palmar crease that ends between the second and third fingers)
sandal gap deformity of the first two toes
syndactyly (partial) of toes two and three
long middle toe

of the child's attentional behavior. Most of the items represent an increasing order of difficulty: children with ADHD are more likely to make errors on the easier earlier items and then improve as the item difficulty increases and demands greater attention. This erratic performance is often unpredictably mirrored in day-to-day school performance as well as on the Wechsler subscales where such dissociation can be remarked.

Drawing tests. Drawing tests can be useful from two different perspectives. First, they can provide an excellent brief psychiatric screening in those cases where associated emotional pathology is suspected. A bright, happy Draw-A-Person (DAP) and a similar Kinetic-Family Drawing (KFD) can tip the balance when the examiner is concerned about some vague emotional symptoms. Drawings can also be used to explore poor visual motor skills associated with both attentional disorders and right brain learning disabilities.

Laboratory

In the training of physicians, medical students are first taught that the history, carefully elicited, provides the diagnosis in most cases of illness. A physical examination is meant to confirm the diagnostic impression and only occasionally to correct it. Laboratory investigations should never offer any surprises to these results. Having been educated in this manner, residents are then counter-trained to rely more and more on the results of increasingly esoteric laboratory studies and refined non-invasive imaging scans—to the point of sometimes missing the patient who resides not in the lab values but in the history. It is then both excusable and understandable for miseducated parents who have been further misled by the scientific disinformation provided via the media and the internet to fall into this same trap and expect that the true diagnosis of ADHD lies in some type of "brain scan." There is no eletroencephalogram (EEG), CT, MRI, or SPECT scan that has a routine place in the assessment of ADHD (Doughtery et al. 1999; Accardo 2000a).

CONCLUSION

The data to be collected in order to identify a neurobehavioral condition such as ADHD can appear diffuse and confusing to the neophyte, but with a little practice, patterns emerge that will markedly facilitate the diagnosis. Aase (1990; Accardo 2000b) categorized the way physicians approach the diagnostic process according to the detective methods in the Sherlock Holmes Canon in the form of the following three processes:

The Scotland Yard (or Inspector Lestrade) method: a linear, left brain, detailed, "no stone left unturned" massive collection of data to then be sifted via an excruciatingly slow team process. This is the way the typical third year medical student painstakingly approaches a clinical problem; it remains appropriate for the novice or beginner. Duration for assessment: very long.

The Doctor Watson method: a right brain pattern approach to diagnosis. Such a visual gestalt approach works best for common conditions with common presentations; it is the way of the experienced practitioner. Duration for assessment: very brief.

The Sherlock Holmes method: this method combines "the worst" of the previous two approaches and is best suited for relatively rare conditions or uncommon presentations of more common disorders. It represents the experienced clinician's judgment in applying elements from both alternative methods. Duration for assessment: variable.

According to the Doctor Watson method, if (1) a child presents with a long history of symptoms compatible with ADHD, and these are reported by both the parent and the school, (2) there are no symptoms of anxiety or depression, no oppositional behavior or global sadness (or if the latter only developed after a protracted history of inappropriate responses to the child's attentional problems), (3) the presence of a neurobehavioral syndrome is supported by a positive family history, fetal hyperactivity, infant colic, dysmorphic features, or soft neurological signs, and (4) the impact of attentional and impulsive behaviors can be found in language, social, and academic areas, then a diagnosis of ADHD can be presumed. Such a simplified approach is more effective with younger children. Undiagnosed adolescents and adults may require more of a Scotland Yard approach simply because of an accumulation of historical garbage and the translation of interpretation into "fact" (such as when the patient has internalized the reading of laziness into his or her own experience of symptoms).

If a child presents with parent or teacher concerns about "inattention," "hyperactivity," struggling in school, failing in school, or at risk for retention, then the chances are close to two out of three (Accardo, Blondis, and Whitman 1990) that that child will, if appropriately assessed, qualify for a diagnosis of ADHD, and close to 90% that he will qualify for a diagnosis of ADHD, NBSLD or CD. This recommendation might be considered almost as striking as being told that a chief complaint of "headache" with no other specification indicated a brain tumor in two out of three cases, or that a chief complaint of "cough" with no other specification indicated lung cancer in two out of three cases. It is intended to be as striking, because it is true.

ACKNOWLEDGMENTS

The preparation of this chapter was supported in part by Grant #MCJ-369029 from the Maternal and Child Health Bureau (Title V, Social Security Act), Health Resources and Services Administration, Department of Health and Human Services.

REFERENCES

Aase, J. M. 1990. *Diagnostic Dysmorphology*. New York: Plenum Press.

Accardo, P. J. 1994. Conduct disorder versus oppositional defiant disorder: End point of learning disabilities. In *Learning Disabilities Spectrum: ADD,*

ADHD, & LD, eds. A. J. Capute, P. J. Accardo, and B. K. Shapiro. Parkton, MD: York Press.

Accardo, P. J. 1997. The "Expanded" Strauss Syndrome. In *Behavior Belongs in the Brain: Neurobehavioral Syndromes*, eds. P. J. Accardo, B. K. Shapiro, and A. J. Capute. Baltimore: York Press.

Accardo, P. J. 1998. ADHD: Clinical considerations. In *Consensus in Child Neurology*, ed. B. L. Maria. Hamilton, Ontario: B. C. Decker, Inc.

Accardo, P. 1999. A rational approach to the medical assessment of the child with Attention-Deficit/Hyperactivity Disorder. In *Attention Deficit Hyperactivity Disorder*, ed. A. Morgan. *Pediatric Clinics of North America* 46: 845–56.

Accardo, P.J. 2000a. SPECT scans for ADHD. *AAP Grand Rounds* 3:27–28.

Accardo, P.J. 2000b. The medical models for Sherlock Holmes. In *Sherlock Holmes Meets Father Brown and His Creator*, eds. P. J. Accardo, J. Peterson, and G. Hasnes. Shelburne, Ontario: Battered Silicon Dispatch Box.

Accardo, P. J., Blondis, T. A., and Whitman, B. Y. 1990. Disorders of attention and activity level in a referral population. *Pediatrics* 85:426–31.

Accardo, P. J., Haake, C., and Whitman, B.Y. 1989. The learning disabled medical student. *Journal of Developmental and Behavioral Pediatrics* 10:253–58.

Accardo, P. J., and Lindsay, R. L. 1998. Learning disabilities just don't add up. *Journal of Pediatrics* 133:320–21.

Accardo, P. J., Painter, M., and Capute, A. J. 2000. Neurodevelopmental disabilities in pediatrics and child neurology: The creation of a new pediatric subspecialty. *Journal of Pediatrics* 136:266–67.

Accardo, P. J., Tomazic, Morrow, J., Haake, C., and Whitman, B. Y. 1991. Minor malformations, hyperactivity, and learning disabilities. *American Journal of Diseases of Childhood* 145:1184–7.

Accardo, P. J., Tomazic, T., Fete, T., Heaney, M. S., Lindsay, R., and Whitman, B. Y. 1997. Maternal report of fetal activity levels in developmental disabilities. *Clinical Pediatrics* 36:279–83.

Blondis, T. A., and Chisolm, J. J. 2000. Plumbism. In *Attention Deficits and Hyperactivity in Children and Adults*, eds. P. J. Accardo, T. A. Blondis, B. Y. Whitman, and M. Stein. New York: Marcel Dekker.

Clarren, S. K. 2000. Attention deficit and hyperactivity in the context of alcohol exposure in utero. In *Attention Deficits and Attention Deficits and Hyperactivity in Children and Adults*, eds. P. J. Accardo, T. A. Blondis, B. Y. Whitman, and M. Stein. New York: Marcel Dekker.

Doughtery, D. D., Bonab, A. A., Spencer, J. J., Rauch, S. L., Madras, B. K. and Fischman, A. J. 1999. Dopamine transporter density in patients with attention deficit hyperactivity disorder. *Lancet* 354:2132–3.

LeFever, G., Dawson, K., and Morrow, A. 1999. The extent of drug therapy for attention deficit-hyperactivity disorder among children in public schools. *American Journal of Public Health* 89: 1359–64.

Zito, J. M.,Safer, D. S., dos Reis, S., Gardner, J. F., Boles, M., and Lynch, F. 2000. Trends in the prescribing of psychotropic medications to preschoolers. *Journal of the American Medical Association* 283:1025–30.

Chapter • 4

ADHD in Primary Care

Over diagnosed, Under treated, and Frequently Misunderstood

Mark A. Stein

Attention deficit hyperactivity disorder (ADHD) is an increasingly common referral problem for children, adolescents, and adults. Previous diagnostic terms for ADHD include: MBD (minimal brain dysfunction), hyperactivity, hyperkinesis, and ADD (attention deficit disorder). Diagnosis is complicated because the symptoms of this disorder overlap and co-occur with a variety of psychiatric, learning, medical, and social problems, and because currently the diagnosis is based primarily on a clinical description of ADHD symptoms. Clinicians vary significantly in diagnostic practices and the extent to which other explanations or "mimics" of ADHD have been ruled out.

Clinically significant attention deficits and hyperactivity appear to be prevalent, affecting 3% to 6% of American school children (Barkley 1991). More recent studies using DSM-IV criteria suggest that the prevalence may be increasing (Wolraich et al. 1996). Symptoms of ADHD include developmentally inappropriate over activity, short attention span, impulsivity, and distractibility, which must have an early onset, chronic course of at least 6 months, and be associated with significant impairment. Individuals with ADHD and their families frequently suffer from many related behavioral, social, learning, and medical problems, particularly academic underachievement, difficulties in peer relationships, disturbed parent-child relationships, adaptive dysfunction, and sleep difficulties (Barkley 1991; Cantwell and

Baker 1991; Henker and Whalen 1989; Lambert and Sandoval 1980; Stein et al. 1995; Stein 1999). Adolescents with ADHD also display increased rates of high-risk health behaviors, such as early smoking and poor driving (Stein and Roizen 1999).

In contrast to earlier views that most children "grow out" of these symptoms, evidence from several prospective studies indicate that significant emotional, behavioral, and academic problems continue into and through adolescence for 50% to 80% of ADHD youth (Fischer et al. 1990; Mannuzza et al. 1991). Moreover, for a small but significant subgroup of approximately 20%, ADHD is strongly associated with severe antisocial behavior and substance abuse (Lambert 1988; Gittelman et al. 1985; Satterfield, Satterfield, and Cantwell 1981; Hechtman and Weiss 1986; Weiss et al. 1979). This worrisome association is with ADHD, not treatment of ADHD. Importantly, several recent studies suggest that stimulant treatment is associated with decreased risk of later substance abuse (Biederman et al. 1997; Paternite et al. 1999). Thus, childhood hyperactivity is a serious, often chronic, neurobehavioral disorder and represents a prevalent and significant public health problem.

Children with suspected ADHD have constituted one of the most common referral problems in psychiatric outpatient clinics for several decades. However, during the previous decade, ADHD has become one of the most common disorders treated by primary care physicians (PCPs). Multiple factors including manpower issues, training, and changes in special education services and health insurance have all contributed to this change.

IF ALL YOU HAVE IS A HAMMER, EVERYTHING LOOKS LIKE A NAIL

Diagnosis of ADHD is strongly correlated with treatment with stimulant medications. Stimulant medications, such as methylphenidate (Ritalin), have a variety of non-disorder specific beneficial effects and are among the most studied and safest psychotropic medications (Klein and Wender 1995). At present, the majority of stimulant prescriptions in the United States are now written by primary care providers (PCPs) (data recently presented at the NIH Consensus Development Conference on ADHD; National Ambulatory Medical Care Survey 1994; Zito et al. 1999).

Recently, stimulant prescriptions have risen from about one-half to three-quarters of all pediatric office visits for ADHD (Swanson, Lerner, and Williams 1995). Safer and colleagues (Safer and Krager 1985, 1988, 1994; Safer, Zito, and Fine 1996) found increased levels of prescribing for all ages of children. Of recent concern, children below the age of 5 are more likely to be prescribed stimulant medications than in the past, despite decreased efficacy for this age group (Zito, et al. 1999). There is a paucity of studies of ADHD in this age group, and diagnosis appears to be much more difficult relative to school age children due to the overlap of ADHD with normal development and consequent decreased stability of ADHD symptoms from the preschool period.

To date, there have been only a few studies that have looked at community prescribing practices for ADHD (Angold et al. 2000; Jensen et al. 1999). The NIMH Multimodal Treatment Study of ADHD (MTA), provided a glimpse of community treatment. In this study, the children referred for community-based treatment improved less than did children receiving medication management or combined medication and psychosocial treatment. Children in the community group were likely to receive medications, but at lower daily dosages and fewer doses than those in the more effective treatment groups who typically received three times a day treatment. Nationally, it is unclear what percentages of children currently taking stimulant medication are appropriately diagnosed, as there are major regional and interregional differences in prevalence (Rappley 1997). It appears that ADHD is often under-diagnosed in inner city and rural areas where there is less access to treatment, and where numerous economic and sociocultural barriers to treatment exist, such as clinician and parent biases against stimulant treatment for behavior disorders such as ADHD. Moreover, there is some evidence to suggest that African-American children are less likely to receive or possibly accept recommendations for stimulant medication relative to SES matched controls, even when covered by insurance (Zito et al. 1998).

Over-diagnosis, on the other hand, may be more common in middle-class and upper middle-class areas where mental health services and pediatric care for school problems are more accepted, when parent and school tolerance for disruptive behavior is low, and where there is easy access to a prescribing physician. Often, consultation from a pediatric subspecialist (i.e., child psychiatrist, psychologist, developmental pediatrician, neurologist, or multidisciplinary team) is not available or covered by insurance carriers. These evaluation services may identify other problems or additional forms of treatment besides stimulant treatment. Although an earlier study by Jensen found that about half of children with significant ADHD symptom levels were receiving stimulant treatment (1999), a more recent study found that many children who were sub-threshold for ADHD were receiving stimulants (Angold et al. 2000). Clearly, much more needs to be learned about current management of ADHD in primary care. Several professional groups, including the American Academy of Pediatrics and American Academy of Child and Adolescent Psychiatry have come out with treatment guidelines for ADHD (Jensen et al. 1999;

Dulcan and Benson 1997). How often these guidelines are followed and, more importantly, if following these guidelines results in improved care, as yet has not been established. For example, the American Academy of Pediatrics recommends following DSM-IV criteria. However, it is unclear how often or how accurate primary care physicians are in identifying coexisting conditions such as learning disorders or evaluating school data.

The purpose of this chapter is to describe diagnostic and treatment practices for ADHD developed by the author and his colleagues, which can be applied by PCPs. Common problems in diagnosis and recommended practices are highlighted. According to Cantwell and Baker (1987), the evaluation and differential diagnosis of childhood psychopathology involves at least three steps: the diagnostic process itself; the use of diagnostic instruments to collect information; and a classification system. The goal of the research diagnostic process is to answer the following questions for each case:

1. Does the child have ADHD (Any Subtype) using DSM-IV criteria?
2. How severe are the disorder and the impairment?
3. What comorbid conditions and associated problems are present?
4. Are the symptoms primarily the result of normal development or a different pediatric or psychiatric disorder, condition, or treatment that may mimic ADHD?
5. What are the child and families' strengths and competencies?

Answering these questions will help educate the family and the patient, prepare and calibrate caregivers' expectations, correct misconceptions, and allow probabilistic statements to be made about prognosis and cost/benefits of treatment. It is also our experience that parents are more willing to follow treatment recommendations after a careful evaluation and diagnostic feedback session which demonstrates knowledge of the child, family, and the environment versus a quick diagnosis and prescription. Due to increasing and biased media attention targeting stimulant medication use, it is important for families to have confidence in the treatment team as well as the diagnosis. Unfortunately, this simply cannot be done in a 15-minute office visit. Although the diagnosis of ADHD may be accurate, lack of family confidence and the sensitive issues regarding medication use in children will increase the likelihood of inadequate and failed treatment.

Communicating diagnostic findings to the family and pediatrician is the initial step which should lay open a "blue print" for coordinated treatment of the multiple symptoms, problems, and impairments which characterize this heterogeneous disorder (Stein and Pearl 1998). In providing feedback, it is important to recognize that the severity of ADHD varies considerably, depending on the number of symptoms, degree of impairment and settings where impairment presents, and the number and types of co-morbid disorders. The majority of children with mild or moderate ADHD will not display symptoms during a brief office visit. It is helpful to convey and describe this to families. Myths persist about children with ADHD being unable to attend for short periods of time, watch TV, or play Nintendo. Almost all children with ADHD have difficulty paying attention at school and in other situations that require sustained mental effort, resulting in significant impairment.

The vast majority of clinic-referred children are present with co-morbid psychiatric and learning disorders (see figure 1). Assessment of co-morbidity is important since co-morbid psychiatric disorders are strongly related to persistence of impairment (Biederman et al. 1996), and should lead to the development of an appropriate treatment plan. Although co-morbid disorders may have similar etiologies, a comprehensive evaluation should also address potential etiological factors for each problem. For example, we recently saw a 9-year-old girl with poor attention, daytime tiredness, and snoring. The diagnosis of ADHD is deferred pending ENT intervention and monitoring of sleep. Outcome of ADHD youth is frequently dependent on treating the co-morbid disorder (e.g., Depression, Conduct Disorder, Learning Disability) as well as the ADHD symptoms. Given the poor prognosis of children with ADHD and co-morbid Conduct and Learning Disorders (Klein 1987), certainly more aggressive and intensive treatment should be considered for these children (i.e., darker shaded areas).

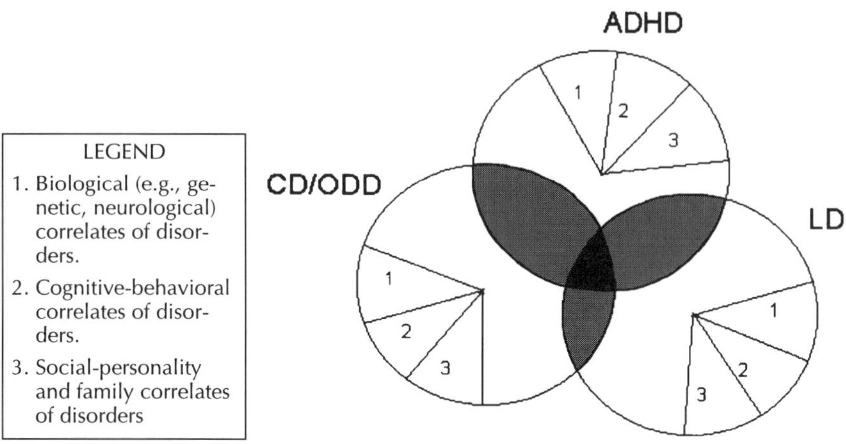

Figure 1. The "Olympic Circles" of Children who Present with Attentional Problems

QUANTIFYING SYMPTOMS AND SEVERITY

A diagnosis of ADHD should not be confused with a chief complaint of attention problems or impulsivity. We have found that 30% of children and 60% of adults who present with ADHD do not meet DSM-IV criteria for the disorder after undergoing a thorough evaluation which includes diagnostic interviews, rating scales, psychological testing, and a physical examination. Attention problems and over activity are nonspecific complaints that occur in a wide range of psychiatric and pediatric disorders, as well as in normal children. It is the clinician's job, based upon all the information available and his or her judgment, to determine if ADHD symptoms are developmentally appropriate, clinically significant, occur in more than one setting, and not primarily due to another pediatric or psychiatric disorder or social condition. If so, then a diagnosis of ADHD should be considered and a treatment plan developed.

There are many diagnostic instruments that may assist the clinician in the diagnostic process. Currently, the *gold standard* for diagnosis is a well-informed and experienced clinician who obtains relevant information from several informants, who knows the family and community, and has appropriate developmental norms. This is important because young children will display more ADHD symptoms than older children, adolescents, or adults.

RATING SCALES

For children, a well-normed rating scale can be extremely helpful in evaluating symptoms relative to age and gender expectations. For adults, it is more complicated as there are fewer validated instruments and often no informants other than the patient. Rating scales are inexpensive, efficient for the practitioner, and can provide a quick estimate of specific symptoms from the rater's perspective. It is important to emphasize that the validity of ratings is quite variable and that behavior ratings are primarily tools which clinicians should utilize. They are not a substitute for clinical judgement. In many, but not all cases, teacher ratings provide key information on ADHD symptoms in an environment that almost all children with ADHD display significant impairments. Since parent and teacher rating agreement is not as high as agreement between parents, it is important to determine reasons for lack of agreement. These may include rater bias, lack of familiarity with age appropriate behavior, or setting requirements that may mask ADHD symptoms (e.g., affluent family with nanny, decreased expectations on child, Montessori classroom). The clinician must evaluate the reliability of all information that is obtained and make a "best estimate" based upon that judgement.

Diagnostic Validity of Rating Scales

To evaluate the diagnostic accuracy of a brief screening procedure, parent- and teacher-ratings were compared with clinical diagnosis in a sample of 416 children referred to the Hyperactivity, Attention, and Learning Problems Clinic at the University of Chicago. A positive ADHD screen required significant scores on both parent (CBCL Attention T-score > 65 or CPRS Hyperactivity Index >15) and teacher (ACTeRS Attention or Hyperactivity < 20 percentile) ratings. Clinical diagnoses were based upon a multidisciplinary team consensus after a 6-hour evaluation consisting of diagnostic interviews, psychological tests, and a physical exam. Of those referred with a chief complaint of ADHD, 69% met diagnostic criteria for ADHD. Of those with ADHD, 65% received clinically significant ratings (sensitivity) on both parent and teacher ratings of ADHD symptoms. However, *almost half of those who were not diagnosed with ADHD* (n = 125) had a positive screen for ADHD. Thus, diagnosis should not be based exclusively on rating scales. Most common false-positives included children with Pervasive Developmental Disorder (38%), Mental Retardation (33%), Borderline IQ (24%), Oppositional-Defiant Disorder (18%), and Overanxious Disorder (12%). These results suggest only moderate sensitivity (0.65) and poor specificity (0.49) for an ADHD screen based upon rating scales. Rating scales are particularly helpful in measuring severity and impairment, as well as response to treatment.

ASSESS THE IMPAIRMENT ASSOCIATED WITH ADHD SYMPTOMS

Most people display ADHD symptoms at various times in their lives. This does not mean that everyone has ADHD. We do distinguish those with only a few persistent ADHD symptoms which have not adversely affected them (i.e., ADHD personality) from those who have displayed many ADHD symptoms along with associated impairment (i.e., ADHD, the psychiatric disorder). In children, this impairment is often demonstrated in areas such as academic underachievement, social difficulties, and sometimes demoralization or low self-esteem.

One way of quantifying impairment is by measuring the adaptive skills of ADHD children. "Adaptive skills" refers to the key social, communicative, and daily living skills that are required for independent functioning. Moderate to severe deficits in adaptive functioning are characteristic of clinic-referred children with ADD and ADHD (Barkley 1991; Roizen and Stein 1999; Stein et al. 1995). These deficits do not just affect school performance but virtually all areas of a child's life. Previous treatment strategies focusing on just treating ADHD in school or which involved parents performing the adaptive skill for the child are clearly not recommended, as discrepancies between adaptive functioning and IQ appear to increase with age (see figure 2).

In order to examine the specific adaptive skills that individuals with ADD/ADHD are typically deficient in performing, we examined the Vineland Adaptive Behavioral Scales (VABS) raw scores for 12- to 15-year olds with ADD or ADHD to determine the specific skills they were deficient in performing. As shown in table I, many individuals with ADHD infrequently make their bed, initiate phone calls, write letters, have hobbies, look after their own health, or develop long range plans. The prognostic significance of these performance deficits is obvious. Clinicians should develop treatment plans with adaptive prescriptions to gradually increase expectations and opportunities to perform adaptive skills.

While epidemiological studies of adaptive functioning of non-referred ADHD children are needed to insure that the results are not an artifact of clinic referral rather than ADHD per se, these data nonetheless provide convincing evidence that adaptive skills dysfunction is an important characteristic in children with ADD/ADHD who present for treatment. Clinically, adaptive skills may also highlight treatment relevant strengths. For example, a child with ADHD and strong social skills may have a better prognosis and would profit from opportunities to utilize this skill.

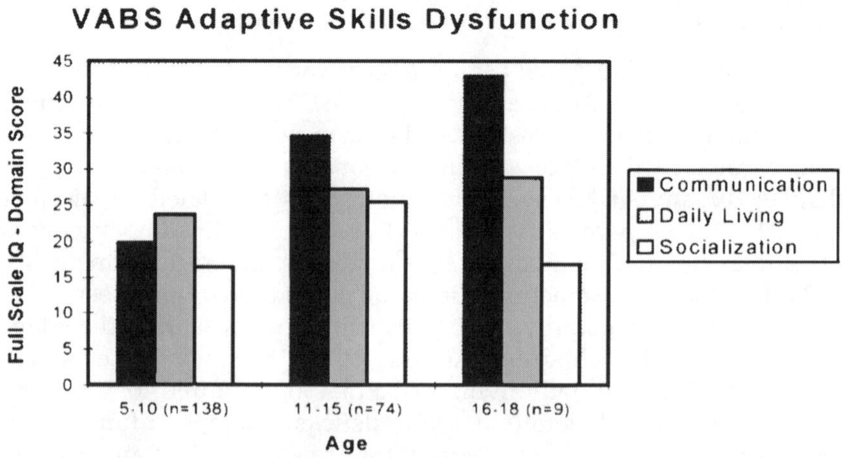

Figure 2. Adaptive functioning and ADHD

Table I. VABS Adaptive Skills Profile for Adolescents between 12 and 15 with ADHD[1]

Starting Age	Item number and description	No, never (%)	Sometimes, Partially (%)	Yes, Usually (%)
Communication Domain				
7, 8	48-prints/writes simple sentences of 3-4 words	0.0	3.4	96.6
	49-Attends to lecture more than 15 minutes	46.4	35.7	17.9
	50-Reads on own initiative	39.4	21.2	39.4
	52-Arranges items/words alphabetically	12.5	3.1	84.4
	53-Prints/writes short notes or messages	25.0	25.0	50.0
9	54-Gives complex directions	40.6	15.6	43.8
	55-Writes beginning letters	60.6	3.0	36.4
	56-Reads books of at least 4th grade level	5.9	0.0	94.1
	57-Writes in cursive most of the time	33.3	6.1	60.6
10-18	58-Uses a dictionary	45.5	33.3	21.2
	60-Writes reports/compositions	34.4	12.5	53.1
	61-Addresses envelopes completely	67.7	0.0	32.3
	62-Uses index in reading materials	36.4	22.7	40.9
	63-Reads adult newspaper stories	31.8	45.5	22.7
	64-Has realistic long-range goals and describes in detail plans to achieve them	63.6	22.7	13.6
Daily Living Domain				
	48-Initiates telephone calls to others	5.0	5.0	90.0
	49-Obeys traffic lights and Walk/Don't Walk signs	8.7	0.0	91.3
	50-Dresses self completely	4.5	0.0	95.5
	51-Makes own bed when asked	19.0	28.6	52.4
	52-States current day of the week when asked	8.3	4.2	87.5
	53-Fastens seat belt in automobile independently	29.2	16.7	54.2
7	54-States value of penny/nickel/dime/quarter	4.2	4.2	91.7

[1]Starting points were selected on the basis of the age at which 70% of the national standardization sample scored 2 (indicating "yes, usually"). Items in each domain are arranged in developmental order (Sparrow, Balla, and Cicchetti 1984).

Starting Age	Item number and description	No, never (%)	Sometimes, Partially (%)	Yes, Usually (%)
	55-Uses basic tools	13.0	21.7	65.2
	56-Identifies left/right on others	16.7	4.2	79.2
	57-Sets table without assistance when asked	8.0	28.0	64.0
8	58-Sweeps/mops/vacuums floor carefully	16.0	20.0	64.0
	59-Uses emergency phone number in emergency	0.0	4.2	95.8
	60-Orders own complete meal in restaurant	0.0	0.0	100.0
	61-States current date when asked	14.3	10.7	75.0
	62-Dresses in anticipation of weather changes	25.9	11.1	63.0
	63-Avoids persons with contagious illnesses	44.0	0.0	56.0
9, 10	64-Tells time by five-minute segments	21.9	9.4	68.8
	65-Cares for hair without being reminded	10.0	3.3	86.7
	66-Uses stove/microwave oven for cooking	10.0	13.3	76.7
	67-Uses household cleaning products correctly	31.0	24.1	44.8
11, 12	68-Correctly counts change from purchase over $1	20.0	3.3	76.7
	69-Uses phone for all kinds of calls	10.0	16.7	73.3
	70-Cares for own fingernails	51.6	6.5	41.9
	71-Prepares foods requiring mixing/ cooking	12.1	21.2	66.7
13-15	72-Uses a pay telephone	3.4	3.4	93.2
	73-Straightens own room	71.9	18.8	9.4
	74-Saves for/has purchased major recreational item	40.6	15.6	43.8
	75-Looks after own health	15.6	18.8	65.6
16	76-Earns spending money on a regular basis	40.6	25.0	34.4
	77-Makes own bed/changes bedding routinely	76.7	6.7	16.7
	78-Cleans room other than own	89.7	3.4	6.9
	79-Performs routine household repairs	87.0	13.0	0.0

Starting Age	Item number and description	No, never (%)	Sometimes, Partially (%)	Yes, Usually (%)
Socialization Domain				
	37-Has a best friend of the same sex	22.7	9.1	68.2
7, 8	39-Makes/buys small gifts	34.5	10.3	55.2
	40-Keeps secrets or confidences for more than a day	19.4	6.5	74.2
	41-Returns borrowed possessions	46.4	35.7	17.9
	42-Ends conversations appropriately	22.6	19.4	58.1
9	43-Follows time limits set by caregiver	37.5	15.6	46.9
	44-Refrains from embarrassing statements	25.0	28.1	46.9
	45-Controls anger when denied own way	75.0	9.4	15.6
	46-Keeps secrets/confidences for as long as appropriate	23.3	10.0	66.7
10, 11	47-Uses appropriate table manners	50.0	6.3	43.8
	48-Watches TV/listens to radio for information about a particular area of interest	25.0	9.4	65.6
	49-Goes to evening school/facility events with friends when accompanied by an adult	29.0	29.0	41.9
	50-Weighs consequences of actions	64.5	32.3	3.2
	51-Apologizes for mistakes	21.9	46.9	31.3
12-14	52-Remembers birthdays of family members	50.0	13.3	36.7
	53-Initiates conversations on topics of particular interest to others	17.9	28.6	53.6
	54-Has a hobby	37.9	13.8	48.3
	55-Repays borrowed money	48.1	18.5	33.3
15-18	56-Responds to hints in conversation	33.3	33.3	33.3
	57-Participates in non-school sports	25.0	7.1	67.9
	58-Uses TV/radio for information	37.0	18.5	44.4
	59-Makes and keeps appointments	40.0	16.0	44.0
	60-Watches TV/listens to radio for news	33.3	9.5	57.1

CO-MORBIDITY AND PSYCHOLOGICAL TESTING

In children, learning and behavioral problems commonly co-occur with ADHD. These learning and behavior problems always require additional interventions (e.g., school consultation, instruction in behavior modification or parenting skills, speech therapy). A smaller percentage of children with ADHD (10%–15%) may have co-morbid anxiety or mood disorders. In adults, co-morbid mood and anxiety symptoms occur in approximately half of those referred. Personality disorders and substance use disorders are also common. The differential diagnosis of ADHD, including mimic and co-morbid symptoms is displayed in table II.

Although a team approach to diagnosis is optimal, *the primary health provider can initially* evaluate for ADHD by reviewing rating scales for ADHD and other disorders; obtaining a history from parents, teachers, and the child; screening for non-psychiatric medical disorders (see shaded region in table II); and estimating developmental status. When there is significant psychiatric co-morbidity or family problems, the primary care provider may want to involve other professionals in questions of differential diagnosis (e.g., Tourette's,

Table II: Differential Diagnosis of ADHD[2]

Learning/ Developmental/ Social Disorders	Psychiatric Disorders	Medical Disorders/ Mimic Conditions
*Learning Disabilities (Reading Disorder, NVLD)	*Oppositional Defiant Disorder	*Sensory/Motor Impairments (hearing, vision); poor sleep or nutrition
Age-appropriate high activity level (in preschoolers)	Conduct Disorder	Chronic Illness (e.g. hypo, hyperthyroid, diabetes)
Speech and Language	**Mood or Anxiety Disorder	Seizures (absence)
Mental Retardation or Borderline IQ	Pervasive Developmental Disorder	Drug induced changes (e.g., anticonvulsants, steroids)
*Poor fit/improper expectations	**Situational Stress	Post-traumatic encephalopathy
*Chaotic School or home	**Substance Abuse (including stimulants)	Other genetic syndromes (Fragile X, FAE)
"ADHD Personality"	**Personality Disorders	CNS Infection
	Psychoses/Bipolar Disorder	Constipation/encopresis

[2]*occurs in at least 25% of ADHD children;
**occurs in at least 25% of ADHD adults

Anxiety, Resistance to Thyroid Hormone), such as psychologists, psychiatrists, neurologists, behavioral pediatricians, endocrinologists, speech pathologists, and educational consultants.

Identification of co-morbid symptoms and medical, psychiatric, and cognitive "mimic" conditions is the first step in treating ADHD. Due to the high rate of co-morbid learning disorders, in most cases *an individually administered IQ and achievement* test should be administered by a school or clinical psychologist, as misdiagnosis will lead to inadequate treatment. Schools can provide this, although there is often reluctance and a tendency to rely on screening tests which may not detect specific learning disorders. Figure 3 depicts a sample letter the primary care physician (PCP) can send to a child's school district to request testing. In many cases, the family may prefer independent testing which may not be covered by the child's insurance plan. This can be appealed, or the family can decide to pay out of pocket for this important activity, as treatment is clearly dependent on the adequacy of an evaluation. A multidisciplinary evaluation should be considered in cases that appear complex due to the degree of co-morbidity, potential mimics, or that have not responded to several interventions. These are usually provided at academic medical centers. The cost of such an evaluation at our center ranges from $1100 to $1700 and requires one day of testing and a feedback session a week later. Figure 4 contains a sample letter for insurers explaining why such care is needed.

To assist the clinician in considering possible mimic conditions, it is useful to begin with pediatric or medical mimic conditions first. Table II contains a list of potential mimic conditions. It is by no means exhaustive, as there are numerous medical conditions that can contribute to attention problems, hyperactivity, or impulsivity (Accardo et al. 1999; Pliszka, Carlson, and Swanson 1999).

To the Principal

Case Elementary School

One of your pupils, ______________________________, was referred to our practice for evaluation of ADHD. Since there are many learning problems that can mimic or coexist with ADHD, please administer an individually based intelligence test (such as the WISC-III) and an achievement test. This will help me in determining whether the child may also have ADHD and whether medical treatment is warranted at this time. The family will be in contact with you and sign a consent form so that I can be sent the results directly.

Thank you in advance for your assistance,

Dr. Stein

Figure 3. School District Letter

ADHD IN PRIMARY CARE

Indirect evidence suggests that primary care treatment may be less effective than other forms of treatment which have demonstrated short term effectiveness, such as structured medication management of behavior modification. The Multimodal Treatment Study of ADHD (MTA) study has provided one of the first glimpses of the effectiveness of community treatment of ADHD. Unfortunately, this first look suggests that non-standardized community treatment is significantly less effective than all other treatments in the MTA study, including medication management alone. With the reporting of the findings of the MTA, it is clear that there is a significant gulf between optimal treatments, such as the MTA Medication and Behavioral Treatment protocols, and community treatment (MTA Group 1999a, b). At first look, community treatment seems to consist of fragmented services and lower and fewer doses of stimulant medications. According to the MTA study design, 1/4 of families who contacted the research team were randomly assigned to the community control group, given a list of community referrals, and then followed up. Such a sample of patients and providers may differ significantly from how ADHD is treated in everyday clinical practice. It is unclear how closely the community treatment represents treatment by PCPs of their own patients.

There are many advantages to primary-care based programs, including: fewer barriers and stigma associated with primary care versus psychiatric settings; increased manpower in primary care versus subspecialty care; opportunities for earlier intervention which may reduce cumulative effects of the disorder; opportunities for coordination of mental health and health care; and opportunities for early intervention before co-morbid disorders and impairment have developed. Often times, PCPs are placed in the role of providing medication treatment, but given few resources for diagnosis, consultation, or management. Many managed care plans do not cover "counseling" or educational activities of the PCP, and mandate referral to "mental health carve outs" for psychosocial treatment. This is likely to reduce PCPs involvement in treating ADHD. Diagnostic evaluations are inconsistently covered, and often excluded. However, parents can often appeal, and a letter such as that contained in figure 4 may be helpful. Some insurers mandate referral to "mental health carve outs" for psychosocial treatment. The PCP may or may not have a relationship with the professional doing the evaluation recommended by the insurance company. Sometimes diagnostic evaluations are covered, often they are not and it is suggested by managed care companies that this is the responsibility of the school. Figure 3 contains a sample letter the PCP can send to the school. Even when there is cooperation between the

Dear Insurer:

I am employed by ____ and currently have chosen ____ 's plan as my current health care plan. We would like you to authorize payment for a multidisciplinary evaluation for my child such as those conducted at Children's National Medical Center Hyperactivity, Attention, and Learning Problems (HALP) Clinic.

I am writing to familiarize you with ADHD, which is a complex, frequently misdiagnosed childhood disorder that is viewed as biological in origin and whose treatment includes both medication and psychosocial interventions, such as behavior modification or school consultation. ADHD varies widely in severity: some children are affected predominantly in school, while others display the effects of this condition in a variety of settings. ADHD is also a chronic condition: approximately two-thirds of individuals diagnosed with ADHD continued to display the primary symptoms into adolescence. While there is general agreement among professionals as to the primary symptoms of ADHD, diagnosis is complicated by the wide range of severity and lack of a single diagnostic test. There are many biological factors (e.g., poor hearing, lead poisoning, seizures, genetic syndromes), behavioral and emotional factors (e.g., depression, anxiety) and social problems (e.g., inadequate fit between child and school, inadequate supervision) that can cause attention problems which must be distinguished from ADHD before treatment recommendations can be made. In addition, children with intellectual deficits and other types of learning disorders can also display attentional problems, further complicating diagnosis and treatment. Thus, the most accurate and most cost-efficient diagnostic and treatment approach for ADHD is a multidisciplinary approach involving physicians and psychologists who work together to evaluate children with suspected ADHD.

ADHD is a disorder whose diagnosis and treatment often does not fit neatly within managed care programs which require evaluation by a single provider, because its symptoms and associated problems overlap and often extend into different areas, some of which have traditionally been covered by medical insurance plans (i.e., prescriptions, blood tests, physical exams), while others (e.g., evaluation of learning disorders) have not. We are most concerned that our child receive appropriate and cost-effective care. According to my child's pediatrician, as well as my reading on the subject, ADHD evaluations should be conducted by someone experienced in ADHD, as well as other pediatric and psychiatric disorders. Certainly, referral to a mental health "carve out" service that is better suited to substance abuse or family interaction problems is inadequate and probably inappropriate for evaluation of ADHD. Also inadequate is diagnosis or empirical treatment with medication in lieu of an evaluation by a child-clinical psychologist, pediatric neurologist, developmental pediatrician, or child psychiatrist who can consult with my child's pediatrician.

I understand that the information gathered from multiple sources during one six-hour HALP-Clinic appointment will lead to the development of a diagnostic formulation and initial treatment plan that can assist us greatly and be followed up on by a child's pediatrician and us. The cost of the evaluation ranges from $650 - $1,500. Should you have questions about the procedure utilized or fees, contact ____________________.

Thank you for your interest in my child.

Sincerely,

cc: Company benefit coordinator

Pediatrician

Figure 4. ADHD letter for multidisciplinary evaluation

PCP, school, and mental health provider, these scenarios lead to *fractionated* care, which may significantly reduce effectiveness and consumer satisfaction.

Many PCPs have had little formal training in managing developmental disorders such as ADHD. As delineated by Rappley (1997), a variety of factors such as limited access to school and mental health resources and failure of insurance plans to recognize ADHD as a medical problem, contribute to a truncated diagnostic process for ADHD, and possible over-reliance on stimulant medication. ADHD is an example of a disorder with a relatively inexpensive treatment, stimulant medication, which is markedly effective in the short term. As a result, it is difficult to improve upon the effects of stimulant medication in short-term efficacy studies. ADHD psychosocial services provided outside of primary care are often "carved-out" to low cost providers. Such models may not be optimal for complex and chronic disorders such as ADHD, which require close collaboration between primary care and mental health providers. Also, the burden on families, costs, and consumer satisfaction of the carve-out model has not been experimentally evaluated. Thus, longitudinal effectiveness trials are needed such as this one which go beyond short-term efficacy studies to assess "real world" applicability and effectiveness.

SURVEY OF PEDIATRICIANS AND FAMILY PRACTITIONERS IN ILLINOIS

To assess provider attitudes toward ADHD and its treatment, a questionnaire survey of PCPs in Illinois regarding their ADHD practices was conducted by Darcy Bittner in 1996. When commenting on possible changes in the future of primary care treatment for ADHD, pediatricians and family practitioners who completed the survey made suggestions alluding to improved training and increased treatment possibilities for their ADHD patients. One family practitioner wrote, "I feel more primary care provider education would be a great boost to ADHD [diagnosis and prescription]." Five others gave similar responses. Some pediatricians were instead interested in seeing increased education of school officials about the nature of ADHD. Family practitioners also suggested standard assessments and use of a diagnostic team: "access to team evaluation of ADHD of multiple disciplines to try to avoid overdiagnosis." Pediatricians also wanted to see a team approach to diagnosis and treatment ("Low cost, comprehensive 'one stop shopping' evaluation by trained psychologists and social workers to help us with [evaluation]"), especially involving school personnel, and to see improved availability of psychological testing and services for needy families. Pediatricians and family practitioners were also interested in greater use of parent training in treatment of ADHD: "Increase access to parenting groups targeted to behavioral issues in ADHD families"; "Require that parents attend counseling sessions and try to get insurance to cover as preventative care." These comments highlight the difficulties of PCPs who are on the front lines of identifying and possibly treating ADHD, yet are hampered by limited training, time constraints, and restricted abilities to consult or refer for psychosocial treatments.

TREATMENT INNOVATIONS

Despite a long record of safety and short-term efficacy, stimulant medications have remained controversial (Swanson et al. 1993). There have been several treatment innovations and more are on the horizon that should increase the accessibility, acceptability, and ultimately, the effectiveness of treatment.

Several new, longer acting medications have been developed which may preclude the use of a noon dose at school, increasing the acceptability to children and parents who do not want others to know they are taking a medication. Adderall has been demonstrated to be as effective as short acting stimulants given twice daily (Pelham et al. 1999). However, most children with moderate to severe ADHD still require two doses of Adderall to target attention problems in the later afternoon or early evening. Concerta is a long acting methylphenidate-based drug delivery system that provides active treatment for up to 12 hours, which is comparable to three times a day methylphenidate in effects and side effects (Pelham and Gnagy 1999). The ascending patterned drug delivery profile may also have some advantages in terms of reducing or eliminating "stimulant rebound" symptoms or side effects as the medication wears off. Additionally, the once a day dosing should reduce opportunities for drug diversion or stimulant abuse as parents can supervise administration directly. Since many children with ADHD display impairments throughout the day, these longer acting treatments may facilitate improvement in other domains, such as social functioning (Stein et al. 1996). Due to less frequent dosing, treatment adherence may be significantly greater than with the short acting stimulants and consequently result in greater effectiveness.

There are also several new medications currently in the development phase. Tomoxetine hydrochloride, a selective noradrenergic reuptake inhibitor shows promise as a nonstimulant treatment for ADHD (Spencer et al. 1998). It will take several years, however, to assess the impact of these medications on the outcome of children and adolescents with ADHD.

Perhaps most encouraging are novel service delivery programs which attempt to reduce fractionated care by providing coordinated psychosocial and pharmacologic treatment services in the same setting. We have begun piloting such a program in Washington, D.C., *Novel and Effective Treatment for ADHD-Primary Care (NET-PC)*. In NET-PC, a pediatric psychologist spends one day per week in a pediatric office setting, conducting collaborative, interdisciplinary evaluations, screening children who should see a subspecialist, running parent training groups, and helping the pediatrician conduct titration trials. To date, we have been impressed by the high levels of consumer and pediatrician satisfaction. The challenge for this type of care will be convincing insurers that it is cost effective in the long run. Efforts are currently underway to determine this.

CONCLUSION

ADHD remains a common and often misunderstood condition. Considerable research suggests that ADHD is a complex, heterogeneous, highly familial condition whose symptoms are ameliorated or normalized with concurrent stimulant medication treatment. To date, the long-term outcome for the disorder has not changed. ADHD persists or is associated with a negative outcome approximately 20% to 30% of the time. ADHD is not just a childhood disorder, nor a disorder whose impact is limited to school hours. After school activities, homework, and family conflicts are part and parcel of the disorder and its treatment for most individuals. Consequently, a chronic illness model may be most appropriate for ADHD, whose symptoms, impairments, and need for treatments may change significantly over time. Treatment response could well be related to the ability to develop coping skills, compensatory strengths, protection from the cumulative effects of "undertreated" ADHD, and protection from environments which are toxic to individuals with ADHD. The pediatrician is in a unique position to identify children at risk for ADHD and to serve as "master of ceremonies" for directing coordinated evaluation and treatment services. Changes in pediatric training, our health care system, and the educational system are needed to optimally treat ADHD and make better use of existing resources, while decreasing fragmentation and inefficiencies in service delivery for this important disorder.

ACKNOWLEDGMENTS

This work was supported by grant K23-NHO-01823 from the National Institute of Mental Health and by grant MOI-RR13297 from the General Clinical Research Center Program of the National Center for Research Resources, National Institutes of Health. The author wishes to acknowledge the editorial assistance of Christopher Sarampote,

Ph.D. Much of the work described herein is the result of numerous clinical and research collaborations with Nancy Roizen, M.D. and Emily Szumowski, Ph.D.

REFERENCES

Accardo, P., Blondis, T., Whitman, B. Y., and Stein, M. A. (eds.) 1999. *Attention Deficits and Hyperactivity in Children and Adults.* New York: Marcel Dekker.

Angold, A., Erkanli, A., Egger, H. L., and Costello, E. J. 2000. Stimulant treatment for children: A community perspective. *Journal of the American Academy of Child and Adolescent Psychiatry* 39(8):975–84.

Barkley, R. A. 1991. *Attention-Deficit Hyperactivity Disorder: A Handbook for Diagnosis and Treatment.* New York: Guilford.

Biederman, J., Faraone, S., Milberger, S., Curtis, S., Chen, L., Marrs, A., Oullette, C., Moore, P., and Spencer, T. 1996. Predictors of persistence and remission of ADHD into adolescence: Results from a four-year prospective follow-up study. *Journal of the American Academy of Child and Adolescent Psychiatry* 35(3):343–51.

Biederman, J., Wilens, J., Mitch, E., Faraone, S., Weber, W., Curtis, S., Thornell, A., Pfister, K., Jetton, J., and Sorinao, J. 1997. Is ADHD a risk factor for psychoactive substance use disorders? Findings from a four-year prospective follow up study. *Journal of the American Academy of Child and Adolescent Psychiatry* 36:21–29.

Cantwell, D. P., and Baker, L. 1987. Differential diagnosis of hyperactivity. *Journal of Developmental Behavioral Pediatrics* 8(3):159–70.

Cantwell, D. P., and Baker, L. 1991. Association between attention deficit hyperactivity disorder and learning disorders. *Journal of Learning Disabilities* 24(2):88–95.

Dulcan, M., and Benson, R. 1997. AACAP official action. Summary of the practice parameters for assessment or treatment of children, adolescents, and adults with ADHD. *Journal of Child and Adolescent Psychiatry* 36(9): 1311–17.

Fischer, M., Barkley, R. A., Edelbrock, C. S., and Smallish, L. 1990. The adolescent outcome of hyperactive children diagnosed by research criteria: II. Academic, attentional, and neuropsychological status. *Journal of Consulting and Clinical Psychology* 58(5):580–8.

Gittelman R., Mannuzza S., Shenker R., and Bonagura N. 1985. Hyperactive boys almost grown up. I. Psychiatric status. *Archives of General Psychiatry* 42(10):937–47.

Hechtman, L., and Weiss, G. 1986. Controlled prospective fifteen-year follow-up of hyperactives and adults: Non-medical drug and alcohol use and anti-social behavior. *Canadian Journal of Psychiatry* 31(6):557–67.

Henker, B., and Whalen, C. K. 1989. Hyperactivity and attention deficits. *American Psychologist* 44(2):216–23.

Jensen, P. S., Kettle, L., Roper, M. T., Sloan, M. T., Dulcan, M. K., Hoven, C., Bird H. R., Bauermeister J. J., and Payne J. D. 1999. Are stimulants over-prescribed? Treatment of ADHD in four communities. *Journal of the American Academy of Child and Adolescent Psychiatry* 38:797–804.

Klein, R. 1987. Prognosis of attention deficit disorder and its management in adolescence. *Pediatrics in Review* 8(7):216–22.

Klein, R., Wender, P. 1995. The role of methylphenidate in psychiatry. *Archives of General Psychiatry* 52:429–33.

Lambert, N. M. 1988. Adolescent outcomes for hyperactive children. Perspectives on general and specific patterns of childhood risk for adolescent educational, social, and mental health problems. *American Psychologist* 43(10):786–99.

Lambert, N. M., and Sandoval, J. 1980. The prevalence of learning disabilities in a sample of children considered hyperactive. *Journal of Abnormal Clinical Psychology* 8:33–50.

Mannuzza, S., Klein, R. G., Bonagura, N., Malloy, P., Giampino, T. L., Addalli, K. A. 1991. Hyperactive boys almost grown up. V. Replication of psychiatric status. *Archives of General Psychiatry* 48(1):77–83.

MTA Group 1999a. A 14-month randomized clinical trial of treatment strategies for attention-deficit/hyperactivity disorder. *Archives of General Psychiatry* 56:1073–86.

MTA Group 1999b. Moderators and mediators of treatment response for children with attention-deficit/hyperactivity disorder. *Archives of General Psychiatry* 56:1088–96.

National Ambulatory Medical Care Survey 1994. Hyattsville, MD: Department of Health and Human Services, National Center for Health Statistics.

Paternite, C., Loney, J., Salisbury, H., and Whaley, M. A. 1999. Childhood inattention-overactivity, aggression, and stimulant medication history as predictors of young adult outcome. *Journal of Child and Adolescent Psychopharmacology* 9(3):169–84.

Pelham, W. E., Aronoff, H. R., Midlam, J. K., Shapiro, C. J., Gnagy, E. M., Chronis, A. M., Onyango, A. N., Forehand, G., Nguyen, A., and Waxmonsky, J. 1999. A comparison of Ritalin and Adderall: Efficacy and time-course in children with attention deficit hyperactivity disorder. *Pediatrics* 103(4):e43.

Pelham, W. E., Gnagy, E. M. 1999. Once-a-day Concerta (methylphenidate HCI) extended release tablets versus tid methylphenidate in natural settings: Safety and efficacy. Paper presented at the annual meeting of the American Academy of Child and Adolescent Psychiatry, Chicago, IL.

Pliszka, S. R., Carlson, C. L., and Swanson, J. M. 1999. *ADHD with Co-morbid Disorders: Clinical Assessment and Management.* New York: Guildford.

Rappley, M. D. 1997. Safety issues in the use of methylphenidate: An American perspective. *Drug Safety* 17:143–8.

Roizen, N., and Stein, M. A. 1999. Adaptive function in children with ADHD. In *Attention Deficits and Hyperactivity in Children and Adults,* eds. P. Accardo, T. Blondis, B. Whitman, and M.A. Stein. New York: Marcel Dekker.

Safer, D. J., and Krager, J. M. 1985. Prevalence of medication treatment for hyperactive adolescents. *Psychopharmacology Bulletin* 21(2):212–5.

Safer, D. J., and Krager, J. M. 1988. A survey of medication treatment for hyperactive/inattentive students. *Journal of the American Medical Association* 260(15):2256–8.

Safer, D. J., and Krager, J. M. 1994. The increased rate of stimulant treatment for hyperactive/inattentive students in secondary schools. *Pediatrics* 94:462–4.

Safer, D. J., Zito, J. M., and Fine, E. M. 1996. Increased methylphenidate usage for attention deficit hyperactivity disorder in the 1990s. *Pediatrics* 98: 1084–8.

Satterfield, J. H., Satterfield, B. T., and Cantwell, D. P. 1981. Three-year multimodality treatment study of 100 hyperactive boys. *Journal of Pediatrics* 98(4):650–5.

Sparrow, S. S., Balla, D. A., and Cicchetti, D. V. 1984. *Vineland Adaptive Behavioral Scales.* Circle Pines, MN: American Guidance Service.

Spencer, T., Biederman, J., Wilens, T., Prince, J., Hatch, M., Jones, J., Harding, M., Faraone, S., and Seidman, L. 1998. Effectiveness and tolerability of tomoxetine in adults with attention deficit hyperactivity disorder. *American Journal of Psychiatry* 155(5):693–5.

Stein, M. A., Blondis, T. A., Schintzler, E., O'Brian, T., Fishkin, J., Blackwell, B., Szumowski, E., and Roizen, N. 1996. Methylphenidate dosing: Twice a day daily versus three times a day daily. *Pediatrics* 98:748–56.

Stein, M. A., and Pearl, P. 1998. Conducting the feedback session. *The ADHD Report* 9:10–13.

Stein, M. A. 1999. Unraveling sleep problems in treated and untreated children with ADHD. *Journal of Child and Adolescent Psychopharmacology* 9:157–68.

Stein, M. A., and Roizen, N. 1999. Adolescent transitions and ADHD. In *Attention Deficits and Hyperactivity in Children and Adults*, eds. P. Accardo, T. Blondis, B. Whitman, and M. A. Stein. New York: Marcel Dekker.

Stein, M. A., Szumowski, E., Blondis, T., and Roizen, N. 1995. Adaptive skills dysfunction in ADD and ADD children. *Journal of Child Psychology and Psychiatry* 36(4):663–70.

Swanson, J., Lerner, M., and Williams, L. 1995. More frequent diagnosis of attention deficit hyperactivity disorder. *New England Journal of Medicine* 333(14):944.

Swanson, J., McBurnette, K., Wigal, T., Pfiffner, L., Lerner, M., Williams, L., Christian, D., Tamm, L., Willcut, E., Crowley, K., Clevenger, W., Khouzam, N., Woo, C., Crinellla, F., and Fisher, T. 1993. Effects of stimulant medication on children with attention deficit disorder: A review of reviews. *Exceptional Children* 60:154–62.

Weiss, G., Hechtman, L., Perlman, T., Hopkins, J., and Wener, A. 1979. Hyperactives as young adults: A controlled prospective ten-year follow-up of 75 children. *Archives of General Psychiatry* 36(6):675–81.

Wolraich, M. L., Hannah, J. N., Pinnock, T. Y., Baumgaertel, A., and Brown, J. 1996. Comparison of diagnostic criteria for attention deficit hyperactivity disorder in a county-wide sample. *Journal of the American Academy of Child and Adolescent Psychiatry* 35(3):319–24.

Zito, J. M., Safer, D. J., dosReis, S., Magner, L. S., Gardner, J. F., and Zarin, D. A. 1999. Psychotherapeutic medication patterns for youths with attention-deficit hyperactivity disorder. *Archives of Pediatrics and Adolescent Medicine* 153(12):1257–63.

Zito, J. M., Safer, D. J., dosReis S., and Riddle, M. A. 1998. Racial disparity in psychotropic medications prescribed for youths with Medicaid insurance in Maryland. *Journal of the American Academy of Child and Adolescent Psychiatry* 37:179–84.

Chapter • 5

The Use and Abuse of Behavior Checklists

Bruce K. Shapiro

Attention-deficit/hyperactivity disorder (ADHD) is a neurobehavioral syndrome, brain based in its mechanism, but expressed in behavioral terms. The mechanisms of ADHD have not been defined because this disorder is associated with many different etiologies. Even though ADHD exhibits no pathognomonic signs or laboratory findings, the disorder and its manifestations have been described for over 150 years. Attention deficit hyperactivity disorder is the most common disorder seen by child psychiatrists, neurologists, and psychologists. Children with ADHD consume more health resources (inpatient and outpatient hospitalizations, emergency department visits, and total medical costs) than children who do not have ADHD (Leibson et al. 2001).

Diagnostic criteria for ADHD are listed in table I. Attention deficit hyperactivity disorder represents a spectrum of dysfunction and not a categorical diagnosis. Thus, ADHD is not a disorder but a syndrome. Attention deficit hyperactivity disorder is diagnosed in two dimensions: the number of behaviors and the degree of impairment that results from each behavior. Individual behaviors are relatively insignificant because a single behavior, even to an extreme degree does not equate to the diagnosis.

In ADHD there are three distinct roles for behavioral measurement: diagnosis, evaluating management, and describing other conditions that may simulate ADHD. There are several methods for

Table I. Attention-Deficit/Hyperactivity Disorder

A. Either (1) or (2):

(1) six (or more) of the following symptoms of inattention have persisted for at least 6 months to a degree that is maladaptive and inconsistent with developmental level:

Inattention

(a) often fails to give close attention to details or makes careless mistakes in schoolwork, work, or other activities.
(b) often has difficulty sustaining attention in tasks or play activities
(c) often does not seem to listen when spoken to directly
(d) often does not follow through on instructions and fails to finish schoolwork, chores, or duties in the workplace (not due to oppositional behavior or failure to understand instructions)
(e) often has difficulty organizing tasks and activities
(f) often avoids, dislikes, or is reluctant to engage in tasks that require sustained mental effort (such as schoolwork or homework)
(g) often loses things necessary for tasks or activities (e.g., toys, school assignments, pencils, books, or tools)
(h) is often easily distracted by extraneous stimuli
(i) is often forgetful in daily activities

(2) six (or more) of the following symptoms of hyperactivity-impulsivity have persisted for at least 6 months to a degree that is maladaptive and inconsistent with developmental level:

Hyperactivity

(a) often fidgets with hands or feet or squirms in seat
(b) often leaves seat in classroom or in other situations in which remaining seated is expected
(c) often runs about or climbs excessively in situations in which it is inappropriate (in adolescents or adults, may be limited to subjective feelings of restlessness)
(d) often has difficulty playing or engaging in leisure activities quietly
(e) is often "on the go" or often acts as if "driven by a motor"
(f) often talks excessively

Impulsivity

(g) often blurts out answers before questions have been completed
(h) often has difficulty awaiting turn
(i) often interrupts or intrudes on others (e.g., butts into conversations or games)

B. Some hyperative-impulsive or inattentive symptoms that caused impairments were present before age 7 years.

C. Some impairment from the symptoms is present in two or more settings (e.g., at school [or work] and at home).

D. There must be clear evidence of clinically significant impairment in social, academic, or occupational functioning.

E. The symptoms do not occur exclusively during the course of a pervasive developmental disorder, schizophrenia, or other psychotic disorder and are not better accounted for by another mental disorder (e.g., mood disorder, anxiety disorder, dissociative disorder, or a personality disorder) (American Psychiatric Association 1994 pg 63–65) quantifying behavior: observation, direct measurement, interview, and behavioral checklists. Although one method may be of greater utility for a specific purpose, no method provides universal functionality. Attention deficit hyperactivity disorder is two inter-related behavioral syndromes: one of hyperactivity/impulsivity and another of inattention. For most children, both syndromes are present. Some children, however, only manifest the inattentive form of ADHD.

Observation of children in a number of settings by an experienced observer would be the "gold standard" for diagnosing ADHD. Direct observation is quite costly in terms of time, personnel and recording equipment, and the child may alter responses due to the presence of the observer. Sampling of school behavior should be performed in structured settings, such as the classroom, as well as unstructured conditions, such as the playground or cafeteria. Direct observation is further complicated by the need to obtain consent to observe other children interacting with the patient. Office observation is not the same as observation in more natural settings of school and play. Office observation is a poor method of diagnostic decision making. "If he is not hyperactive in my office, he is not hyperactive," has been disproved (Sleator and Ullmann 1981).

Behavior may be directly measured. Some examples of techniques that directly measure behavior are actigraphs to measure extremity movements, strain gauges that record seat-fidgeting, and rooms that count and map the number of times a preschool child crosses a light beam. Direct measurement of behaviors is relatively expensive because of the cost of the recording equipment. In contrast to direct observation, the observer does not know the context of the recording. High actigraph readings when a child is in church are quite different than when she is in gymnastics. Most of the research on direct measurement compares groups of "normals" to groups of children with ADHD, but the utility of direct measurement to diagnose individuals with ADHD has not been demonstrated (Dane et al. 2000).

Interviews depend upon an observer, usually the parent or teacher, to report behaviors of interest. The interviewer and the observer must coordinate their schedules to permit the transfer of data. Typically this is more difficult for teachers than parents. Observers may have their own agendas (e.g., are opposed to using stimulants), may not possess the information queried, or may be trying to please the interviewer. They may obscure their responses because the data is requested in an unfamiliar format, or they choose not to share the information, or they may report in excessive detail. Skilled interviewers inquire about key points in several ways to assure data accuracy.

Behavioral checklists are the most commonly used means of measuring behavior. They are quick, inexpensive, and do not require scheduling of interviews. Originally checklists were developed to measure the response of research subjects to medications. Recently, behavioral checklists have assumed a greater role in the diagnosis of ADHD.

This chapter considers the proper use of behavioral checklists for children with ADHD. Specifically we seek to answer the question, "Is it reasonable to use behavioral checklists to diagnose ADHD?" To answer this question requires the development of two arguments. The first focuses on the disorder. Is ADHD definable? The second focuses on the method. If either argument does not support the use of behavioral checklists, then there is no justification for the procedure.

DIAGNOSTIC ISSUES

Different aspects of attention dysfunction may be exhibited by children with ADHD. ADHD is not simply a lack of attention. Attention is a complex neuropsychological construct with multiple dimensions. Attentional capacity is influenced by memory/encoding abilities, timing characteristics (speed of presentation), spatial characteristics, cognitive resources of the subject, processing speed, arousal, effort generation, and motivation (Cohen and O'Donnell 1993). Measurement of attention is confounded by a number of cognitive and emotional processes: language, auditory processing, memory, anxiety, and depression. Some have suggested that attention is normal in ADHD and the deficit is in behavioral inhibition (Barkley 1997)

The diagnosis of ADHD is established by a series of behaviors that are functionally impairing, independent of the mechanism. This requires answering the question, "Is ADHD a homogenous syndrome?" If it is not, then it is doubtful whether a single checklist can capture sufficient information to diagnose the varied types of ADHD. Further, it is unlikely that sufficient diagnostic reliability can be achieved if there is substantial heterogeneity of the syndrome.

The diagnosis of ADHD is independent of mechanism, but defining the relationship between brain mechanisms and behavioral manifestations is not irrelevant. Mechanism-based diagnosis is necessary to advance the diagnosis of ADHD beyond a behavioral syndrome. Moving from a behavioral- to mechanism-based diagnosis will enable us to delineate which brain mechanisms result in an aberrant behavior (e.g., poor attention, language processing, or hearing may result in "failure to follow directions") and which behaviors may be the result of an aberrant brain mechanism (e.g., poor organization and forgetfulness).

Most children with ADHD do not exhibit all of the behavioral characteristics of the diagnostic criteria. Furthermore, the behaviors listed in the diagnostic criteria are not specific and may be seen in some children who are developing in a typical fashion, or in children with other disorders (e.g., language disorders, cognitive dysfunction, adjustment, anxiety, or affective disorders). A major task in the diagnosis of ADHD is distinguishing ADHD from secondary forms of inattention. Children with specific learning disabilities, receptive expressive language disorders, and pervasive developmental disorders may be misdiagnosed as having ADHD because their inattention and increased activity is generated from inability to perform the target work. Anxiety is commonly misconstrued as hyperactivity, affective disorder as inattention.

Not only are there differences between children but there is substantial variation within individuals. Individual children may manifest attentional dysfunction variably. Some children manifest more difficulty with attention in some situations than in others. For example, most children with ADHD adequately watch television or play video games. Many children with ADHD show inexplicable temporal variability. Some days children are functioning on "all eight cylinders" while on other days only "three cylinders" are firing. This gives rise to a common complaint that the child's decreased performance is volitional.

Existing information suggests that ADHD is expressed variably and that subgroups of children with ADHD can be defined (Fletcher 1991). Attention deficit hyperactivity disorder varies with age: younger children have increased hyperactivity while adults are more likely to present with inattention/disorganization. Sex differences have lead to longstanding under-diagnosis of girls (Gaub and Carlson 1997). There are cultural and socioeconomic influences on the expression of ADHD (Reid 1995). The absence of behavioral homogeneity would be less confounding if there were critical aspects that define the disorder.

Not only is there variation in the expressions of the disorder, there is also substantial variability in the diagnosis of ADHD. Without a pathognomonic finding, the diagnosis is a relative judgement. Most professionals exhibit adequate reliability when diagnosing ADHD, however, there is a substantial number of children who fall into a gray zone. Some professionals adhere to a very restricted view of ADHD and exclude these children. Others test the margins of the disorder. There is no clear point when a behavior transforms from annoying into impairing. To increase diagnostic reliability, the observed dysfunction must be present in a pervasive fashion. Practically, this requires ADHD to be present in more than two settings—home, school, play.

CHECKLISTS

Checklists that are used to quantify behavior in children may be grouped by those that are ADHD specific and those that are more general in approach. Table II lists the checklists, subscales, and conditions addressed.

ADHD Specific Checklists

The ADD-H: Comprehensive Teacher Rating Scale (ACTeRS)(Ullman et al. 1997) was developed for use with children 5 to 12 years of age. It consists of 24 questions that are relevant to classroom performance.

Table II. Behavioral Checklists

ADHD Specific Checklists	Subscales	Other Diagnoses Addressed
ADD-H:Comprehensive Teacher Rating Scales (ACTeRS)	Attention, Hyperactivity, Social skills, Oppositional Behavior, Early Childhood	Oppositional Defiant Disorder
Attention Deficit Disorders Evaluation Scale (ADDES)	Inattention, Hyperactive-Impulsive, Total	
Broad-Band Checklists		
Behavior Assessment System for Children (BASC)	Aggression, Hyperactivity, Conduct Problems, Anxiety, Depression, Somatization, Attention Problems, Learning Problems, Atypicality, Withdrawal, Adaptability, Social Skills, Study Skills, Behavioral Symptoms Index	Anxiety, Conduct Disorder, Depressive Disorder, Learning Disability
Child Behavior Checklist (Parent and Teacher Versions)* *Adaptive behaviors scales differ. Parent version has additional "sex problems" subscale.	Adaptive Scales, Withdrawn, Somatic Complaints, Anxious/depressed, Social Problems, Thought Problems, Attention Problems, Delinquent Behavior, Aggressive Behavior, Internalizing Composite, Externalizing Composite, Total Problem Scales	Anxiety, Conduct Disorder, Depressive Disorder, Learning Disability, Oppositional Defiant Disorder
Conners Rating Scales, 1997 Revised Version	Oppositional, cognitive problems, hyperactivity, anxious-shy, perfectionism, social problems, psychosomatic, Conners' global index (restless-impulsive, emotional lability), ADHD index, DSM-IV symptoms (inattentive, hyperactive-impulsive)	Anxiety, Depressive Disorder, Learning Disability, Oppositional Defiant Disorder

Questions are quantified on a 1 to 5 scale ranging from (1) being "almost never" to (5) "almost always." There is no frequency reference to any of the quantifiers. Summary scores are reported as percentiles or T-scores. Separate profiles exist for boys and girls. This measure has proved to be useful in monitoring medication effects. Because it was based on DSM-III criteria, the behaviors addressed do not directly map to the DSM-IV ADHD. The checklist does not identify other behaviors that may mirror ADHD. Companion Self Report and Parent forms were added subsequent to the second edition.

The Attention Deficit Disorders Evaluation System (ADDES) (McCarney 1995a,b) was standardized on a population of 4.5 to 19 year olds. Most of the data were collected from 6 to 16 year old children. Home versions (parent report) and school versions (teacher report) are available. Questions are quantified on a 0 to 4 scale: does not engage in behavior (0), behavior occurs one to several times per month (1), week (2), day (3), or hour (4). Scores are reported as standard scores and an overall percentile. Norms are reported by age and sex. The ADDES is not referenced to DSM IV criteria. It does not identify behaviors that may simulate ADHD. Separate checklists for adults have been developed.

Broad-Band Behavioral Checklists.

The Behavior Assessment System for Children (BASC) (Reynolds and Kamphaus 1992) was standardized on almost 10,000 children from ages 4 to 18 years. Parent (138 items), teacher (138 items), and self report (152 items) scales are available. A student observation system and a structured developmental history complete the system. Questions are quantified "never" (N) , "sometimes" (S) , "often" (O), "almost always" (A). Positive and negative dimensions of behavior are included. Scores are reported as percentiles or T-scores. Norms exist for age groups, sex, and clinical and general populations. The BASC maps to DSM criteria.

The Child Behavior Checklist for Ages 4 to 18 (CBCL4/18) is based on a principal components analyses of parents' ratings of 4,455 clinically referred children and normed on 2,368 children aged 4 to 18 (Achenbach 1991). It includes 118 items that describe specific behavioral and emotional problems, plus two open-ended items for reporting additional problems. Parents are asked to rate on a three point scale how well each item describes their child at the time of evaluation or within the past six months. Quantifiers are: "not true," "somewhat" or "sometimes true," and "very true" or "often true." The quantifiers are not frequency referenced. Percentiles and T-scores are reported. The teacher form has 93 items in common with the parent report form but ratings are based on a two-month period of observation. The CBCL/4-18 is not referenced to DSM criteria.

The Revised Conners Teacher Rating Scale (CTRS-R) (Conners et al. 1998a) was developed using 1,702 students ages 3 to 17 years. The checklist scores 38 behaviors of the previous month are scored on a 4 point Likert scale. Problems are rated as "not at all" (never, seldom), "just a little true" (occasionally), "pretty much true" (often, quite a bit), or "very much true" (very often, very frequent). Boys and girls are scored separately. Scoring was collapsed into three age groups: 3 to 7 years, 8 to 12 years, and 13 to 17 years. T-scores are reported and some DSM criteria are referenced.

The Revised Conners Parent Rating Scale (CPRS-R) (Conners et al. 1998b) was developed using a sample of 2,200 students from 3 to 17 years old. It is an 80 item scale that scores behaviors of the previous month on a 4-point Likert scale. Problems are rated as "not at all" (never, seldom), "just a little true" (occasionally), "pretty much true" (often, quite a bit), and "very much true" (very often, very frequent). Fourteen subscales including an ADHD index, DSM-IV symptoms result, and T-scores are reported.

CHECKLIST ISSUES

Measurement

Checklists must meet the same standards of reliability and validity as other clinical assessment instruments. Reliability can refer to three separate conditions: test/retest, multiple assessors, and stability across time. Most reliability testing is conducted in a test/retest fashion, where a checklist is administered at a point in time and repeated at a later time. The degree to which responses agree between test administrations is a measure of reliability. Most behavior checklists are not developed for use in a longitudinal or predictive fashion. Thus, the instability of these measures over time may be related to the changes that occur with ADHD or the alterations/accommodations that occur in the environment after the diagnosis is made. Reliability also refers to the ability of multiple assessors to come to the same conclusion at the same time. Common examples of this include parents and teachers rating the same child, or assessments from multiple teachers.

Validity is the degree to which a test actually measures what it purports to measure. For ADHD, studies have found that checklists correspond fairly well to each other (Bussing et al. 1998; Cohen 1990). Other studies compared behavior checklists of children to their performance on continuous performance tasks, actigraphs, matching familiar faces, and other questionnaires (Barkley 1991; DuPaul et al. 1992,

Reichenbach et al. 1992). In composite, the studies report a disparity between checklists and other measures of cognition and attention.

Another measure of validity is internal consistency. Internal consistency is a measure of the correlation of the component questions to the total score. Although commonly used as a measure of validity, in the absence of external validation, internal consistency reveals little of what a test measures.

In addition to having adequate validity and reliability, behavioral checklists must distinguish children with ADHD from those without ADHD. Classification abilities include sensitivity, specificity, and predictive value. Sensitivity is the ability to detect a child with ADHD. Specificity is the ability to correctly classify children who do not have ADHD within the general population. Positive predictive value is the proportion of children who have ADHD of the total number of children who have positive tests (*Children with ADHD*/Total number of positive tests). This latter statistic is a measure of false positives. Predictive values are dependent upon the number of affected children within the study population. In clinically derived populations with higher than normal prevalence of ADHD, predictive values are larger. Kappa is a statistic that accounts for the prevalence of a disorder in the sample. Alternatively, in the case of ADHD, one can assume a population of 1,000 children with an ADHD prevalence of 6% (see table III for example). Table IV lists the sensitivity, specificity, and calculated positive predictive value based on these assumptions for the ADDES, CPRS-R, CTRS-R. Generally the ADHD-specific checklists did fairly well. The ADHD Index and DSM-IV Symptoms subscales of the CPRS-R and CTRS-R were particularly good in distinguishing subjects with ADHD from those without ADHD but the ACTeRS was poor (Wong et al. 1999). Statistics are not presented for the BASC or CBCL4/18. The broad band behavioral checklists did not provide data to determine their ability to diagnose ADHD.

Table III. Classification abilities of the ADDES

	ADHD POSITIVE	ADHD NEGATIVE	TOTAL
ADDES POSITIVE			
	28.8	103.4	132.2
	(48%)	(11%)	PPV = 21.8%
ADDES NEGATIVE			
	31.2	836.6	867.8
	(52%)	(89%)	NPV = 96.4%
TOTAL	60	940	1,000

Sensitivity 48%, Specificity 89%, Prevalence 6%, Population size 1,000 (sensitivity and specificity data from Bussing 1998). PPV= predictive value of a positive test. NPV = predictive value of a negative test.

Table IV. Classification abilities of Behavioral Checklists

Checklist	Sensitivity	Specificity	Positive Predictive Value
ADDES	0.48	0.89	0.218
CPRS-R	0.923	0.945	0.517
CPTR-R	0.781	0.91	0.364

Good reliability, validity and classification abilities obtained in the research setting are not guarantees that behavioral checklists will be effective in clinical use.

Why Checklists Fail: Test Characteristics

Inadequate definition of the quantifiers, variable time of observation, absent referents, vague questions and lack of assignment of the relative importance of symptoms to the diagnosis are some of the test characteristics that trouble behavioral checklists. Most of the checklists do not present enough information to allow respondents to interpolate the extremes of the scale. Does several times an hour exclude several times a day (ADDES)? How do you distinguish between "very much" and "pretty much" (CTRS-R, CPRS-R)? Is "almost never" "somewhat true"?

Behavior checklists also are inconsistent in the time span used to sample behavior. The only checklist that assesses the length of time stipulated in the diagnosis of ADHD is the CBCL4/18. In others, the range of observation extends a month (ADDES, CTRS-R, CPRS-R). The BASC and ACTeRS do not stipulate a time of observation.

The structure of the questions is troublesome. Most questions are worded in the negative. Only the BASC assesses positive aspects of behavior. Some questions are difficult to quantify because the comparative reference is not identified; e.g., impulsive, does not listen to what others are saying, restless, or overactive.

The content of the questions are also problematic. Age is an important factor in ADHD, yet the wide age of sampling, approximately 4 to 17 years, does not permit evaluation of age-specific behaviors. Using behaviors that span such a wide age range hinders the ability to discern the immaturity that is commonly seen in children with ADHD. Assessing all behaviors as equal leads to "right column kids," but no data is available that would permit quantifiable differentiation of individual behaviors to improve the classification by checklists.

Consequently, the ranges that separate normal from abnormal behavior are restricted and children are over-identified. For example, a 10 year old girl who scores one point responses—"Just a little true" (occasionally)—on all 12 behaviors of the CTRS-R ADHD Index will have a T-score of 63. (A score of 14 will yield a T-score of 70). If a child has a few behavioral characteristics that are present to a great degree (3 point responses) he will likely be assigned into the ADHD category (see Reid and Maag 1994).

Why do checklists fail: Reporting characteristics

Interviews are strengthened by the ability of the interviewer to clarify, validate, and translate the responses of the respondent. Behavioral checklists do not have that safety net and, therefore, rely on the ability of the respondent. Those abilities may be limited because the respondents see different behaviors, view the same behavior differently, or are limited in their ability to report.

The most common reporting differences are seen between parents and teachers. Many studies show that the agreement between parents and teachers on the same checklists is less than those of parents or teachers on different checklists (Cohen 1990; Mitsis 2000). These differences are attributed to teachers and parents observing different behaviors. However, this does not explain the differences seen when checklists are completed by multiple teachers (as in the case of middle school). Speculation may attribute the variance in this condition to time of day, subject content, and the teacher's tolerance for deviation.

Some observers see the same behavior and interpret it differently. One person's hyperactivity is another's enthusiasm. This is not uncommon between parents and extended family members, and occasionally seen between fathers and mothers. These differences emphasize that behavior is not quantified in isolation. Behavior is interpreted within a context. Checklists cannot use context to interpret the results. As an example, one parent reported no hyperactivity for her son who was jumping off the examination table. When queried about her response she replied, "His brother is worse."

Behavioral checklists may fail because of blunted reporting or defensiveness. Respondents may be unwilling or unable to call behavior extreme. Thus, the questionnaire reports middle of the road responses that may or may not place a child into a clinically significant category. Sometimes respondents minimize or maximize behavior because of an external agenda, e.g., sidestepping the diagnosis of ADHD to avoid the use of stimulant medication. Finally, some respondents are defensive about reporting because they feel that a poor score on the behavior checklist reflects poor teaching or poor parenting abilities.

Limitations of the respondent also limit the ability of checklists to quantify behavior. This may be the result of contamination by recent events, severity of the behavior, or the "piling on" phenomenon. The "piling on" phenomenon is noted when a positive response generates more positive responses. Parents may struggle to decide whether the checklist is seeking a report of behavior before the treatment program started at school. Trying to quantify six months' worth of behavior with a single checklist may be impossible for the parent of a child who manifests variable behavior. Severe behavior also may contaminate responses. Yesterday's behavior flare may offset the good progress of the past month. Concomitant aggression tends to increase all negative behavioral responses (Abikoff et al. 1993). Finally, some respondents cannot read the questionnaire but will complete it.

CONCLUSIONS

Behavioral checklists have many positive attributes to commend them. They are time efficient, are inexpensive and are easily scored. However, they cannot be endorsed as a primary means of diagnosing ADHD. The lack of homogeneity of the ADHD syndrome mandates that symptoms must be obtained through skillful history taking and then interpreted by knowledgeable professionals to establish the proper diagnosis. The degree to which behavioral checklists aid clinical care has yet to be determined (Power and Ikeda 1996). There is not enough data to determine how well checklists reflect change nor how well they predict later behavior.

ACKNOWLEDGMENTS

Supported in Part by Grant MCJ 249149, MCH Training Program in Neurodevelopmental Disabilities, Maternal and Child Health Bureau of the Health Resources & Services Administration, Department of Health and Human Services. The author acknowledges the editorial assistance of Melissa Shapiro in the preparation of this manuscript.

REFERENCES

Abikoff, H., Courtney, M., Pelham, W. E., and Koplewicz, H. S. 1993. Teacher ratings of disruptive behaviors: The influence of halo effects. *Journal of Abnormal Child Psychology* 21:519–33.

Achenbach, T. M. 1991. *Manual for the Child Behavior Checklist/4–18 and 1991 Profile*. Burlington, VT: University of Vermont Department of Psychiatry.

American Psychiatric Association 1994. Quick Reference to the diagnostic criteria from DSM-IV. Washington, D.C: *American Psychiatric Association*.

Barkely, R. A. 1991. The ecological validity of laboratory and analogue assessment methods of ADHD symptoms. *Journal of Abnormal Psychology* 19:149–78.

Barkley, R. A. 1997. Behavioral inhibition, sustained attention, and executive functions: Constructing a unifying theory of ADHD. *Psychological Bulletin* 121:65–94.

Bussing, R., Schuhmann, E., Belin, T. R., Widawski, M., and Perwien, A. R. 1998.Diagnostic Utility of two commonly used ADHD screening measures among special education students. *Journal of the American Academy of Child and Adolescent Psychiatry* 37:74–82.

Cohen, M., Becker, M. G., and Campbell, R. 1990. Relationships among four methods of assessment of children with attention deficit-hyperactivity disorder. *Journal of School Psychology* 28:189–202.

Cohen, R. A., and O'Donnell, B. F. 1993. Models and mechanisms of attention: A summary in *The Neuropsychology of Attention,* ed. R. A. Cohen. New York: Plenum

Conners, C. K., Sitarenios, G., Parker, J. D. A., and Epstein, J. N. 1998a. Revision and restandardization of the Conners Teacher Rating Scale (CTRS-R): Factor structure, reliability, and criterion validity. *Journal of Abnormal Child Psychology* 26:279–91.

Conners, C. K., Sitarenios, G., Parker, J. D. A., and Epstein, J. N. 1998b. The Revised Conners' Parent Rating Scale (CPRS-R): Factor structure, reliability, and criterion validity. *Journal of Abnormal Child Psychology* 26:257–68.

Dane, A. V., Schachar, R. J., and Tannock, R. 2000. Does actigraphy differentiate ADHD subtypes in a clinical research setting? *Journal of the American Academy of Child and Adolescent Psychiatry* 39:752–60.

DuPaul, G. J., Anastopoulos, A. D., Shelton. T. L., Guevremont, D. C., and Metevia, L. 1992. Multimethod assessment of attention-deficit hyperactivity disorder: The diagnostic utility of clinic-based tests. *Journal of Clinical Child Psychology* 21:394–402.

Fletcher, J. M., Morris, R. M., and Francis, D. J. 1991. Methodological issues in the classification of attention-related disorders. *Journal of Learning Disabilities* 24:72–77.

Gaub, M., and Carlson, C. L. 1997. Gender differences in ADHD: A meta-analysis and critical review. *Journal of the American Academy of Child and Adolescent Psychiatry* 36:1036–45.

Leibson, C. L., Katusic, S. K., Barbaresi, W. J., Ransom, J., and O'Brien, P. C. 2001. Use and costs of medical care for children and adolescents with and without attention-deficit/hyperactivity disorder. *JAMA* 285: 60–66.

McCarney, S. B. 1995a. *The Attention Deficit Disorders Evaluation Scale.* 2nd ed. [home version technical manual]. Columbia, MO: Hawthorne Educational Services, Inc.

McCarney, S.B. 1995b. *The Attention Deficit Disorders Evaluation Scale.* 2nd ed. [school technical manual]. Columbia, MO: Hawthorne Educational Services, Inc.

Mitsis, E. M., McKay K. E., Schulz, K. P., Newcorn, J. H., and Halperin, J. M. 2000. Parent-Teacher concordance for DSM-IV attention-deficit/hyperactivity disorder in a clinic-referred sample. *Journal of the American Academy of Child and Adolescent Psychiatry* 39:308–13.

Power, T. J., and Ikeda, M. J. 1996. The clinical utility of behavior rating scales: Comments on the diagnostic assessment of ADHD. *Journal of School Psychology* 34:379–85.

Reichenbach, L. C., Halperin, J. M., Sharma, V., and Newcorn, J. H. 1992. Children's motor activity: Reliability and relationship to attention and behavior. *Developmental Neuropsychology* 8:87–97.

Reid, R., and Maag, J. W. 1994. How many fidgets in a pretty much: A critique of behavior rating scales for identifying students with ADHD. *Journal of School Psychology* 34:339–54.

Reid, R. 1995. Assessment of ADHD with culturally different groups: The use of behavioral rating scales. *School Psychology Review* 24:537–60.

Reynolds, C. R., and Kamphaus, R. W. 1992. *BASC, Behavioral Assessment System for Children* [manual]. Circle Pines, MN: American Guidance Services, Inc.

Sleator, E. K., and Ullmann, R. K. 1981. Can the physician diagnose hyperactivity in the office? *Pediatrics* 67:13–17.

Ullmann, R. K., Sleator, E. K., Spraguc, R. L., and MetriTech Staff. 1997. *ACTeRS* Teacher and parent forms manual. Champaign, IL: MeriTech, Inc.

Green, M., Wong, M., Atkins, A., Taylor, J., and Feinleib, M. 1999. Diagnosis of Attention-Deficit/Hyperactivity Disorder. Technical Review Number 3. (Prepared by Technical Resources International , Inc. under Contract No. 290–94–2024) AHCPR Publication No. 99–0050. Rockville, MD: Agency for Health Care Policy and Research.

Chapter • 6

Clinical Diagnosis of ADHD
A Medical Perspective

Larry B. Silver

At this time there are no formal tests to establish the diagnosis of attention deficit hyperactivity disorder (ADHD). Unfortunately, there are no specific physical examination findings or blood, urine, brain imaging, brain wave, or other neurological findings that establish the diagnosis, although there are excellent psychological tests, computer-based tests, and rating scales in use today. Each will be discussed later in this chapter. The data collected from these assessment instruments might clarify that a child or adolescent is hyperactive and/or inattentive/distractible, and/or impulsive. However, none of these evaluations will clarify the reason that this individual has one or more of these behaviors. The clinical problem in establishing a diagnosis is that there are many causes of hyperactive, distractible, and impulsive behaviors with children, adolescents, and adults. The reason for the behaviors must be clarified to make the diagnosis.

The only way we currently have for finalizing the proper diagnosis is by taking a *clinical history*. A history is information obtained from the individual, parents, teachers, others, and previous records that lead to a diagnosis. This chapter will focus on this diagnostic process.

Some say that ADHD is the "disease of the 90s." Everyone seems to have it, thinks he or she has it, or wishes he or she had it so there would be an explanation for his or her problems. It is true that the number of individuals diagnosed with ADHD has increased significantly over the past 10 to 15 years. However, the reason for this is an increasing awareness of this disorder as a result of specific educational efforts focused on parents and teachers. Through the efforts of parent organizations, the print and electronic media, and a plethora of books, more parents and classroom teachers have learned about ADHD and what behaviors suggest that the child or adolescent might have this disorder. Thus, more students have been recognized and referred for evaluation. Also, more physicians have learned about ADHD and make this diagnosis rather than a behavioral diagnosis. Further, in the past 10 years the concept that adults can have ADHD has been recognized; therefore, more adults are now diagnosed.

Part of the difficulty is that there are many reasons for the behaviors seen with ADHD. The most common cause of hyperactivity, distractibility, or impulsivity with children, adolescents, and adults, is *anxiety* which makes them unable to sit still or pay attention, and they may be irritable or snap at others. The second most common cause of these behaviors in any age group is *depression*. Individuals may have agitated depression, in which case they are restless, have difficulty maintaining focus on anything, and may be irritable. Others may have psychomotor retardation. They will be withdrawn and may not want to get out of bed or leave home. When with other people, they feel that they are walking around in clouds and have difficulty listening or talking to others. They appear to be inattentive and not focusing. The third most common cause of hyperactivity, distractibility, and impulsivity in any age group is one of the other *neurologically based disorders*. A child with learning disabilities might appear to be not paying attention or not staying on task because of the impact these disabilities have on learning. A child with sensory integration disorder and tactile sensitivity might be fidgety and squirmy. A child or adolescent who has obsessive compulsive disorder might be distracted by her or his intrusive thoughts or behaviors. *The least common cause of hyperactivity, distractibility, and/or impulsivity in any age group is ADHD.*

Perhaps the reason some children and adolescents are misdiagnosed with ADHD is that the clinician involved does not know of this differential diagnostic issue and does not use the appropriate approach for making the diagnosis. A teacher tells a parent that his or her child can not sit still and pay attention. This parent goes to the family doctor and repeats these concerns. The family doctor prescribes Ritalin. I often say to family doctors, if a child came in with the complaint of lack of energy and listlessness and you noticed that the inner lining of his eyelids are pale, would you conclude that the child was anemic and start treatment? No, you would get the necessary blood work and other studies done first so that the correct diagnosis can be made. The same approach must be made with children or adolescents who come into the family doctor's office with the complaint that they are overactive, inattentive, or impulsive. This information starts a diagnostic process. It is necessary to collect the other essential information before making the diagnosis.

I will review the official criteria for diagnosing ADHD. Then I will review the differential thinking to clarify if the person with these behaviors has an anxiety disorder, depression, another neurologically based disorder, or ADHD. Or, to clarify if the person has ADHD plus one or more of these other areas of difficulty.

THE OFFICIAL CRITERIA FOR ADHD

The official guidelines used by health and mental health professionals to diagnose ADHD is found in *The Diagnostic and Statistical Manual of Mental Disorders*. This is published by the American Psychiatric Association. This manual is now in a fourth edition; thus, the brief name for it is DSM-IV.

Some parents become upset that ADHD is listed as a mental disorder in a psychiatric publication. It is often helpful to explain to these parents how this process happened. The World Health Organization consists of representatives from each nation represented in the United Nations. One of the goals of this organization is to have a common definition of all medical disorders with specific criteria for diagnosing each. In this way there can be uniformity around the world in diagnosing diseases; thus, there can be uniform data collected on diseases. These guidelines are developed and finalized by committees made up of representatives from around the world. Once agreed upon, each member nation must follow these guidelines. About every ten years, the World Health Organization publishes an updated set of guidelines called the *International Classification of Diseases*. The current form is the 10th edition, called ICD-10. Once published, each nation must modify its own classification system to conform with the ICD. In the United States, the American Medical Association is given this task. The edition of the ICD modified for the United States is called the *International Classification of Diseases—Clinically Modified* or *ICD-CM*. The current one, the 10th edition, is the *ICD-CM-10*. The American Medical Association assigns different parts of the diagnostic system to the appropriate specialty organization to prepare this revised publication. The World Health Organization defines what is a "mental disorder." The American Medical Association assigns these disorders to the American Psychiatric Association to update the existing guidelines in the United States to conform with the new guidelines from the ICD. These changes are published as the *Diagnostic and Statistical Manual of Mental Disorders*. As mentioned, DSM-IV reflects ICD-CM-10.

Much of what we knew and practiced in the past when working with mental disorders was based on our understanding of the mind. Knowledge of the brain was not yet available. With the major explosion, over the past 20 to 30 years, of knowledge of the brain and of the mind-brain relationships, many mental disorders once thought of as psychologically based are now understood to be neurologically based with possible psychological consequences. Attention deficit hyperactivity disorder is one of these disorders. Thus, it may not be inappropriate to have ADHD listed in this manual.

In DSM-IV, ADHD is clarified using five major steps, each with specific criteria:

ATTENTION DEFICIT HYPERACTIVITY DISORDER

A. Presence of either (1) or (2) as listed below:

(1) Six (or more) of the following symptoms of inattention have persisted for at least 6 months to a degree that is maladaptive and inconsistent with developmental level:

Inattention

(a) often fails to give close attention to details or makes careless mistakes in schoolwork, work, or other activities
(b) often has difficulty sustaining attention in tasks or play activities
(c) often does not seem to listen when spoken to directly
(d) often does not follow through on instructions and fails to finish schoolwork, chores, or duties in the workplace (not due to oppositional behavior or failure to understand instructions)
(e) often has difficulty organizing tasks and activities
(f) often avoids, dislikes, or is reluctant to engage in tasks that require sustained mental effort (such as schoolwork or homework)
(g) often loses things necessary for tasks or activities (e.g., toys, school assignments, pencils, books, or tools)
(h) is often easily distracted by extraneous stimuli
(i) is often forgetful in daily activities

(2) Six (or more) of the following symptoms of hyperactivity-impulsivity have persisted for at least 6 months to a degree that is maladaptive and inconsistent with developmental levels:

Hyperactivity

(a) often fidgets with hands or feet, or squirms in seat
(b) often leaves seat in classroom or in other situations in which remaining seated is expected

(c) often runs about or climbs excessively in situations in which it is inappropriate (in adolescents or adults, may be limited to subjective feelings of restlessness)
(d) often has difficulty playing or engaging in leisure activities quietly
(e) is often "on the go" or often acts as if "driven by a motor"
(f) often talks excessively

Impulsivity

(g) often blurts out answers before questions have been completed
(h) often has difficulty awaiting turn
(i) often interrupts or intrudes on others (e.g., butts into conversations or games)

B. Some hyperactive-impulsive or inattentive symptoms that caused impairment were present before age 7 years.
C. Some impairment from the symptoms is present in two or more settings (e.g., at school [or work] and at home).
D. There must be clear evidence of clinically significant impairment in social, academic, or occupational functioning.
E. The symptoms do not occur exclusively during the course of a pervasive developmental disorder, schizophrenia, or other psychotic disorder and are not better accounted for by another mental disorder (e.g., mood disorder, anxiety disorder, dissociative disorder, or a personality disorder.)

In DSM-IV, three subtypes of ADHD are noted. The clinician is to clarify which type the individual has:

1. **Attention Deficit Hyperactivity Disorder, Combined Type:** To be used if both Criteria A1 and A2 are met for the past 6 months.
2. **Attention Deficit Hyperactivity Disorder, Predominantly Inattentive Type:**
   To be used if Criterion A1 is met but Criterion A2 is not met for the past 6 months.
3. **Attention Deficit Hyperactivity Disorder, Predominantly Hyperactive-Impulsive Type:**
   To be used if Criterion A2 is met but Criterion A1 is not met for the past 6 months.

One word of caution before moving on. There are many books available today for parents to read about ADHD. Most are good. Some are excellent. Popular books do not have to meet the same standards as professional books. Thus, a parent might read a book that uses the terms attention deficit hyperactivity disorder or attention deficit disorder.

However, the author presents his or her own criteria for this diagnosis. Some authors let it be known in the beginning that they do not follow the DSM-IV guidelines; however, some do not. There are books that do an excellent job of describing many aspects of ADHD. However, the criteria used for saying that someone has ADHD is not the same as the official guidelines. It is not infrequent for me to see an adult or parent who read one of these books and concluded that he/she or the son/daughter has ADHD. The individual meets the characteristics described in the book but does not meet the official criteria; therefore, I cannot make the diagnosis.

THE DIFFERENTIAL DIAGNOSTIC PROCESS

The three presenting behaviors are hyperactivity, inattention, and/or impulsivity. Let me review again each of these behaviors before focusing on the diagnostic process.

Hyperactivity

Most hyperactive children and adolescents are not running around the room or jumping on the furniture; some might be, but most are not. What we see is fidgety and/or squirmy behavior. Their fingers are tapping, their pencils are moving, their legs are swinging, they are up and down from their desk or the dinner table. Something is always in motion. Parents may report that the child is equally restless at night, moving about the bed. Some may show what appears to be "verbal hyperactivity." They seem to talk constantly.

Inattention

In all previous editions of the *Diagnostic and Statistical Manual of Mental Disorders*, this behavior was listed as distractibility. In DSM-IV, the name was changed to inattention. There is no clear explanation of the difference between these two terms. Many use them interchangeably.

Before being specific about inattention, it is important to review the broader concept of attention and attentional disorders. Researchers on attentional disorders clarify that there are three tasks involved in attending: (1) the ability to seek out what needs to be attended to and attend to it; (2) once attending, the ability to maintain this attention; and (3) once the task is complete, the ability to stop attending and move on to something else.

The most common cause of problems with the first task, *seeking out and attending*, is avoidance. The child or adolescent knows there is homework to do but keeps putting off (procrastinating with) the task.

"I just want to watch one more TV show," or "I'll do it soon. I promise." Or, he or she might start to do the homework, then get up to get a drink, later to get a snack, later to call a friend, and later to take a break. (When you have several tasks to do, somehow the one you least want to do keeps being bumped to the bottom of the list.) Avoidance is best understood by looking at what is being avoided. Perhaps the student does not know how to do the homework or has learning disabilities. Avoidance is not ADHD.

The second task is the ability to *sustain one's attention* once the task is initiated. Children and adolescents who are anxious, worried, or depressed might have difficulty maintaining attention. If the environment is too noisy or stimulating (doing homework at the kitchen table as dinner is being prepared, or trying to work in a classroom that is too noisy), it will be difficult to concentrate. If the work is too hard or not understood, attention will wander. If the individual has difficulty screening out unimportant stimuli from what is being focused on, sustaining attention will be hard. Only the last of these examples might be ADHD.

Inability to complete the third task, *breaking away from the task and moving one's attention to another task*, might be a result of the current task being too much fun. A child is watching TV and is told it is time to go to bed so the TV has to be turned off. The child will not want to do so. Or, the child is playing a computer game and is told to turn it off and start homework. There are neurological disorders that result in difficulty with stopping one task to start another. This difficulty is called perseveration. A child or adolescent with obsessive compulsive disorder may have difficulty stopping one task to move onto another until the necessary thoughts or behaviors are completed.

Looking at the full picture of attentional problems, it is clear that ADHD is one of the possible causes for difficulty with the second task, sustaining attention once a task is started. Often avoidance or not wanting to stop something that is more pleasant is misinterpreted as ADHD.

There appear to be two general groups of problems as far as inattention or distractibility are concerned. Some people may show evidence of external distractibility and others may show evidence of *internal distractibility*.

External Distractibility. Some children have difficulty screening out unimportant sounds or sights. They have *auditory* or *visual* distractibility. A child or adolescent (or adult) with auditory distractibility seems to hear everything. She or he is sitting in a room doing homework and hears a car going by outside, a sister talking in the next room, the phone ring, or the dog's tale wagging. In school, this child is distracted by the sound of footsteps in the hall. College students often say they have to study in a small room on the top floor of the library with the door shut. If they study in the main area of the library, they hear the person next to them turn the page or the sound of the pencil on the page. Adults report that they can only work when their door is shut or they wait until everyone goes home to work. The sound of talking, the computer, the printer, each distracts them.

Individuals with visual distractibility will notice everything around them. A student is working and starts to look at the design of a rug, or a poster, or out of the window. She or he is talking to friends in the cafeteria and begins to look at what other people are wearing. A child is playing soccer and looking into the sky or at the grass. Parents may report that their child has difficulty getting dressed in the morning. He or she starts to dress and the parent leaves the room. Then the child sees something and starts to play with it. Then they see something else and their attention changes. This parent comes back in and finds the child playing and begins to yell, "I told you to get dressed." A child or adolescent is sent to get something by a parent or teacher and never seems to get there. On the way, he or she sees something (a book or game) and starts to use it. Then, something else is seen and attention changes again.

I am reminded of a mother who described what had happened several days prior to our meeting. She went into the kitchen to start dinner, and as she walked in she saw some papers on the kitchen table and decided to sit down and go over them. While she was working on these papers she looked up and noticed a yellow stickum attached to her phone and remembered that she needed to make a phone call. While she was on the phone, she looked across and saw something on a counter. When she got off the phone she went to the counter. At this time, her children came in and asked when dinner would be ready.

Some children with both auditory and visual distractibility might show what is called "sensory overload" when in a very stimulating environment—a birthday party, a busy shopping mall, the circus. It is as if so much is coming in and bombarding the brain that these children are overloaded. They might be irritable, cry, hold their ears, or want to leave.

Occasionally parents describe their adolescent's study habits and question how they could have auditory distractibility. Their teen can only study with music playing in the background. I have had so many adolescents describe in the same way why they do this that I believe their reason. If they study in total silence, they hear every little blip or sound in the house. The music acts as white noise. They get used to it and do not pay attention to it. The music helps them not be distracted by other sounds.

Internal Distractibility. This form of distractibility is not fully understood; thus, different professionals may define it differently. It is more commonly found with adolescents and adults, and seen less with children. I will share my understanding of this problem. I see two types of internal distractibility. For want of a term to describe what I hear described, I coin these two types as *drifting* and *jumping*.

Drifting means daydreaming. We all daydream at times. However, for these individuals, the daydreaming occurs all of the time—in school (or at work), with friends, or with family. Each example given might be experienced by all people. It is the consistency over time that is different. The adolescents or adults might start to read a page. Their eyes go down the page but their mind is someplace else. They have no idea what they read. They are in class and the teacher is talking. They wander off and miss what is said. They are with friends and everyone is talking. Their thoughts wander off and they do not hear what is said. Parents, teachers, friends, (and employers) might see that "glassy" or blank look in their eyes. Some are called "airheads" or "space cadets." One girl joked that her friend often said, "Earth to Susan. Earth to Susan. Come in Susan." Any of these examples might be seen with everyone. Again, it is the consistency over time in all situations that distinguishes drifting from normal daydreaming.

Jumping behavior is something that confuses others and frustrates the person with the problem. Our mind is always busy. We have many thoughts going on at the same time. Most people can screen out all but the thoughts that need to be focused on. Individuals with the jumping form of internal distractibility cannot. They have multiple thoughts going on at the same time. They might make a comment from three thoughts away and everyone looks puzzled about what the comment has to do with what is being talked about. This person may start to do something, then his or her thoughts jump to something else. Thus, their activity shifts to another task or activity. Another jump and they change again. Their life is full of piles of incomplete activities.

Impulsivity

Impulsive behavior is usually described as the inability to stop or difficulty with stopping to reflect before speaking or acting. Some will have difficulty stopping to think before speaking. Others may have difficulty stopping to think before acting. Most have both problems.

These children or adolescents might interrupt in class, calling out before being called on. Or they might blurt out an answer or interrupt a teacher while he or she is working with another student. At home, this is the son or daughter who continues to interrupt parents while they are on the phone or talking to someone else. These people may say something to a friend before thinking and hurt the friend's feelings. As soon as they say it they are sorry; but, it is too late. Adolescents and adults often become aware of this problem and work at controlling it.

Some act before thinking. A young child might grab something, knock someone else's blocks down, push into line, or hit. Older children might continue these behaviors, or they might write down or say the first answer they think of without reflecting first. Older individuals might do dangerous behaviors because they do not think before they act. Adults might buy something before thinking through if they can afford it, or they might quit a job before getting another. Adolescents and adults with ADHD might have a poor driving record with more accidents than most.

Children and adolescents who are impulsive are at risk for certain other behaviors. We do not always understand the connection, but we look for them. They might still be bed wetters, be fascinated with fire or matches, or they might have a problem with stealing.

MAKING THE DIAGNOSIS

As is clear by now, the main difficulty in making the diagnosis is differentiating between the many causes of these behaviors. The first step is data collection. The interview with parents and with the child or adolescent, psychological test results, data from specially designed computer performance tests, and scores on rating scales will help to clarify if someone has one or more of these three behaviors. But this information will only lead to the diagnosis of ADHD if the clinical history can document that the presenting behaviors of hyperactivity, distractibility, and/or impulsivity have a chronic and pervasive history. Let me clarify why this is essential.

The "Other" Causes of These Three Behaviors

Anxiety. The most common cause of hyperactivity, inattention/distractibility, or impulsivity is anxiety. Anxiety can be a reflection of psychological stress or conflict or reflective of a specific anxiety disorder. This psychological stress might be the result of an academic problem. When anxious, the child or adolescent might be physically active. As with adults, anxious feelings result in the need to be active. Also as with adults, when anxious, it is hard to pay attention or to maintain focus. Daydreaming or escaping into TV are not uncommon. If children or adolescents have learning disabilities, they might become anxious when asked to perform in their areas of weakness. Thus, during reading group they begin to fidget. When sitting at the desk doing a worksheet, they become frustrated and look around the room or out of the window. They might have no problems sitting or attending when the tasks relate to their strengths. For example, they might have excellent language skills and have no problem sitting still and attending during periods of class discussion.

Depression. Again, depression might reflect a psychological conflict or stress or might reflect a specific mood disorder. This psychological stress might be reflected by a poor self-image and low self-esteem resulting from learning disabilities. Depression can be experienced at all ages. Sometimes it is difficult to clarify whether the child or adolescent is primarily depressed; whether the depression is a result of learning disabilities; or, whether both are present, possibly along with ADHD.

> Chris was 10 years old and in the fifth grade when I was asked to do a consultation. He had been in individual and group therapy for two years because of emotional problems and depression. He was unhappy in school and not doing his class work or his homework. A psychological and educational evaluation was done by his school system 18 months earlier that showed evidence of learning disabilities. However, the team of evaluators concluded that "his weaknesses were not great enough nor his skill levels behind enough to qualify for services."
>
> A review of his school records plus the history provided by his parents revealed that he had been labeled as hyperactive and distractible in preschool and kindergarten. The first grade teacher described him as overactive and unable to stay on task. The second grade teacher made the same comments. Third grade was described as terrible. He got into fights, disrupted the classroom, and did not complete his work. Fourth grade was similar. He was falling further behind in school skills and strategies. The teachers blamed this on his behavior and his "refusal to sit still and pay attention."
>
> The clinical history added to the diagnostic process. Chris was adopted by his family at age four and a half. He had been in a foster home for one year prior to this adoption. He was removed from his mother because her boyfriend had sexually abused him. His mother was neglectful and often left him alone. The social service agency's records noted that mother had used alcohol and drugs during this pregnancy. Chris was in both individual and group therapy to help him cope with his past. All of his academic and behavioral problems were seen as secondary to his emotional problems.
>
> During my assessment sessions with Chris he spoke openly of his past. He knew about it and felt that he no longer worried about it. "I talked it all over in my therapy. It is behind me and this is my family now and forever. I like them." I could find no evidence of emotional conflicts relating to his past. He did speak of his frustrations in school. He did not like school and he knew he was not as smart as the other kids. Chris was aware that it was difficult to sit still in class. He also was aware of

his easy distractibility by any noise or activity. He blamed the fighting on the other kids teasing him.

I found Chris to have a chronic and pervasive history (as far as such a history could be obtained) of hyperactivity, distractibility, and impulsivity. Thus, I had to consider the diagnosis of ADHD. The alcohol and drugs his mother used during her pregnancy with Chris certainly placed him at risk for ADHD and/or learning disabilities. However, his history also suggested that he might still be dealing with what is called a "post-traumatic stress disorder." The hyperactivity, distractibility, and impulsivity might be reflective of anxiety and/or depression.

After discussing the clinical issues with his therapist, I presented these diagnostic questions to Chris and his parents. We agreed to a trial on medication to help clarify the issues. He was started on Ritalin. The dose was adjusted. He became calmer, more on task, and less impulsive at home and in school. All of his teachers, as well as his parents, noticed the significant improvement. His level of work at school improved as well.

After helping his parents request more services, his school professionals agreed to identify him as having learning disabilities. He began to receive services and classroom accommodations. His grades went up. The fighting and other disruptive behaviors stopped.

In conclusion, Chris may be struggling with anxiety and depression relating to his past life experiences. But, he also has ADHD and learning disabilities.

Diagnosing ADHD

The clinical history becomes critical to the diagnosis of ADHD. If the behaviors observed and documented *started at a certain time or occur in certain situations*, the clinician must think of anxiety, depression, or another neurologically based disorder. Billy was first described as hyperactive and impulsive in third grade. We learned that his parents separated during the summer before a favorite grandmother died. Allison is only inattentive/distractible in reading group or when sitting at her desk working on a report. She is very attentive when there is class discussion. Jose seems to be distracted when doing homework, but at no other home time.

Attention deficit hyperactivity disorder is present at birth or during the early years of life. Thus the history of the behaviors is both *chronic and pervasive*. This makes sense. The child is born with the problem and the brain is with him or her throughout life; thus the behaviors are seen year after year. This brain is with the child or adolescent every minute of every day; thus, the behaviors occur all day.

The history is chronic. A mother might say that her child was more active in utero or has been active all of his or her life. "He started walking at 10 months and at 10 months and one minute my life became hell. He never stopped running." A mother might go to a school conference for her third grade daughter. The teacher comments that she does not stay in her seat or pay attention. The mother says, "You think you have problems. Her second grade teacher complained. Her first grade and kindergarten teachers complained. She was kicked out of nursery school because she would not sit in circle time and pay attention." Adults will describe their problems as being present since adolescence or childhood. With some effort, the clinician can usually find evidence to support the chronic nature of the problems.

The problems are pervasive. The morning teachers complain about the behaviors. The lunch room monitor complains, as do the afternoon teachers. The tutor complains. The piano teacher complains. The soccer coach complains. Sunday School teachers are not allowed to complain; but, they let you know. These behaviors are not just school problems. They interfere with friends, family life, and after school activities.

To make the diagnosis, then, the following steps must be taken: (1) Confirm the presence of the criteria in DSM-IV to establish the presence of one or more of the three behaviors; (2) show, through the clinical history, that these behaviors have been present throughout life—they are chronic; and (3) show through the clinical history that these behaviors are present throughout the person's present life—they are pervasive.

Diagnostic and Statistical Manual of Mental Disorders-IV guidelines require this chronic and pervasive history. The behaviors identified must have been present before age six, and these behaviors must interfere with functioning in two or more areas of the person's life.

FORMAL INSTRUMENTS OFTEN USED AS PART OF THE DIAGNOSTIC PROCESS

Rating Scales

Rating scales are popular when assessing children's behaviors. These behavioral rating scales might be completed by parents, teachers, and/or the child or adolescent being evaluated. The results can be analyzed and compared to established norms. Important information can be obtained in an efficient way, and these findings provide a baseline so that any changes can be compared.

The difficulty is in using the results to make the diagnosis. The results will clarify if the individual is hyperactive, inattentive/distractible, or impulsive. However, the results will not clarify the reason for these behaviors.

My bias is not to use rating scales. I have great respect for them; however, I learn more by collecting the information asked for in the rating scales directly from the parents and child or adolescent, followed by talking to the teacher or teachers by phone. This process might take more time, but it is worth it. I can learn more by talking with a teacher for five minutes than I can learn from any rating scale.

Rating scales are two-dimensional. The results are reported as a behavior or behavioral cluster being present at a significant level or not, but when I talk to the teacher I can pick up more. For example, the teacher might report to me that the child is hyperactive and inattentive. She or he would have marked the rating scale accordingly, but, as we discuss the child, I learn that these behaviors are only noticed during certain activities and not during others. Or, they occurred after something happened at home or they are more likely to be seen during the time the child is at one parent's home than when at the other's home. I also can pick up the teacher's affect. How upset or angry is he or she about these behaviors. "He is so disruptive that I can't teach my class!!!" tells me more than a check on a rating scale saying that the child is impulsive.

I must admit that I am in the minority. Most professionals like rating scales and use them as part of the diagnostic process. These scales operationalize the DSM criteria. The Conners series of parent and teacher rating scales are probably the most popular, although there are other behavioral rating scales in use. New rating sheets are developed all of the time and some professionals have their own. Some school systems use standard rating scales that have been modified to fit the school's needs.

Computer-based Tests

Several tests have been developed using the computer to assess the child's or adolescent's ability to pay sustained attention. The results will suggest that this individual has difficulty sustaining attention or that he or she shows evidence of impulsivity.

There are professionals who insist that they can make the diagnosis of ADHD based on the results of these studies. They cannot. The presence of difficulty maintaining attention or of impulsivity only confirms the presence of these behaviors. Unless the clinical history shows that these behaviors have been both chronic and pervasive, the diagnosis cannot be finalized. The results are to be used as part of the diagnostic process, not as the diagnostic process. The results might provide an excellent baseline to be used later in assessing the impact of medication on these behaviors.

The *Continuous Performance Test* (CPT) and the *Test of Variables of Attention* (TOVA) are the most frequently used. For each, vigilance is assessed by having the child respond to an auditory or visual stimulus by pressing a button. The stimulus may be in the background of similar signals. For example, visual stimuli appear on a screen and the child is asked to respond when a certain stimulus appears or when two appear in a specific sequence (for example, follow each other). The tasks are monotonous and require constant attention. The speed or complexity of the task can be increased. Children or adolescents with ADHD perform more poorly than normal children. They might make more errors of omission (missed signals) and/or make more errors of commission (pressing the button in error). Errors of omission are seen as reflective of inattention. Errors of commission are seen as reflective of impulsivity.

IN SUMMARY

All children, adolescents, and adults who are hyperactive, inattentive/distractible, and/or impulsive do not have ADHD. In reality, ADHD is probably the least most common cause for these behaviors. A clear differential diagnostic process that takes into account all possible causes for these behaviors is needed before a diagnosis can be made. A diagnosis of ADHD requires a chronic and pervasive history of the hyperactivity and/or inattention/distractibility and/or impulsivity.

Because individuals with ADHD have a higher likelihood of having learning disabilities than other children and adolescents, if someone is diagnosed with ADHD, the possibility of a learning disability must be considered. So, too, the possibility of one of the modulating disorders or a tic disorder must be considered. If there are emotional, social, or family problems, the clinician must help in deciding if these problems are causing the behaviors or if these problems are secondary to the ADHD and the resulting emotional and behavioral problems.

Only by understanding the total child or adolescent in his or her total world can the full clinical picture be seen. And, only when the full clinical picture is known can a comprehensive treatment plan be developed.

This chapter was taken, in part, from *Attention-Deficit/Hyperactivity Disorder: A Clinical Guide to Diagnosis and Treatment for Health and Mental Health Professionals*, 2nd edition, by Larry B. Silver, M.D. Washington, D.C.: American Psychiatric Press, Inc., 1999.

Chapter • 7

Interaction of Disorder of Vigilance and Learning Disabilities

Warren A. Weinberg, Caryn R. Harper, and Roger A. Brumback

This chapter will discuss vigilance in relationship to clinical neuropsychiatric syndromes including learning disabilities. The meaning of the term *vigilance*, its historical background, as well as current ideas about the neural substrates responsible for vigilance, will be presented.

> Precision is the essence of scientific observation; semantic precision is the essence of scientific communication. (Sarnat 1995, p. 178).

Sir Henry Head (1926) used the term *vigilance* in reference to a state of maximum physiological efficiency. Alluding to the concept of an individual's being in the state of optimal receptivity (alertness), Head states, "I would suggest that we employ the word vigilance for this state of high grade physiological efficiency" (Head 1926; Brain 1958; Davies and Parasuraman 1982). *Vigilance* is thus defined as steady state wakefulness/alertness (tonic arousal) the state of being alert, awake, and watchful (Dorland's Illustrated Medical Dictionary 1974, p. 1715). When vigilance is being lost the individual will have difficulty attending to tasks requiring continuous mental performance. The loss of *vigilance* results in motor restlessness, including fidgeting, dawdling, moving about (minor busyness), yawning, stretching, talkativeness, or a combination of these minor ("mini") motor activities. Motor restlessness represents an attempt by an individual to improve his or her vigilance or wakefulness/alertness. If not allowed to be active ("restless") in order to stay awake (alert), the individual with lowered vigilance will stare off, daydream, exhibit minor hyperactivity, and ultimately fall asleep (Weinberg and Brumback 1990; Weinberg and Harper 1993; Weinberg, Harper, Brumback 1998).

Unfortunately, the term *vigilance* has been variously used in the literature of physiological, behavioral psychology, and neurology to describe sustained, directed, and selected attention rather than tonic arousal/alertness/wakefulness (Arruda et al. 1999; Billingsley et al. 2000; Blanco and Leiros 2000; Byrne et al. 1998; DeWolfe et al. 1999; Dimond and Beaumont 1973; Dinges and Broughton 1989; Koelega 1993; Manly et al. 1999; Mass et al. 2000; Moray 1969; Pribram and McGuiness 1975). Attention is the "concentration of the mental powers upon an object; a close or careful observation or listening" (American Heritage Dictionary 1991, p.139). Sir William James (1890 p.403) wrote "Everyone knows what attention is" and D. O. Hebb (1949) wrote, "Since everyone knows that attention exists, we had better get the skeleton out of the closet and see what can be done with it" (p. 4-5). While an alert, wakeful (vigilant) state is required in order to achieve the sustained, directed, and continuous performance necessary for "close or careful observing or listening" of sustained attention, attention is also influenced by other variables such as primary sensory input, motivation, diligence, volition, intelligence, and the presence of distracting stimuli (Weinberg and Brumback 1990; Weinberg and Harper 1993; Weinberg, Harper, and Brumback 1998). Vigilance is thus only one variable of attention, but loss of vigilance diminishes the ability to maintain the alert, awake state necessary to sustain attention.

Based upon the studies of the British neurologist N. H. Mackworth in the 1940s, 1950s, and 1960s (1944, 1948, 1950, 1957, 1965, 1968) psychological investigations of "vigilance" have employed "vigilance tasks," also called "monitoring tasks" or "watchkeeping tasks" (Belyavin and Wright 1987; Davies and Parasuraman 1982; Dinges and Broughton 1989; Koelega 1993; Pribram and McGuiness 1975; Weitkunat and Bestler 1990), which measure "sustained attention directed toward one or more sources of information over varying periods of time detecting small changes in the presented information" (Davies and Parasuraman 1982; Herman et al. 1989, 1990; Hirshkowitz and Herman 1989; Hirshkowitz et al. 1993; Lichstein et al. 2000; Mackie 1977; Mackworth 1970; Moray 1969; Weitkunat and Bestler 1990). In 1943, Mackworth was commissioned by the Royal Air Force and the English Coastal Command to find out why radar screen operators were not detecting German U-boats (submarines) (Davies and Parasuraman 1982; Mackie 1977; Mackworth 1950; Moray 1969). He applied the term vigilance in studies of specific stimulus-response tasks requiring continuous mental performance (i.e., Clock Test, Synthetic Radar Test) (Mackworth 1944). Mackworth reported that the within-session deterioration in efficiency found on the Clock Test (the "vigilance decrement": deterioration in performance over time) could be prevented by allowing a rest period during the task and by offering 10 milligrams of oral Benzedrine (amphetamine sulfate) one hour before testing (Davies and Parasuraman 1982; Mackworth 1948, 1950, 1957, 1965). Mackworth (1957) defined vigilance as "a state of readiness to detect and respond to certain specified small changes occurring at random timed intervals in the environment." Like Head (1926), Mackworth considered arousal (alertness) to be a possible theoretical basis for vigilance but emphasized an inhibition (habituation) explanation for this observation (Mackworth 1968). At present there are no tests that measure pure vigilance (Berger et al. 2000; Conradt et al. 1999; Weinberg and Brumback 1990; Weinberg and Harper 1993; Weinberg, Harper, and Brumback 1998) since these psychological measures derived from Mackworth and others are actually measuring attention rather than vigilance. Performance on such tasks is not synonymous with steady state wakefulness/alertness or vigilance (Weinberg and Brumback 1990; Weinberg and Harper 1993; Weinberg, Harper, Brumback 1998), but instead represents generic attention influenced by the multiple variables of intelligence, motivation, primary sensory input, distractions, and vigilance.

NEUROBIOLOGY OF VIGILANCE (WAKEFULNESS/TONIC AROUSAL)

Kleitman included in his text, *Sleep and Wakefulness* (1939 and 1963), references to early 1700s describing individuals with intractable daytime sleepiness. Lavie (1991) in his review of pre-20th century accounts of patients included a report of a physician with incapacitating daytime sleepiness. Lavie described the following in the June 3, 1884 minutes of the New York Neurological Society:

Jay Morton, President of the Society, presented a case of morbid somnolence . . . the patient, a 32-year old physician gave the following description of himself: "I began the study of medicine, and it was during the lectures' hours that I was first troubled with my inability to keep awake. During the 3 years of my attendance upon medical lectures I do not think there was a single day when I did not at least once during the lectures either go soundly asleep or pass into a state of semi-unconsciousness . . . . This condition of things has grown steadily worse, until now I seldom can read more than half an hour often not longer than 15 minutes without falling asleep. I would often, thinking it might only be a mental habit which could be broken by opposition, fight against this sleepiness for hours . . . I have gone to sleep while making a vaginal examination in case of labour. Three times during the writing of a single prescription I have nodded off in a momentary doze. I have gone to sleep in a dental chair while the pounding of gold filling was going on" (Lavie 1991, p. 1841).

Neurophysiology of Vigilance

Basic neurophysiological studies of sleep-wakefulness, including the growth of sleep medicine (Sinton and McCarley 2000), has further confounded the terms vigilance, attention, and wakefulness. Terms such as "directed," "selected," "sustained attention," "vigilance," "arousal," and "watchfulness" are often used interchangeably without distinct definitions. One possible dogma dating to the studies of Moruzzi and Magoun (1949) and Magoun (1952) designated arousal as a function of an ascending reticular "activating system" (a portion of the mesencephalic reticular formation). This ascending reticular activating system was initially defined in cats as the brain stem nuclei which, when stimulated, were associated with EEG desynchronization (production of low-voltage, fast EEG activity) (Magoun 1952; Moruzzi and Magoun 1949). A correlation between similar EEG desynchronization (low-voltage, fast wave beta activity: 14-21 Hertz) and states variously termed "attention," "arousal," and "vigilance" have been found in neurophysiological studies of human subjects in a variety of stages of wakefulness and sleep. A recent study of the "vigilance state" (as defined as arousal/alertness) concluded that slow eye movements are a more sensitive and consistent indication of excessive daytime sleep-related performance impairment than changes in EEG activity (Kinnari et al. 2000). Dimond and Beaumont (1973) hypothesized that the right cerebral hemisphere is responsible for tonic, or steady-state, vigilance, whereas the left hemisphere is more active in phasic vigilance. Heilman and Valenstein (1993), comparing EEG findings from awake patients with right or left temporo-parietal infarcts, suggested that the right cerebral hemisphere might have a special role in mediating both central and peripheral arousal. Similar results have been noted in studies that use galvanic skin response as a measure of arousal (Heilman et al. 1978; Schrandt et al. 1989).

In an excellent review, Posner and Petersen (1990) highlighted the influence of the right cerebral hemisphere, particularly the right parietal and pre-striate cortex, with the physiological property of norepinephrine pathways that arise in the locus ceruleus as being responsible for the state of "high priority visual information" processing. Cherry and Hellige (1999) offered further support for cerebral arousal (vigilance) being a function of the posterior right cerebral hemisphere utilizing a visual field inter-hemispheric transfer paradigm. Fernandez-Duque and Posner (1997) reported that alertness (vigilance) is consistent with a broad axonal distribution of the noraderenergic system whereas the orienting mechanism may be modulated by the basal forebrain cholenergic system, supporting Posner and Petersen's (1990) delineation of an anterior and posterior attention systems in both cerebral hemispheres (figure 1). The various properties of the generic term "attention" may be further delineated by these frontal (anterior) and posterior systems of attention (Berger and Posner 2000) with the cognitive, emotional, motivational, diligence, and orienting/planning/preparation variables being anterior (frontal), and vigilance (tonic arousal/alertness/wakefulness) being a fundamental property of the posterior (parietal) system of "attention."

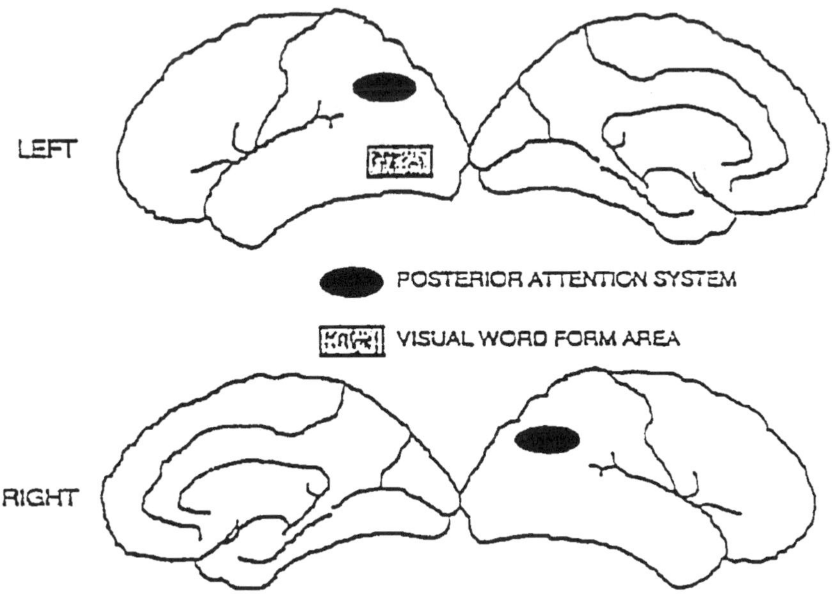

Figure 1. The posterior attention system. The upper two drawings are the lateral (left) and medial (right) surfaces of the left hemisphere. The lower two drawings are the medial (left) and lateral (right) surfaces of the right hemisphere. The location of the posterior visual spatial attention system is shown on the lateral surface of each hemisphere as determined by blood flow studies. The location of the visual word form area on the lateral surface of the left hemisphere is also depicted (from Posner and Petersen 1990)
From: Harris J. C.: *Developmental Neuropsychiatry, The Fundamentals, Volume 1.* New York , Oxford University Press, 1995, p. 116. Used with permission.

Neuroanatomy of Vigilance (Weinberg and Brumback 1990; Weinberg and Harper 1993; Weinberg, Harper, and Brumback 1998)

Several neuroanatomic schemas have been proposed to explain the normal mechanisms involved in sustained or directed attention and arousal (Posner 1994; Posner and Driver 1992). Mesulam (1981, 1985, 1990) has suggested the term *attentional matrix* to describe the mechanisms responsible for attention, arousal, affect, memory, motivation, and perception. The neuroanatomic network for the *attentional matrix* involves afferent pathways from the brain-stem reticular system (including the mesenecephalic reticular formation, locus coeruleus, and brain-stem raphe nuclei), the thalamic nucleus reticularis and other thalamic nuclei, and the limbic system (including the cingulate cortex, the parietal sensory association cortex, and the polymodal cortex of the inferior parietal lobule and cortex at the depths of the superior temporal sulcus). Efferent pathways involve the frontal eye fields, the superior colliculus, the striatum, and the thalamic pulvinar nuclei (figure 2).

On the basis of investigations of the neglect syndrome in humans and of ablation experiments in monkeys, Heilman and co-workers (Heilman and Valenstein 1993; Heilman et al. 1970, 1983, 1985, 1986; Voeller 1991; Voeller and Heilman 1988) have emphasized the importance of the right cerebral hemisphere as the neuroanatomic substrate for neglect and tonic arousal. In both humans and monkeys, the classic neglect syndrome along with hypoarousal (hypovigilance) (Heilman and Van Den Abell 1979; Heilman et al. 1983, 1985; Mountcastle et al. 1975) results from lesions of the right posterior parietal cortex, inferior parietal lobule, and cortex at the depths of the superior temporal sulcus. According to schema of Heilman and colleagues, the brain-stem reticular formation has direct input to the inferior parietal lobule, polymodal association cortex (prefrontal cortex, cortex at the depths of the superior temporal sulcus, and cortex of the posterior cingulate [limbic] gyrus), sensory cortex, and sensory association cortex (figure 3). The inferior parietal lobule has reciprocal interaction with the polymodal association cortex. The polymodal association cortex and the inferior parietal lobule have efferent interaction with the thalamic nucleus reticularis. The thalamic nucleus reticularis inhibits the diencephalic nuclei that relay primary sensory information to the cerebral cortex (Watson et al. 1981).

In extending the concepts of Mesulam and of Heilman and colleagues, we have hypothesized that cerebral alerting is a widely distributed function located mainly within the cerebral hemispheres, the right more than the left. The function of the brain-stem reticular formation is to place both cerebral hemispheres into the state of sleep.

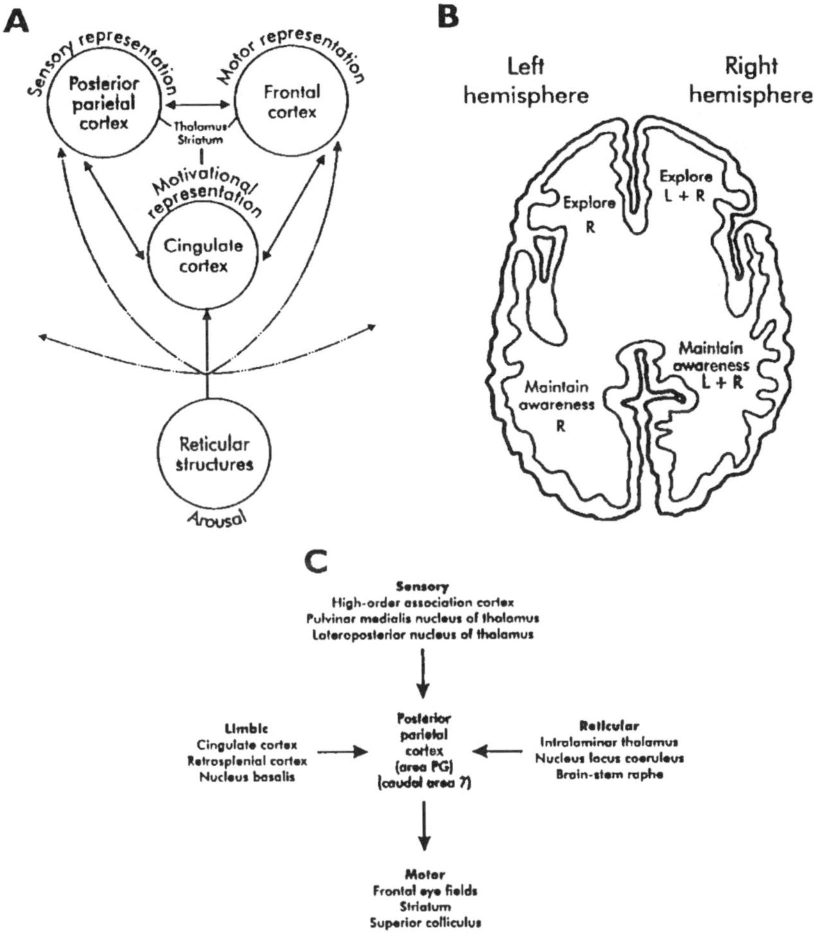

Figure 2. (A) Network involved in the distribution of attention to extrapersonal targets. (B) Model for the right hemisphere specialization in directed attention. (C) Summary of the connections of area PG (posterior parietal cortex in the rhesus monkey.

Source: Reprinted from Mesulam M-M: "Attention, Confusional States, and Neglect," in *Principles of Behavioral Neurology*. Edited by Mesulam, M-M. Philadelphia, PA, F. A. Davis, pp. 157, 152, 159. Copyright 1985, F. A. Davis Company. Used with permission.

Modulation, primarily from the right inferior parietal lobule, is necessary to decrease this effect of the brain-stem reticular formation on the thalamic nucleus reticularis (Weinberg and Brumback 1990; Weinberg and Harper 1993; Weinberg, Harper, and Brumback 1998). When the influence of the right inferior parietal lobule is removed, the cerebral

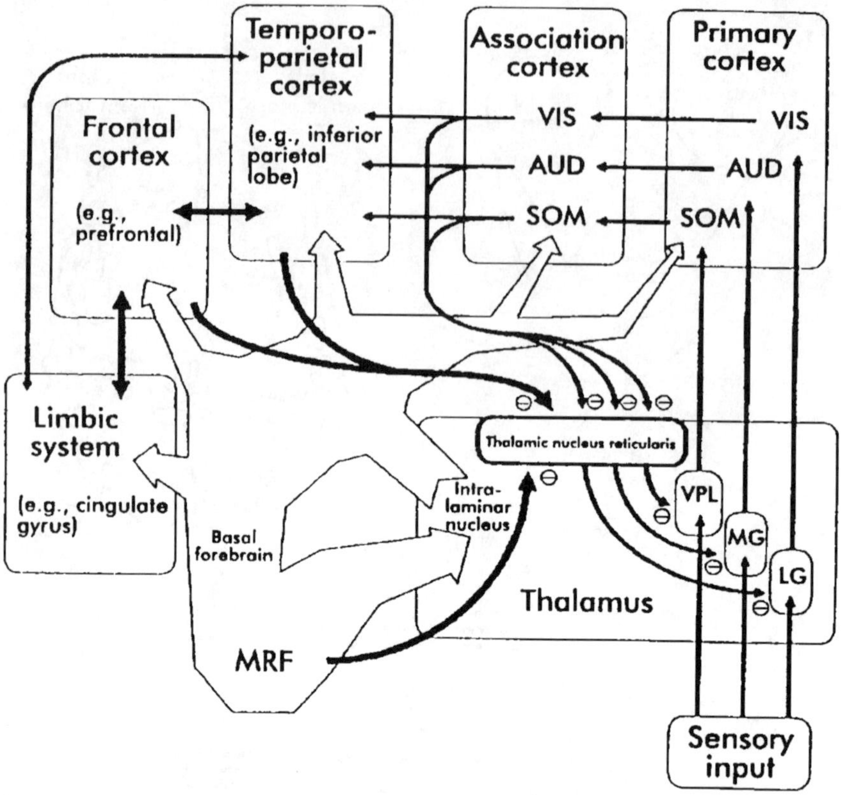

Figure 3. Schematic representation of pathways important in sensory attention and tonic arousal. MRF = mesencephalic reticular formation; VIS = visual; AUD = auditory; SOM = somesthetic. Within the thalamus, sensory relay nuclei are indicated; VPL = ventralis posterolateralis; MG = medial geniculate; LG = lateral geniculate.
Source: Reprinted from Heilman K. M., Watson R. T., Valenstein E.: "Neglect and Related Disorder," in *Clinical Neuropsychology*, 3rd Edition. Edited by Heilman K. M., Valenstein E. New York, Oxford University Press, p. 294. Copyright 1993, Oxford University Press. Used with permission.

alerting necessary to prevent sleep is readily overcome, and brain stem-induced sleep ensues (figure 4). According to this hypothesis, the cerebral hemispheres (the right more than the left) have specialization for steady-state wakefulness and alertness (vigilance) (Weinberg and Brumback 1990; Weinberg and Harper 1993; Weinberg, Harper, and Brumback 1998). In this context, narcolepsy would represent a primary disease of brain-stem reticular formation (Weinberg and Brumback 1990). Coma is physiologically different from sleep (Galassi

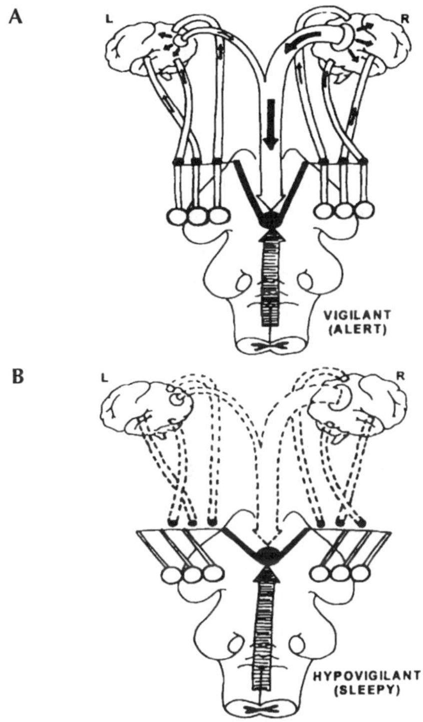

Figure 4. Schematic representation of major pathways involved in the maintenance of vigilance. (A) In the vigilant (alert) state, the inferior parietal lobule of each cerebral hemisphere (right more than left) sustains cerebral hemispheric alerting (and directed attention) and influences the thalamic nucleus reticularis, which is the controller ("on-off switch") of sensory input from diencephalic sensory relay nuclei (depicted by circles representing the ventralis posterolateralis, which projects to the sensory cortex of the postcentral gyrus; the medial geniculate nucleus, which projects to the auditory cortex of Heschl's gyrus; and the lateral geniculate nucleus, which projects to the visual cortex of the calcarine sulcus). The influence of the inferior parietal lobule overcomes tonic input of the brain-stem reticular formation, thereby placing the thalamic nucleus reticularis in an "on" position that opens sensory input pathways to the cerebral cortex. (B) In the hypovigilant (sleepy) state, the cerebral influence of the inferior parietal lobules on the surrounding cerebral cortex and on the thalamic nucleus reticularis is reduced or absent. Thus, the cerebral alerting function is lost, and the unopposed tonic influence of the brain-stem reticular formation places the thalamic nucleus reticularis in an "off" position, blocking input to the cerebral cortex from the diencephalic sensory relay nuclei.
Reprinted from Weinberg W. A., Harper C. R., Brumback R. A.: Attention-deficit/hyperactivity disorder III: disturbances of vigilance (wakefulness). In Coffey C. E., Brumback R. A.: *Textbook of Pediatric Neuropsychiatry*, American Psychiatric Press, Washington, DC, 1998. p. 509. Used with permission.

et al. 1996; Niedermeyer 1999); it can be considered a state of deafferentation induced by removal of primary sensory input through the diencephalon (Gutling et al. 1996; Singer 1977).

Consistent with this hypothesis is the increasing time spent in wakeful states from infancy to adulthood in relation to the maturation of the brain. Premature infants demonstrate sparse periods of sustained wakefulness. Infants, during the first year of life, sleep 16 to 20 hours per day, and toddlers (ages 1 to 2 years) normally sleep 12 to 14 hours daily (including lengthy naps). Children 2 to 5 years of age have increasingly longer periods of vigilance, evidenced by extended periods of wakefulness and fewer naps. Usually by ages 5 or 6 years, the child no longer takes daytime naps and has prolonged periods of continuous mental task performance.

Term infants have a brain weight of about 500 grams, which increases to 1,200 grams by age 5 years and to about 1,500 grams by age 20 years. A major part of this increase in size relates to greater neuronal arborization and axonal myelination. Although neocortical arborization is minimal at term birth, reasonably mature cortical neuronal arborization is evident by ages 5 to 6 years (Peters and Jones 1988). Myelination of the reticular formation begins at approximately 9 months gestation and myelination of cerebral association areas of the temporal and parietal lobes begins about 2 months later. The reticular formation is 50% myelinated by about 4 or 5 years (Peters and Jones 1988). This growth of the brain correlates with progressive wakefulness, decreasing naptime, and the thesis that the cerebral hemispheres are dominant for vigilant states (Weinberg, Harper, and Brumback 1998).

Support for this hypothesis comes from the work of Heilman, Geschwind, and their colleagues (1978, 1980, 1985, 1993) who emphasized the importance of the right cerebral hemisphere as a neuroanatomic substrate for both neglect and tonic arousal, in particular, the right posterior parietal cortex, inferior parietal lobule, and cortex at the depths of the superior temporal sulcus. Posner and Petersen (1990) noted two cortical systems of attention occurring in both cerebral hemispheres, the anterior and posterior attention systems, with the right posterior cerebral hemisphere being most powerful in producing a state of arousal and sustained attention. (Harris 1995; Posner and Dehaene 1994; Posner and Petersen 1990) (figure 1):

> Lesions of the right cerebral hemisphere cause difficulty with alerting. This has been shown with measurement of galvanic skin responses in humans and monkeys (Heilman et al. 1985) and with heart rate responses to warning signals (Yokoyama et al. 1987). Performance in vigilance tasks is also more impaired with right rather than left lesions (Coslett et al. 1987, Wilkins et al. 1987). It has also been observed in

> split-brain patients that vigilance is poor when information is presented to the isolated left hemisphere, but is relatively good when presented to the isolated right hemisphere (Dimond and Beaumont 1973). In summary, the isolated right hemisphere appears to contain the mechanism needed to maintain the alert state so that when lesioned, it reduces performance of the whole organism (Posner and Peterson 1990).

More recently, Posner and Rothbart (1998) have highlighted the anterior attention system, including the cingulate structures, to regulate cognition and emotion as the executive attention network. Two specific systems of attention are also supported by EEG studies of alpha coherence (Cantero et al. 1999). Stroke patients with aphasia (left cerebral hemisphere lesions) do not show attention deficits, again suggesting the importance of the right cerebral hemisphere (Korda and Douglas 1997).

Crick (1984) had previously suggested the role of thalamic reticular complex as the "search-light attention hypothesis." Crick's (1984) emphasis on the reticular complex of the thalamus, and Posner and Petersen's review (1990) of blood flow and metabolic studies delineating a posterior attention system with right cerebral hemisphere dominance, are consistent with our proposal of the anatomic substrate for tonic arousal (vigilance) being a function of the right inferior parietal lobules resultant influence on the nucleus reticularis of the thalamus and inhibition of the mesencephalic reticular formation (Weinberg and Brumback 1990; Weinberg and Harper 1993; Weinberg, Harper, and Brumback 1998).

Neuropsycho-pharmacology of Vigilance

The effects of a variety of stimulant drugs (amphetamines, methylphenidate, caffeine, nicotine) have been studied on various so-called "vigilance" tasks (sustained attention tasks). A comprehensive review of these studies by Koelega (1993) resulted in the following conclusions: (1) stimulants improve "vigilance" performance both by enhancing the overall level of performance and by preventing decrements in performance over time; (2) effects of "false alarms" on results are negligible; (3) "vigilance tasks" appear to be more sensitive tests for detecting the effects of stimulants; (4) stimulant-induced improvements are not restricted to fatigued subjects and protracted sessions; (5) improvements do not occur only in subjects with sleep deprivation-induced impairments; and (6) simple neurotransmitter models of attention and information processing may be untenable. Clinically, the stimulant agents improve arousal (vigilance) and sustained attention if intelligence, motivation, diligence, and the avoidance of distractions are appropriate for the task (Weinberg, Harper, and Brumback 1998).

Several neurotransmitters (norepinephrine, dopamine, and acteylcholine) are positively involved in the EEG aspects of wakefulness (arousal) (Gaillard 1985; Hilakivi 1987; Nicholson and Pascoe 1990; Rammsayer 1989; Saletu and Grunberger 1985; Svensson 1987). Low levels of norepherine are associated with rapid eye movement (REM) sleep. Serotonin is involved in the storage and release of sleep-inducing factors and in the rhythmicity of sleep (Nakamura and Kurasawa 2000). Serotoninergic antidepressant medications (amitriptyline, doxepin, fluoxetine, and trazodone, but not sertraline) often promote hypovigilance whereas noradrenergic antidepressant medications (imipramine, desipramine, bupropion, venlafaxine) can improve vigilance (Gaillard 1985; Hilakivi 1987; Hollister 1978; McCracken 1991; Svensson 1987; Weinberg, Harper, and Brumback 1998). Unfortunately, because these studies actually evaluated sustained attention rather than pure vigilance, the psychopharmacology of vigilance remains poorly understood (Biederman and Spencer 1999; Brumback 2000; Head 1926; Weinberg and Brumback 1990; Weinberg and Harper 1993; Weinberg, Harper, and Brumback 1998; Weinberg and McLean 1986).

PRIMARY DISORDER OF VIGILANCE

Vigilance (tonic arousal) can be disturbed by a number of common medical conditions (table I). A prominent cause of disturbed vigilance, in otherwise healthy individuals, is the primary disorder of vigilance (Weinberg and McLean 1986; Brumback and Weinberg 1990). Table II presents the diagnostic criteria for the primary disorder of vigilance that may be responsible for a significant proportion of attention deficit hyperactivity disorder (ADHD), inattentive type, in patients without hyperactivity/impulsivity or mood disturbance. In such patients, the

Table I. Selected causes of disturbed vigilance

Primary disorder of vigilance
Affective illness
Learning disabilities
Narcolepsy
Sleep deprivation (including obstructive sleep apnea syndrome)
Epilepsy
Drugs
Medications
Toxins
Structural brain lesions (midbrain or right cerebral hemisphere)
Hormonal or metabolic disorders

Adapted from Weinberg, W. A., and Harper, C. R. 1993. Vigilance and its disorders. *Neurologic Clinics* 11:59–78. Used with permission.

Table II. Primary Disorder of Vigilance

A. Primary disorder of vigilance is a disorder of at least 1 year's duration, with symptoms from all five (5) major symptom categories:

1. decreasing ability to sustain alertness, wakefulness, arousal, and watchfulness during continuous mental (or other task) performance
   a. complaints of tiredness, drowsiness, sleepiness, lethargy
   b. yawning, stretching, sleepy-eyed ("glassy-eyed") appearance
   c. falling asleep; excessive napping
2. decreasing attention to current activities
   a. daydreaming
   b. difficulty focusing attention; tendency to lose place in activities and conversation
   c. poor performance due to inattention
   d. slow, delayed, or incomplete performance of tasks
   e. disorganized
3. avoidance of structured or repetitive activities
   a. loss of interest in structured activities or complaints that such activities are dull, boring, monotonous, tedious, uninteresting (or no longer interesting)
   b. preference for shifting activities that have random or irregular changes in schedule or activity (orderly randomization)
4. use of motor restlessness and behaviors to improve alertness
   a. fidgeting
   b. talkativeness
   c. moving about
   d. busyness
5. possession of a caring, compassionate, affectionate, and kind temperament

B. Presence of a major symptom category is accepted as positive when the symptom or one or more of its behaviors is identified in a semi-structured, closed-end interview of patient and primary caretakers

C. This symptom complex must precede the onset of other conditions (i.e., depression, narcolepsy, various medications, alcohol and drug abuse, hypothyroidism) that can cause secondary hypovigilance

D. Although symptoms may be identified at any age, the disorder generally becomes more symptomatic during school and can result in increasing maladaptation.

Adapted from Weinberg, W. A., and Brumback, R. A. 1990. Primary disorder of vigilance: A novel explanation of inattentiveness, daydreaming, boredom, restlessness, and sleepiness. *Journal of Pediatrics* 116:720–5. Used with permission.

symptoms that seemingly suggest the diagnosis of ADHD (inattentiveness, daydreaming, boredom, restlessness and sleepiness), that results in minor but non-intrusive busyness are actually caused by loss of vigilance during activities requiring continuous mental performance and during repetitive tasks not involving orderly randomization. In the primary disorder of vigilance, these symptoms represent attempts by the hypovigilant individuals to improve alertness and wakefulness. These children must be busy to be alert, to learn, and to perform. Sitting still, excessive time on task, reiterative/repetitive activities, lectures, and prolonged reading act as sedatives. To overcome this transient loss of alertness these individuals doodle, fidget, talk, and move about, thus becoming busy (Weinberg and Brumback 1990; Weinberg, Harper, and Brumback 1995, 1998).

An interesting observation in children and adults with the primary disorder of vigilance is their very kind, affectionate, forgiving nature. They seem to be unable to hold a grudge, and, if free of mood disorders, are not behavior problems. However, as shown in figure 5, mood disorders and learning disabilities are common in children with the primary disorder of vigilance referred to clinical settings.

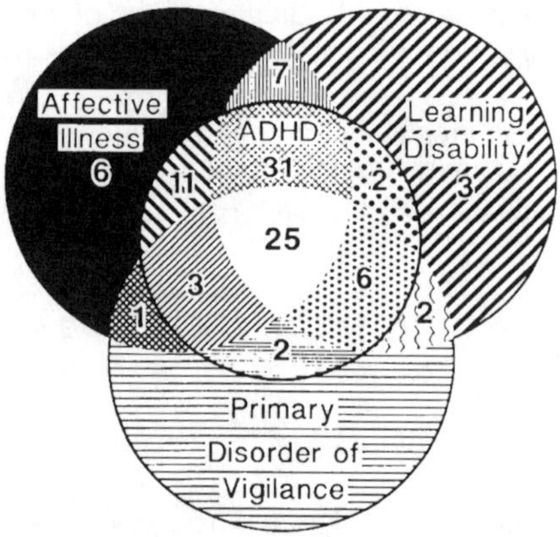

Figure 5. Distribution of diagnoses for 100 children (73 boys, 27 girls) consecutively referred to the outpatient Pediatric Behavioral Neurology Program at the Children's Medical Center of Dallas (only 99 children are represented because 1 child with affective illness, primary disorder of vigilance, and learning disability did not fulfill criteria for attention-deficit/hyperactivity disorder [ADHD]). The mean age of the group was 10.3 years (range = 5 years, 5 months to 18 years, 9 months). Racial distribution of the population was 93 white, 6 black, and 1 Oriental, and all subjects were of at least middle-class socioeconomic status. A large number of the children had more than one specific diagnosis (comorbidity of disease). All ADHD (inner circle) could be explained by one or more of the specific entities of affective disorder, primary disorder of vigilance, and learning disability.
Source: Reprinted from Weinberg W. A., Brumback R. A.: "The Myth of Attention Deficit-Hyperactivity Disorder: Symptoms Resulting From Multiple Causes." *Journal of Child Neurology* 7:431–445, 1992. Used with permission.

The primary disorder of vigilance seems to be a dominantly inherited trait. It often worsens with aging, and adults with the primary disorder of vigilance commonly fall asleep while watching television, reading, sitting in church or lectures, or riding as passengers in automobiles or other modes of transportation. They will manifest difficulty with work tasks requiring continuous mental activity for example, sitting in a confined office, reading and writing reports, and attending board meetings, lectures, or training programs. To remain alert and awake and to perform in an acceptable manner, adults with the primary disorder of vigilance find it necessary to keep busy by arranging their activities in a manner that permits orderly randomization. Naps are generally not described as refreshing for adults with the primary disorder of vigilance. Elderly people with the primary disorder of vigilance are often teased about their excessive naps and accused of "sleeping their lives away." Although the primary disorder of vigilance is a lifelong condition that worsens with age, rarely do adults seek evaluation for hypovigilance. Interestingly, once the disorder has been recognized in their children, symptomatic parents and grandparents, not infrequently, ask for treatment of their primary disorder of vigilance. The most evident clinical neurologic finding associated with the primary disorder of vigilance is minor restlessness. A subtle left-limb hemimotor syndrome characterized by minor clumsiness, minimal tremor, and dishing (spooning) of the extended left hand (but without motor impersistance) may also be evident (Emslie, Weinberg, and Kowatch 1998; Levy et al. 1992; Weinberg and Harper 1993; Weinberg, Harper, and Brumback 1998).

Satterfield and colleagues (Satterfield and Dawson 1971; Satterfield et al. 1974), in studying a heterogeneous group of children manifesting hyperactivity, found that greater severity of hyperactivity correlated with lower arousal states (hypovigilance) as evidenced by EEG, auditory evoked cortical responses, and skin conductance changes. Methylphenidate improved arousal (vigilance) as measured by these physiological parameters. These researchers postulated that hypoarousal (hypovigilance) states are associated with failure of the mechanisms that exert inhibitory control (modulation) over sensory input with the absence of such modulation allowing excessive stimulation, which manifests as clinical hyperactivity.

Because wakefulness is associated with a stable (tonic) pupillary size that can be assessed quantitatively (Korczyn 1987; Pressman et al. 1980; Schmidt 1982; Yoss et al. 1969), Duane and Epcar-Zigler (1991) used pupillometry as a measure of alertness in the evaluation of a cohort of children with diagnoses of ADHD alone, ADHD and reading disorder, and reading disorder alone. They found pupillometric evidence of hypovigilance in 31 of the 50 children with ADHD, 15 of the 24 with ADHD and reading disorder, and 8 of the 18 with reading disorder alone. Subsequently, Duane and Berman (1992) and Duane (1993) reported similar findings in another sample of children and adolescents with ADHD, developmental reading disorder, or both.

Treatment of the primary disorder of vigilance (table III) involves recognizing the need to stay busy, which requires altering the individual's environment (especially school settings) to permit and plan for busyness, and planning activities utilizing context of orderly randomization. Avoiding excessive sameness, reiteration, and structured mundane repetition are central to successful management. Medications with sedative properties also need to be avoided. Stimulant medications (methylphenidate, amphetamines, and possibly modafinil [Ferraro et al. 1999]) are beneficial when the individual is free of depression. Improvement in handwriting by stimulant medication is often noted. This is not surprising since the graphomotor skill of handwriting is also a right parietal cortex function (figure 6).

Hypovigilance is common in depression and is manifested as excessive daytime sleepiness. During a period of depression, tiredness, loss of energy and interest, and dyshedonia can be particularly prominent symptoms in adolescents with the primary disorder of vigilance. Young children with the primary disorder of vigilance and depression often become aimlessly hyperactive, clumsy, and sleepy-eyed as they are wandering about. Some children with the primary disorder of vigilance may only be hyperactive during an episode of depression (Weinberg, Rutman, Sullivan, et al. 1973; Brumback and Weinberg 1990; Weinberg and McLean 1986). Figure 7 presents a biological representation for the interaction of vigilance, affective illness, and the right hemisphere learning/communication disorders. Figure 5 shows the distribution of referred children and adolescents manifesting the primary disorder of vigilance, learning disabilities, and affective illness in association with ADHD (DSM-IIIR).

Table III. Treatment of Primary Disorder of Vigilance

Pharmacotherapy
- Methylphenidate (Ritalin)
- Dextroamphetamine/amphetamine (Adderall, 4-amphetamine salts)
- Dextroamphetamine (Dexedrine)
- Protriptyline (Vivactyl)
- Sertraline (Zoloft)

Environmental manipulation
- Schedule activity in context of orderly randomization
- Avoid sameness, drill, reiteration
- Use "mini" breaks "along the way"
- Keep busy to be alert, to learn, and to perform

Adapted from Weinberg, W. A., and Harper, C. R. 1993. Vigilance and its disorders. *Neurologic Clinics* 11:59–78.Used with permission.

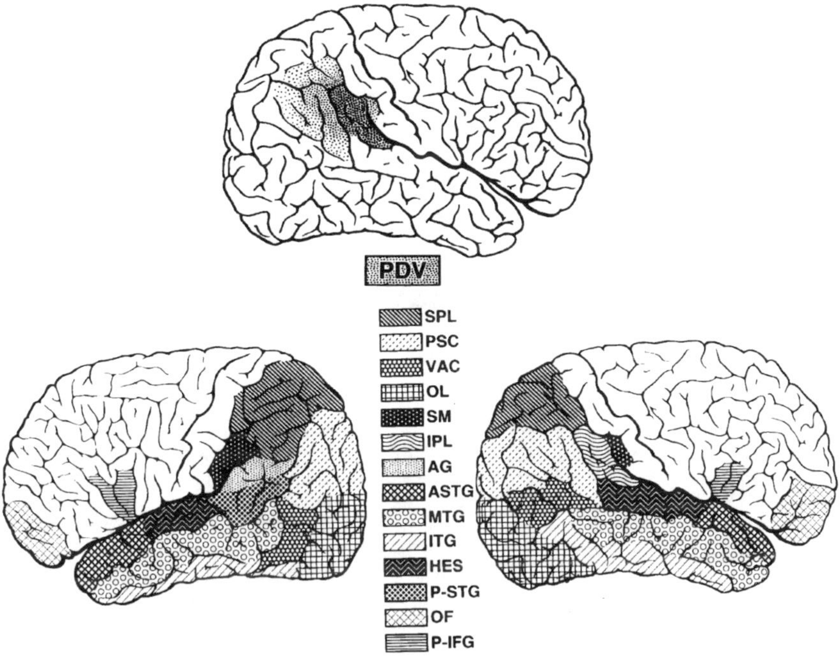

Figure 6. (A) Cerebral localization (inferior parietal lobule and minor influence of surrounding cortical areas; see text) in primary disorder of vigilance (PDV. (B) Line drawing of human cerebral hemisphere with highlighted cytoarchitectonic areas as follows: SPL = superior parietal lobule; PSC = prestriate cortex (posterior parietal cortex); VAC = visual association cortex; OL = occipital lobe; SM = supramarginal gyrus; IPL = inferior temporal gyrus; AG = angular gyrus; ASTG = anterior superior temporal gyrus; MTG = middle temporal gyrus; ITG = inferior temporal gyrus; HES = Heschl's gyrus; P-STG = posterior superior temporal gyrus; OF = orbitofrontal cortex; P-IFG = posterior inferior frontal gyrus.
Source: Reprinted from Weinberg W. A., Harper C. R., Brumback R. A.: "Neuroanatomic Substrate of Developmental Specific Learning Disabilities and Select Behavioral Syndromes." *Journal of Child Neurology* 10 (suppl): 578–580, 1995. Used with permission.

LEARNING DISABILITIES

Hypovigilance that becomes evident and progressive in school is frequently associated with learning disabilities. Figure 5 offers findings gleaned from one of several studies of children and adolescents doing poorly in school (Weinberg and Brumback 1992). In this study 39 of 100 subjects manifested the primary disorder of vigilance. However another 24 of these subjects demonstrated hypovigilance but only on

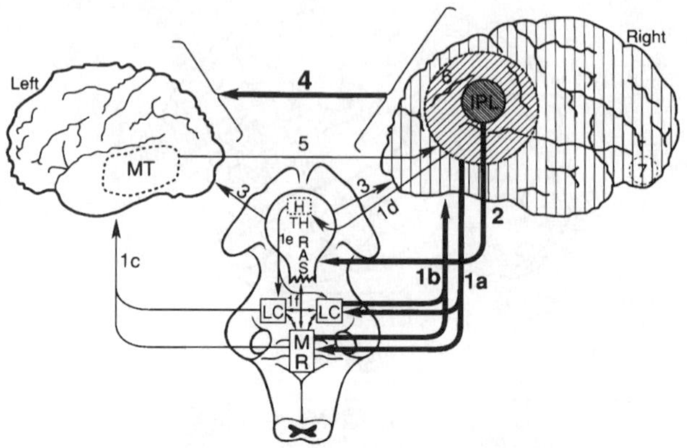

Figure 7. Diagrammatic representation of the anatomic substrate of specific disorders that produce behavioral disturbances in children. Depression relates to the loss of the controlling interaction (1a) of the right parietotemporal cortex (larger hatched circle) on the brain-stem locus coeruleus (LC) and median raphe (MR) nuclei; dysfunction of the right parietal cortex causes a disturbance of function in these nuclei, with resultant reduced norepinephrine (locus coeruleus) and serotonin (median raphe) neurotransmission to the cerebral cortex of both hemispheres (1b and 1c), resulting in the symptomatology characteristic of depression. A disturbance in the controlling influence (1d) of the right parietal cortex on the circadian functions of the hypothalamus (H) also occurs in depression, with resultant abnormalities in biological rhythms (e.g., cortisol secretion) and a secondary disturbance of the diurnal activity of the other brain-stem and diencephalic nuclei (1e) such as the locus coeruleus and median raphe. Interactions (1f) between these nuclei and with the reticular formation (RF) correlate with the disordered sleep/wake cycle characteristic of depression. The primary disorder of vigilance relates to interaction of the right inferior parietal lobule (IPL) on the thalamic nucleus reticularis (TH), diencephalic nuclei that relay primary sensory information to the cerebral cortex, and the reticular formation (RF). With the loss of controlling modulation (2) of the inferior parietal lobule on the thalamic nucleus reticularis (and reticular formation), the cerebral alerting necessary to prevent sleep is lost and the influence (3) of the reticular formation on both cerebral hemispheres induces sleep. In narcolepsy, the influence of the inferior parietal lobule is intact, but the genetically abnormal reticular formation aberrantly influences (3) both cerebral hemispheres, with resultant sleep attacks, hypovigilance, and other narcoleptic symptoms. Although abnormal functioning of the left medial temporal cortex (MT) can present as the clinical syndrome of mania, more often interactions (4 and 5) between the two hemispheres determine the clinical symptomatology of affective illness. Not only does right-hemisphere disorder generate the symptomatology of depression, but its influence (4) on the left hemisphere can result either in mixed symptomatology of depression and mania or, less commonly, in pure mania. Occasionally, primary dysfunction of the left mesial temporal cortex can induce (5) a disturbance on right-hemisphere function that is apparent as either a mixed clinical syndrome of depressed and manic symptoms or a pure major depression. Because right-hemisphere learning disability syndrome principally involves the right parietal cortex (6), all of these interactions may be disrupted by symptomatology such as hypovigilance and dysaffectivity (depression, mania, dysprosody/dysemotionality). In contrast, primary conduct disorder/sociopathy (the disorder of social rules and conduct, diligence, and character) probably relates to dysfunction of the anterior and inferior right frontal cortex (7).
Source: Adapted from Weinberg W. A., Brumback R. A.: "The Myth of Attention Deficit-Hyperactivity Disorder: Symptoms Resulting From Multiple Causes." *Journal of Child Neurology* 7:431–445, 1992. Used with permission.

tasks that targeted their specific areas of difficulty. In this context, hypovigilance is exaggerated or caused by repetitive activities (for example, remediation exercises) that attempt to use these areas of cortical abnormality. In individuals with a primary reading disability, reading results in boredom, daydreaming, and sleepiness as these individuals find themselves struggling to read the words without attending to the content (an example of "task-dependent" hypovigilance). This loss of vigilance is also noted in individuals with dysgraphia and sequencing based dyscalculia (both normally functions of the right parietal lobe). Individuals with the primary disorder of vigilance but no primary reading problem often do not enjoy reading or may use reading as a sedative to initiate bedtime sleep. Attempting to sit quietly through a lecture only results in napping, which is unnecessary and not refreshing, and no information from the lecture is learned. Writing an essay without the presence of a helpful assistant will often not be attempted, or produce either rambling or memo-style output. Homework requiring mundane reading and repetitive drill-type paper-pencil activity is truly problematic, taking an inordinate amount of time to complete, requiring frequent breaks, avoidance due to the discomfort such activity produces, and is often a source of major confrontation with parents (Weinberg, Harper, and Brumback 1998).

It is not uncommon for subtle specific learning disabilities arising from the right parietal cortex (sequencing dyscalculia, event sequencing, graphomotor writing skills, and various other motor coordination skills) to escalate and be problematic in children and adolescents with the primary disorder of vigilance in schools emphasizing "more time on task," reading for quantity (rather than meaningful information), lengthy writing, and homework. Likewise, children and adolescents with learning disabilities of any cerebral location will often lose attention (with some becoming hypovigilant) when required to perform repetitively what they are unable to do ("task-dependent" ADHD). Important in the treatment of the various developmental specific learning disorders, including the dysprosodias (and the primary disorder of vigilance), are bypass/compensatory strategies (table IV) to assure successful learning and acceptable performance and avoidance of hypovigilance in the work/school environment.

Prescription stimulant medications (methylphenidate, amphetamines), caffeine, and nicotine are stimulants that can benefit arousal (Mancuso et al. 1999; Rees et al. 1999; Stolerman et al. 2000), although only transiently. Interestingly, caffeine deprivation in habitual coffee drinkers has been demonstrated to produce "impaired vigilance performance" (that is, attention) and subjective reports of decreased vigor, increased fatigue, sleepiness, headache, and reduced ability to work (Lane and Phillips-Bute 1998). Although stimulants

Table IV. Bypass Compensatory Strategies

Reading	* Listen to "good readers" read age-appropriate (not skill-level) material while eyeing the printed page; avoid listening to poor readers * Use talking books, listen to tapes, and view films and filmstrips for information; if necessary, read salient material using well-prepared course handouts and worksheets * Read silently for meaning, but never read aloud * Test orally and provide a reader and recorder for necessary written test (such as the college entrance examinations and group achievement tests) * Highlighted texts, Cliff notes, Master Plots
Word finding Vocabulary Reading Comprehension	* Use picture-to-word matching tasks (including associating names and faces) for vocabulary development * Test both orally and in writing using multiple choice, true-false, yes-no, or circle-the-correct-answer formats; avoid both oral and written fill-in-the-blank testing situations
Picture-word association	* Avoid practice and reiteration of nouns for recall purposes
Spelling	* Look at word while simultaneously hearing the word spoken * Test spelling by multiple-choice format using age-appropriate (not skill-level) words * Use The Bad Speller's Dictionary 1974. New York: Random House * Use a good speller as a secretary or write using a computer word processor with appropriate spelling-checking software
Writing	* Encourage oral expression or demonstration instead of written tasks * Allow the child to dictate information or answers into a tape recorder or directly to a secretary * Use a circle-the-correct-answer written text format * Provide computer with word processing software that contains a built-in dictionary and thesaurus
Computation Arithmetic	* Pursue instruction of age-appropriate (not skill-level) mathematical concepts and principles, avoiding specific calculations
Mathematics	* For instruction of computation, teach by example showing both correct and incorrect responses * Provide calculators and/or computers with appropriate software to perform the necessary computations at age-appropriate levels * Use the pick-the-correct-answer testing formats
Organization	* Offer one small task at a time or divide larger tasks into

several mini tasks
* As necessary, provide reminders of tasks; avoid nagging and checklists
* Provide a pictorial systems for self-reminding of tasks, chores, and events
* Offer all testing using an untimed format

Adapted from Brumback, R. A., and Weinberg, W. A. 1998. Pediatric behavioral neurology: Update on the neurological aspects of depression, hyperactivity, and learning disabilities. In *Textbook of Pediatric Neuropsychiatry*, eds. C. E. Coffey, and R. A. Brumback. Washington, D. C.: American Psychiatric Press. Used with permission.

seem to improve vigilance (and thus attention), they can induce or promote problematic side effects including depression (particularly in genetically susceptible individuals).

SUMMARY

Vigilance (tonic arousal) appears to be a function of the right cerebral hemisphere inferior parietal lobule. Hypovigilance can be manifested as a primary genetic disorder (the primary disorder of vigilance) and a common cause of the inattentive type of ADHD. Hypovigilance can be secondary to a number of other conditions including depression, various medications, and learning disabilities. We suggest that the treatment for the primary disorder of vigilance is to stay busy, take frequent breaks, and avoid mundane, repetitive activities so popular in school. Stimulant medications are beneficial when the individual is genetically free of depression and when the hypovigilance being treated is due to the primary disorder of vigilance. This chapter highlights the neurophysiology, neuroanatomy, neuropsycho-pharmacology and aspects, as well as what is known about the term "attention," and a specific property of attention, defined as vigilance. Using these understandings and concepts, further research should provide an improved understanding of the clinical issues and management for the primary disorder of vigilance and other neuropsychiatric syndromes (Brumback 2000).

ACKNOWLEDGMENTS

This work was funded by contributions from Caleb C. and Julia W. Dula Education and Charitable Foundations, Mr. and Mrs. Woody Hunt (Cimmaron Foundation), Mr. Morton Meyerson, and the Azoulay family.

REFERENCES

American Heritage Dictionary, 2nd College Edition 1991. Boston, MA: Houghton Mifflin.

American Psychiatric Association: *Diagnostic and Statistical Manual of Mental Disorders*, 3rd edition, revised (DSM-IIIR) 1987. Washington, DC: American Psychiatric Association.

Arruda, J. E., Walker, K. A., Weiler, M. D., and Valentino, D. A. 1999. Validation of a right hemisphere vigilance system as measured by principal component and factor analyzed quantitative electroencephalogram. *International Journal of Psychophysiology* 32:119–28.

Belyavin, A., and Wright, N. A. 1987. Changes in electrical activity of the brain with vigilance. *Electroencephalography and Clinical Neurophysiology* 66:137–44.

Berger, A., Jones, L., Rothbart, M. K., and Posner, M. I. 2000. Computerized games to study the development of attention in childhood. *Behavior Research Methods, Instruments, and Computers* 32:297–303.

Berger, A., and Posner, M. I. 2000. Pathologies of brain attentional networks. *Neuroscience and Behavioral Reviews* 24:3–5.

Biederman, J., and Spencer, T. 1999. Attention-deficit/hyperactivity disorder (ADHD) as a noradrenergic disorder. *Biological Psychiatry* 46:1234–42.

Billingsley, R. L., Smith, M. L., and McAndrews, M. P. 2000. Material specific and non-specific attention deficits in children and adolescents following temporal-lobe surgery. *Neuropsychologia* 38:292–303.

Blanco, M. J., and Leiros, L. I. 2000. Temporal variation in the luminance level of stimuli displayed on a cathode-ray tube monitor: Effects on performance on a visual vigilance task. *Ergonomics* 43:239–51.

Brain, W. R. 1958. The physiological basis of consciousness. *Brain* 81:426–55.

Brumback, R. A. 2000. Weinberg's syndrome: A disorder of attention and behavior problems needing further research. *Journal of Child Neurology* 15:478–80.

Brumback, R. A., and Weinberg, W. A. 1990. Pediatric behavioral neurology: An update on the neurologic aspects of depression, hyperactivity, and learning disabilities. *Neurology Clinics* 8:677–703.

Byrne, J. M., Bawden, H. N., DeWolfe, N. A., and Beattie, T. L. 1998. Clinical assessment of psychopharmacological treatment of preschoolers with ADHD. *Journal of Clinical and Experimental Neuropsychology* 20:613–27.

Cantero, J. L., Atienza, M., Salas, R. M., and Gomez, C. M. 1999. Alpha EEG coherence in different brain states: An electrophysiological index of the arousal level in human subjects. *Neuroscience Letters* 271:167–70.

Cherry, B. J., and Hellige, J. B. 1999. Hemispheric asymmetries in vigilance and cerebral arousal mechanisms in younger and older adults. *Neuropsychology* 13:111–20.

Conradt, R., Brandenburg, U., Pensel, T., Hasan J., et al. 1999. Vigilance transitions in reaction time test: A method of describing the state of alertness more objectively. *Clinical Neurophysiology* 110:1499–1509.

Coslett, H. B., Bowers, D., and Heilman, K. M. 1987. Reduction in cerebral activation after right hemisphere stroke. *Neurology* 37:957–62.

Crick, F. 1984. Function of the thalamic reticular complex: the searchlight hypothesis. *Proceedings of the National Academy of Sciences* 81:4586–90.

Davies, D. R., and Parasuraman, R. 1982. *The Psychology of Vigilance*. New York: Academic Press.

DeWolfe, N. A., Byrne, J. M., and Bawden, H. N. 1999. Early clinical assessment of attention. *Clinical Neuropsychologist* 13:458–73.

Dinges, D. F., and Broughton, R. J. 1989. *Sleep and Alertness: Chronobiological, Behavioral, and Medical Aspects of Napping*. New York: Raven Press.

Dimond, S. J., and Beaumont, J. G. 1973. Difference in the vigilance performance of the right and left hemispheres. *Cortex* 9:259–65.

Dorland's Illustrated Medical Dictionary, 25th edition. Philadelphia: WB Saunders.

Duane, D. 1993. Alertness: Vigilance and wakefulness in developmental disorders of reading and attention. *Annals of the New York Academy of Sciences* 682:333–4.

Duane, D., and Berman, M. B. 1992. Daytime somnolence by pupillometry in developmental disorders (abstract). *Sleep Research* 21:102.

Duane, D., and Epcar-Ziglar, L. 1991. Pupillometry, sleepiness, and vigilance in developmental disorders (abstract). *Neurology* 41:236.

Emslie, G. J., Weinberg, W. A., and Kowatch, R. A. 1998. Mood disorders. In *Textbook of Pediatric Neuropsychiatry*, eds. C. E. Coffey, and R. A. Brumback. Washington, DC: American Psychiatric Press, Inc.

Fernandez-Duque, D., and Posner, M. I. 1997. Relating the mechanisms of orienting and alerting. *Neuropsychologia* 35:477–86.

Ferraro, L., Antonelli, T., Tanganelli, S., O'Connor, W. T. et al. 1999. The vigilance promoting drug modafinil increases extracellular glutamate levels in the medial preoptic area and the posterior hypothalamus of the conscious rat: Prevention by local GABAA receptor blockade. *Neuropsychopharmacology* 20:346–56.

Gaillard, J. M. 1985. Neurochemical regulation of the states of alertness. *Annals of Clinical Research* 17:175–84.

Galassi, R., Morreale, A., Montagra, D., et al. 1996. Fatal familial insomnia: Behavioral and cognitive features. *Neurology* 46:935–9.

Gutling, E., Isenmann, S., and Wichmann, W. 1996. Electrophysiology in the locked-in syndrome. *Neurology* 46:1092–1101.

Harris, J. C. 1995. *Developmental Neuropsychiatry, vol 1. Fundamentals.* Oxford, UK: Oxford University Press.

Head, H. 1926. *Aphasia and Kindred Disorders of Speech.* Cambridge, UK: The University Press.

Hebb, D. O. 1949. *Organisation of Behavior*. London: Wiley.

Heilman, K. M., Bower, D., Valenstein, E., et al. 1986. The right hemisphere: Neuropsychological functions. *Journal of Neurosurgery* 64:693–704.

Heilman, K. M., Pandya, D. N., and Geschwind, N. 1970. Trimodal inattention following parietal lobe ablations. *Transactions of the American Neurological Association* 95:259–61.

Heilman, K. M., Schwartz, H. D., and Watson, R. T. 1978. Hypoarousal in patients with the neglect syndrome and emotional indifference. *Neurology* 28:229–32.

Heilman, K. M., and Valenstein, E. (eds) 1993. *Clinical Neuropsychology*, 3rd edition. New York: Oxford University Press.

Heilman, K. M., and Van Den Abell, T. 1979. Right hemisphere dominance for mediating cerebral activation. *Neuropsychologia* 17:315–21.

Heilman, K. M., Watson, R. T., and Valenstein, E. 1985. Neglect and related disorders. In *Clinical Neuropsychology*, eds. K. M. Heilman, and E. Valenstein. New York: Oxford Press.

Heilman, K. M., Watson, R. T., Valenstein, E., et al. 1983. Localization of lesions in neglect. In *Localization in Neuropsychology*, ed. A. Kertesz. New York: Academic Press.

Herman, J. H., Roffwarg, H. P., Becker, P. M., et al. 1989. The evaluation of daytime vigilance: A new function for sleep disorders centers (abstract). *Sleep Research* 18:120.

Herman, J. H., Steinberg, J. B., Roffwarg, H. P., et al. 1990. Vigilance and sleepiness in the hypersomnolent child (abstract). *Sleep Research* 19:119.

Hilakivi, I. 1987. Biogenic amines in the regulation of wakefulness and sleep. Medical Biology 65:97–104.

Hirshkowitz, M., and Herman, J. 1989. Multiple vigilance test (MVT) (abstract). *Sleep Research* 18:393.

Hirshkowitz, M., de la Cueva, L., and Herman, J. 1993. The multiple sleep vigilance test: Behavior research methods. *Behavior Research Methods, Instruments, and Computers* 25:272–5.

Hollister, L. E. 1978. Drug therapy: Tricyclic antidepressants. *New England Journal of Medicine* 229:1106–71.

James, W. 1890. *The Principles of Psychology*. New York: Holt.

Kinnari, K., Peter, J. H., Pietarinen, A., Groete, L., et al. 2000. Vigilance stages and performance in OSAS patients in a monotonous reaction time task. *Clinical Neurophysiology* 111:1130–6.

Kleitman, N. 1939. *Sleep and Wakefulness.* Chicago: University of Chicago Press.

Kleitman, N. 1963. *Sleep and Wakefulness*, Revised Edition. Chicago: University of Chicago Press.

Koelega, H. S. 1993. Stimulant drugs and vigilance performance: A review. *Psychopharmacology* 111:1–16.

Korczyn, A. D. 1987. The pupil and vigilance. *Functional Neurology* 2:539–44.

Korda, R. J., and Douglas, J. M. 1997. Attention deficits in stroke patients with aphasia. *Journal of Clinical and Experimental Neuropsychology* 19:525–42.

Lane, J. D., and Phillips-Bute, B. G. 1998. Caffeine deprivation affects vigilance performance and mood. *Physiology and Behavior* 65:171–5.

Lavie, P. 1991. The touch of Morpheus: Pre-20th century accounts of sleepy patients. *Neurology* 41:1841–4.

Levy, H. B., Harper, C. R., and Weinberg, W. A. 1992. A practical approach to children failing in school. *Pediatric Clinics of North America* 39:895–928.

Lichstein, K. L., Riedel, B. W., and Richman, S. L. 2000. The Mackworth Clock Test: A computerized version. *Journal of Psychology* 134:153–161.

McCracken, J. T. 1991. A two-part model of stimulant action on attention-deficit hyperactivity disorder in children. *Journal of Neuropsychiatry and Clinical Neuroscience* 3:201–09.

Mackie, R. R. (ed) 1977. *Vigilance: Theory, Operational Performance, and Physiological Correlates*. New York: Plenum.

Mackworth, N. H. 1944. Notes on the Clock Test A new approach to the study of prolonged perception to find the optimum length of watch for radar operators (Air Ministry F.P.R.C. Report No. 586). London: Her Majesty's Stationery Office.

Mackworth, N. H. 1948. The breakdown of vigilance during prolonged visual search. *Journal of Experimental Psychology* 1:6–21.

Mackworth, N. H. 1950. Researches on the measurement of human performance (Medical Research Council Special Report No 268). London: Her Majesty's Stationery Office.

Mackworth, N. H. 1957. Some factors affecting vigilance. *Advancement of Science* 53:389–93.

Mackworth, N. H. 1965. Effect of amphetamine on the detectability of signals in a vigilance task. *Canadian Journal of Psychology* 19:104–10.

Mackworth, N. H. 1968. Vigilance, arousal, and habituation. *Psychological Reviews* 75:308–22.

Mackworth, N. H. 1970. *Vigilance and Attention: A Signal Detection Approach.* Harmondsworth, UK: Penguin.

Magoun, H. W. 1952. An ascending reticular activation system in the brain stem. *Archives of Neurology and Psychiatry* 67:145–54.

Mancuso, G., Andres, P., Ansseau, M., and Tirelli, E. 1999. Effects of nicotine administered via a transdermal delivery system on vigilance: A repeated measure study. *Psychopharmacology* 142:18–23.

Manly, T., Robertson, I. H., Galloway, M., and Hawkins, K. 1999. The absent mind: Further investigations of sustained attention to response. *Neuropsychologia* 37:661–70.

Mass, R., Wolf, K., Wagner, M., and Haasen, C. 2000. Differential sustained attention/vigilance changes over time in schizophrenics and controls during a degraded stimulus Continuous Performance Test. *European Archives of Psychiatry and Clinical Neuroscience* 250:24–30.

Mesulam, M. 1981. A cortical network for directed attention and unilateral neglect. *Annals of Neurology* 10:309–25.

Mesulam, M. 1985. Attention, confusional states, and neglect. In *Principles of Behavioral Neurology,* ed. M. Mesulam. Philadelphia: F. A. Davis.

Mesulam, M. 1990. Large-scale neurocognitive networks and distributed processing for attention, language, and memory. *Annals of Neurology* 28:597–613.

Moray, N. 1969. *Listening and Attention.* Middlesex, UK: Penguin Books.

Moruzzi, G., Magoun, H. W. 1949. Brain stem reticular formation and activation of the EEG. *Electroencephalography and Clinical Neurophysiology* 1:455–73.

Mountcastle, V. B., Lynch, J. C., Georgopoulos, A., et al. 1975. Posterior parietal association cortex of the monkey: Command functions for operations within extrapersonal space. *Journal of Neurophysiology* 38:871–908.

Nakamura, K., and Kurasawa, M. 2000. Serotoninergic mechanisms involved in the attentional and vigilance task performance of rats and the palliative action. Naunyn-Schmiedebergs *Archives of Pharmacology* 361:521–8.

Nicholson, A. N., and Pascoe, P. A. 1990. Dopaminergic transmission and the sleep-wakefulness continuum in man. *Neuropharmacology* 29:411–17.

Niedermeyer, E. 1999. A concept of consciousness. *Italian Journal of Neurological Sciences* 20:7–15.

O'Mara, S., and Walsh, V. (eds) 1994. The cognitive neuropsychology of attention. *Journal of Cognitive Neuropsychology* (special issue).

Peters, A., and Jones, E. 1988. *Development and Maturation of Cerebral Cortex.* New York: Plenum.

Posner, M. I., and Driver, J. 1992. The neurobiology of selective attention. *Current Opinions in Neurobiology* 2:165–69.

Posner, M. I., and Dehaene, S. 1994. Attentional networks. *Trends in Neuroscience* 17:75–9.

Posner, M. I., and Petersen, S. E. 1990. The attention system of the human brain. *Annual Review of Neuroscience* 13:25–42.

Posner, M. I., and Rothbart, M. K. 1998. Attention, self-regulation, and consciousness. *Philosophical Transactions of the Royal Society of London Series B: Biological Sciences* 353:1915–27.

Pressman, M. R., Speilman, A. J., and Korczyn, A. 1980. Pupillometry in normals and narcoleptics throughout the course of a day (abstract). *Sleep Research* 9:218.

Pribram, K. H., and McGuiness, D. 1975. Arousal activation and effort in the control of attention. *Psychological Reviews* 182:116–49.

Rammsayer, T. 1989. Dopaminergic and serotoninergic influence on duration discrimination and vigilance. *Pharmacopsychiatry* 22(suppl):39–43.

Rees, K., Allen, D., and Lader, M. 1999. The influence of age and caffeine on psychomotor and cognitive function. *Psychopharmacology* 145:181–8.

Saletu, B., and Grunberger, J. 1985. Memory dysfunction and vigilance: Neurophysiological and psychopharmacological aspects. *Annals of the New York Academy of Sciences* 444:406–27.

Sarnat, H. B. 1995. Ectopic or heterotopic? An appeal for semantic precision in describing developmental disorders of the nervous system. *Pediatric Neurology* 13:178–9.

Satterfield, J. H., Cantwell, D. P., and Satterfield, B. T. 1974. Pathophysiology of the hyperactive child syndrome. *Archives of General Psychiatry* 31:839–44.

Satterfield, J. H., and Dawson, M. E. 1971. Electrodermal correlates of hyperactivity in children. *Psychophysiology* 8:191–7.

Schmidt, H.1982. Pupillometric assessment of disorders of arousal. *Sleep* 5:S157–64.

Schrandt, N. J., Tranel, D., and Damasio, H. 1989. The effects of the total cerebral lesions on skin conductance response to signal stimuli. *Neurology* 39 (suppl):223–6.

Singer, W. 1977. Control of thalamic transmission by corticifugal and ascending reticular pathways in the visual system. *Physiological Review* 57:386–420.

Sinton, C. M., and McCarley, R. W. 2000. Neuroanatomical and neurophysiological aspects of sleep: Basic science and clinical relevance. *Seminars in Clinical Neuropsychiatry* 5:6–19.

Stolerman, I. P., Mirza, N. R., Hahn, B., and Shoaib, M. 2000. Nicotine in an animal model of attention. *European Journal of Pharmacology* 393:147–54.

Svensson, T. H. 1987. Peripheral, autonomic regulation of locus ceruleus noradrenergic neurons in brain: Putative implications for psychiatry and psychopharmacology. *Psychopharmacology* (Berl) 92:1–7.

Voeller, K. K. S. 1991. What can neurological models of attention, intention, and arousal tell us about attention-deficit hyperactivity disorder? *Journal of Neuropsychiatry Clinical Neuroscience* 3:209–16.

Voeller, K. K. S., and Heilman, K. M. 1988. Attention deficit disorder in children: A neglect syndrome? *Neurology* 38:806–8.

Watson, R. T., Valenstein, E., and Heilman, K. M. 1981. Thalamic neglect: Possible role of the medial thalamus and nucleus reticularis in behavior. *Archives of Neurology* 38:501–6.

Weinberg, W. A., and Brumback, R. A. 1990. Primary disorder of vigilance: A novel explanation of inattentiveness, daydreaming, boredom, restlessness, and sleepiness. *Journal of Pediatrics* 116:720–5.

Weinberg, W. A., and Brumback, R. A. 1992. The myth of attention deficit hyperactivity disorder: Symptoms resulting from multiple etiologies. *Journal of Child Neurology* 7:431–45.

Weinberg, W. A., and Harper, C. R. 1993. Vigilance and its disorders. *Neurology Clinics* 11:59–78.

Weinberg, W. A., Harper, C. R., and Brumback, R. A. 1995. Neuroanatomic substrate of developmental specific learning disabilities and selected behavioral syndromes. *Journal of Child Neurology* 10 Supp 1:S78–S80.

Weinberg, W. A., Harper, C. R., and Brumback, R. A. 1998. Attention-Deficit/Hyperactivity Disorder III: Disturbances of vigilance (wakefulness). In *Textbook of Pediatric Neuropsychiatry*, eds. C. E. Coffey, and R. A. Brumback. American Psychiatric Press.

Weinberg, W. A., and McLean, A. 1986. A diagnostic approach to developmental specific learning disorders. *Journal of Child Neurology* 1:158–72.

Weinberg, W. A., Rutman, J., Sullivan, L., Penick, E. C., and Dietz, S. G. 1973. Depression in children referred to an educational diagnostic center: Diagnosis and treatment. *Journal of Pediatrics* 83:1065–72.

Weitkunat, R., and Bestler, M. 1990. Computerized Mackworth Vigilance Clock Test. *Computer Methods Programs Biomedical* 32:147–9.

Wilkins, A. J., Shallice, T., and McCarthy, R. 1987. Frontal lesions and sustained attention. *Neuropsychology* 25:359–66.

Yokoyama, K., Jennings, R., Ackles, P., Hood, P., et al. 1987. Lack of heart rate changes during an attention-demanding task after right hemisphere lesions. *Neurology* 37:624–30.

Yoss, R. E., Moyer, N. J., and Ogle, K. N. 1969. The pupillogram and narcolepsy. *Neurology* 19:921–8.

Chapter • 8

Attention Deficit Hyperactivity Disorder and Auditory Processing Disorders

Frank E. Musiek, Eliane Schochat, and Jennifer Shinn

Auditory processing disorders (APD), also referred to as central auditory processing disorders (CAPD) (Jerger and Musiek 2000) and attention deficit hyperactivity disorders (ADHD), have become popular diagnoses for school age children. Despite the common use of both terms, the differentiation of these diagnoses for professionals remains a challenge. Indeed, children (and adults) with APD and ADHD have many behaviors in common. Moreover, it has been shown that many individuals with ADHD perform poorly on tests of central auditory function. This has led some investigators to conclusions that are controversial and difficult to understand. In addition to the shared behavioral manifestations, there exists the otitis media link. That is, many children with ADHD have histories of chronic otitis media and these children often perform poorly on tasks of central auditory function. Given these observations, one might question whether otitis media (or other types of auditory disorders) could trigger ADHD.

According to Lazar and Frank (1998), ADHD was first defined more than 30 years ago for infants and teenagers. It is present all over the world. It is defined in the Diagnostic and Statistical Manual of Mental Disorders (DSM IV; American Psychiatric Association 1994) as a persistent pattern of inattention and/or hyperactivity-impulsivity that is more frequent and severe than is typically observed in individuals at a comparable level of development; manifests in at least two settings; interferes with developmentally appropriate social, academic, or occupational functions; and is present since or before 7 years of age. According to the American Academy of Pediatrics (2000), ADHD is the most common neurobehavioral disorder of childhood, as well as the most prevalent chronic health condition affecting school-aged children. Children with ADHD may experience significant functional problems, such as school difficulties, academic underachievement, troublesome interpersonal relationships with family members and peers, and low self-esteem. Individuals with ADHD in childhood may continue to show symptoms as they enter adolescence and adult life.

Recorded prevalence rates for ADHD vary substantially, partly because of changing diagnostic criteria over time, and partly because of variations in ascertainment in different settings and the frequent use of referred samples to estimate rates. A recent review of prevalence rates in school-aged community samples (rather than referred samples) indicates rates varying from 4% to 12%, with estimated prevalence based on combining these studies of 8% to 10%. In the general population, 9.2% (5.8% - 13.6%) of males and 2.9% (1.9% - 4.5%) (American Academy of Pediatrics 2000) of females are found to have behaviors consistent with ADHD. With the DSM-IV criteria (compared with earlier versions), more females have been diagnosed with the predominantly inattentive type.

CHARACTERIZING ADHD AND APD

There are no empirical markers that identify ADHD (Taylor 1986; Gordon 1991; Reid et al. 1993; Chermak et al. 1998). Therefore, diagnosis of ADHD is based on observational criteria defined as a cluster of behaviors involving impaired attention and distractibility, impulsivity, and hyperactivity (APA 1994). Patterns of inattention, hyperactivity, and impulsivity are used to differentiate ADHD into three subtypes. The predominantly inattentive type presents primary symptoms of inattention (APA 1994). The predominantly hyperactive-impulsive type is considered a behavioral regulation disorder (APA 1994). The combined type is characterized by hyperactivity-impulsivity (i.e., behavioral regulation disorder) and inattention (APA 1994).

According to the DSM-IV, impulsivity is characterized by blurting out answers, failing to take turns, and interrupting or intruding on others. Hyperactivity is characterized by fidgeting with hands or feet, squirming in seat, difficulty remaining seated, running or climbing excessively in inappropriate contexts, difficulty engaging in quiet activity, constantly moving or engaging in activity, and talking excessively. Inattention in ADHD is marked by difficulty attending to details, sustaining attention to tasks, listening when spoken to, following through on instructions, finishing or organizing tasks and activities, initiating tasks that require sustained mental effort, keeping track of objects needed for a task, ignoring extraneous stimuli, and remembering routine procedures or familiar information.

Attention deficit hyperactivity disorder subtypes are diagnosed on the basis of behaviors that have persisted for 6 months or longer. They are listed below.

DSM IV Criteria for Diagnosis of ADHD Subtypes:

A Inattention
1. Displays poor attention to details or careless mistakes
2. Has difficulty sustaining attention in tasks
3. Does not listen when spoken to
4. Does not follow through on instructions or tasks
5. Has difficulty organizing tasks
6. Has difficulty with sustained mental effort
7. Loses things necessary for tasks
8. Is often distracted by extraneous stimuli
9. Is often forgetful in daily activities

B Hyperactivity-Impulsivity

Hyperactive
1. Fidgets or squirms
2. Leaves seat in classroom
3. Runs or climbs excessively
4. Has difficulty engaging in quiet activity
5. Is always "on the go" or acts as if "driven by a motor"
6. Talks excessively

Impulsive
1. Blurts out answers
2. Has difficulty waiting turn
3. Interrupts or intrudes on others

DSM-IV criteria for diagnosis of ADHD subtypes requires the presence of six or more symptoms

ADHD Combined Types (meets criteria A and B)

ADHD Predominantly Inattentive Type (meets criterion A but not B)

ADHD Predominantly Hyperactive Impulsive Type (meets criterion B but not A)

In 1996, a description of CAPD was provided by a task force on central auditory processing, convened by the American Speech-Language and Hearing Association (ASHA 1996). Central auditory processing disorder was defined as a noted deficiency in one or more of the following behaviors: sound localization/lateralization; auditory discrimination or pattern recognition; temporal; resolution, masking, integration, or ordering; or auditory performance decrements with competing or degraded acoustic stimuli. More recently, a consensus conference has provided this definition: An auditory processing disorder (APD) is defined as a deficit in the processing of information in the auditory modality (Jerger and Musiek 2000).

Auditory processing disorder results from dysfunction of processes dedicated to audition; however, APD may coexist with more global dysfunction that affects performance across modalities (e.g., attention deficit, neural timing deficits, language representation deficit). Auditory processing disorders have been observed in diverse clinical populations, including those where central nervous system pathology or neurodevelopmental disorder is suspected (e.g., developmental language disorder, dyslexia, learning disabilities, attention deficit disorder) and those where evidence of central nervous system pathology is clear (e.g., aphasia, multiple sclerosis, epilepsy, traumatic brain injury, tumor, and Alzheimer's disease).

It seems plausible that APD and ADHD could be unique clinical entities that co-exist. There also is the distinct possibility that there could be misdiagnoses of the disorders in many instances. That is, some children with APD may actually have ADHD and vice-versa. For the purposes of this chapter, the assumption will be made that APD and ADHD do exist as individual entities, or that at least one of them is the primary deficit that is represented.

Although attention deficits frequently characterize APD and ADHD (particularly the combined and predominantly inattentive types), there are distinctions to be drawn regarding the nature of the inattention observed in the two disorders (Chermak et al. 1999). The attention deficits of ADHD typically are pervasive and supra-modal, having an impact on more than one sensory modality (APA 1994). In contrast, individuals with APD experience attention deficits that may be restricted to the auditory modality (Chermak and Musiek 1997). As noted by Chermak and Musiek, the commonly observed left-ear deficit on dichotic speech tests seen in individuals with APD, as well as their depressed auditory performance under conditions of either contralateral or ipsilateral competition as a function of the level of brain dysfunction, argues against pervasive attention deficit in APD, and helps distinguish APD from ADHD (Musiek et al. 1984, 1994; Jerger et al. 1988). Nonetheless, further research is needed to ascertain the degree to which modality specificity of processing deficits characterizes APD.

Attention deficit hyperactivity disorder is an output disorder, with sustained attention deficits (secondary to disinhibition and poor self regulation) and problems in executive functioning (Barkley 1997). On the other hand, APD is an input disorder with selective and divided attention deficits. Deficits in executive function are a secondary source of listening problems for individual with APD (Chermak et al. 1999).

It should also be noted that there is the possibility of a shared neurological basis for individuals with APD and ADHD. The results of morphological studies of children with attention deficit disorder yield similar morphological and physiological results to those studies involving children with APD and/or language disorders. This may yield important information regarding the high co-morbidity of these disorders and may provide a possible means for differential diagnosis (Riccio et al. 1994). In part, the difficulty in differential diagnosis has been attributed to the number of disorders that historically include attentional problems (Barkley 1990) and the difficulties of defining the concept of attention operationally (Fletcher et al. 1991). Benson (1991) strongly believes, based on evidence of several syndromes of abnormal mental awareness associated with prefrontal brain damage, that the frontal cortex has a special role to play in ADHD. Children with ADHD show decreased blood flow in the frontal lobes and basal ganglia, with increased metabolic activity in the primary sensory and sensorimotor regions.

Typically, according to Riccio and Hynd (1993), the studies hypothesize the involvement of cortical (frontal) and subcortical structures (brain stem, reticular activating system, thalamus, hypothalamus, and basal ganglia). The caudate nucleus also seems to be involved in the neurological basis of ADHD, because of the resemblance of ADHD to the spectrum of behaviors associated with dysfunction in the caudate-frontal axis, a system in the brain known to be important in motor regulation and behavioral inhibition. Evidence to support possible dysfunction of the caudate includes cerebral blood flow studies that found decreased metabolism in the caudate (Lou et al. 1989).

Postmortem and neuroimaging studies reveal some interesting findings in regard to brain morphology in individuals with dyslexia, learning disabilities, ADHD and controls. Post mortem studies by Galaburda et al. (1985) show nests of ectopic cells (misplaced cells) in individuals with dyslexia. Interestingly, these ectopic nests of cells are found in the left hemisphere and mostly in the auditory areas of the cortex and subcortex. It has also been noted in dyslexia and learning disabilities that the planum temporale is more symmetric or smaller on the left side than in controls where the left planum is usually larger (Kaufman and Galaburda 1989; Hynd et al. 1990). Children with ADHD show the left planum commonly larger than the right (similar to the world population) (Hynd et al. 1990). Certain areas of the corpus callosum have been shown to be smaller in brains of children with ADHD than control subjects (Hynd et al 1991).

DIAGNOSTIC ISSUES

There is an abundance of research that documents the difficulty in the differential diagnosis of attention deficit hyperactivity disorder as well as the co-morbidity of ADHD with developmental learning disorders (Cantwell and Baker 1991; Riccio and Hynd 1993). Specifically, co-morbidity has been demonstrated between ADHD and communication disorders.(Baker and Cantwell 1990).

This difficulty in differential diagnosis has become evident with regard to ADHD and central auditory processing disorders. The inclusion of attention in the conceptualization of both APD and ADHD, albeit auditory attention in APD, makes differential diagnosis difficult. In fact, it has been suggested that the diagnosis of APD or ADHD may be largely dependent on whether the child is evaluated by an audiologist or a psychologist (Keller 1992).

The relationship of attention to cognitive and behavioral functioning results in difficulty in disentangling behavioral from cognitive symptoms in children with learning disabilities. Swanson et al. (1991) argued that presumed attentional deficits can be linked neither to specific cognitive operations nor to specific neural systems. Although researchers perceive attention as a unitary process, it appears to be subserved by a number of brain structures with a corresponding variety of symptoms and etiology related to attentional deficits.

Attention can also be triggered by a stimulus to any sensory system. Bottom up attention is attention that is recruited by a stimulus such as a loud sound. When this happens, the brainstem auditory pathway inputs profusely to the reticular activating system. This, in turn, may result in garnering attention to the stimulus as well as triggering the startle and acoustic reflex (if the sound is loud enough) (Musiek and Chermak 1994; Phillips 1990).

Keith and Engineer (1991) studied the effects of methylphenidate (Ritalin) on auditory processing abilities of children with ADHD. All children ($n = 20$) were tested with and without medication. Results showed a significant improvement in performance on measures of auditory vigilance and auditory processing with medication. They concluded that the children with ADHD were functioning at a lower level than their chronological age in areas of auditory attention, auditory processing, and receptive language.

Cook et al. (1993) also studied the relationship between APD and ADHD in a double blind, placebo-controlled, single-cross-over study of methylphenidate. They studied 15 boys who meet the criteria for ADHD and 10 control boys. They concluded that sustained attention is a critical feature of performance on APD tests, and the current diagnostic criteria for APD make a clinical separation of the two disorders problematic. They also concluded that stimulants appear to be a useful treatment for the symptoms of both ADHD and APD. Finally, they concluded that APD tests may be useful measures of ADHD symptomatology and response to stimulants.

Tillery, Katz, and Keller (2000), in a double-blind placebo study, investigated the effects of methylphenidate on three tests of auditory processing in children diagnosed with both ADHD and APD. The results showed that Ritalin did not have a significant effect on any of the three central auditory processing measures, although it was found that their performance improved significantly on the attention/impulsivity test. It should be noted that improvement in the child's attentive ability facilitates the central auditory processing (CAP) evaluation, with less stress on the child and tester.

Hence, the studies above are scattered in terms of the effects of medications on APD or ADHD in regard to differentiating these two entities.

However, we will explore how individuals with mostly APD may differ from those persons with mostly ADHD (this terminology is used because it is the belief of the authors that in some cases APD exists with ADHD). This is indeed a challenge for several reasons. One reason is that the diagnostic efficiency surrounding ADHD is suspect. There is little data that addresses the validity and reliability of the instruments used in the diagnosis of ADHD. This can also be said, but to a lesser degree, about APD. Another reason for the difficulty encountered in attempting to separate ADHD from APD is that there is some common physiology underlying attention and auditory processing. The auditory pathways have profuse neural inputs to the ascending reticular activating system.

Although APD and ADHD have overlapping symptomatologies, they do seem to have behavioral profiles that can be used potentially to distinguish the two. Chermak et al. (1999) found that the rank orderings of behaviors associated with APD and those associated with ADHD were quite different when audiologists and pediatricians were polled (see list below). They asked 100 audiologists and 100 pediatricians, randomly selected from national membership rosters of ASHA (American Speech-Language and Hearing Association) and the American Pediatric Society respectively, to put in order various behaviors compiled from various checklists purportedly reflecting APD and/or ADHD:

ADHD	APD
1. Inattentive	1. Difficulty hearing in noise
2. Distracted	2. Difficulty following instructions
3. Hyperactive	3. Poor listening skills
4. Fidgety/restless	4. Academic difficulties
5. Hasty/impulsive	5. Poor auditory association skills
6. Interrupts	6. Distracted

Although a careful analysis of the above behaviors may help the clinician differentiate ADHD and APD to some limited degree in individual cases, there will continue to exist considerable diagnostic uncertainty regarding differential diagnosis of these two disorders. However, the use of a carefully selected central auditory test battery can help to more accurately separate these two types of diagnoses.

Central auditory tests have been developed based on data that indicates they are reasonably efficient in detecting central auditory dysfunction. It would seem that true APD should result in poorer scores than true ADHD on central auditory tests. Moreover, there are some specific tests and interpretations of auditory tests that may help in the differentiation of APD and ADHD. For example, on dichotic listening tasks, the majority of individuals with APD show a laterality effect (one ear score is significantly different than the other). From an audiological perspective, it seems difficult to understand how a laterality effect would occur with ADHD—an acknowledged global phenomena.

Various tests measure central auditory processing (CAP), but many of them share the common feature of binaural presentation. The task may involve monitoring the target signal in one ear while a competing message is presented to the contralateral ear, or it may require the listener to integrate information presented discretely to the two ears. Pillsbury et al. (1995) compared basic binaural processing between children with ADHD and normal children. They found that although no differences were observed on a detection task, some differences were noted on a recognition task. However, the differences did not seem to be strongly linked to binaural processing. Therefore, a reduction in binaural advantage does not seem to be a necessary contributor to poor CAP performance among children with ADHD.

Additionally, central auditory tests may help in differentiating APD and ADHD by the use of auditory evoked potentials. The auditory brainstem response (ABR) is generated by the auditory nerve and auditory brainstem pathway. Evoked potentials such as the middle latency response (MLR) are generated by auditory regions of the thalamus and cortex, and therefore can provide measures indicative of higher auditory function. Although the MLR can be affected by attention, the effects are minimal. Other test alternatives are the P300 and mismatched negativity (MMN). The P300 is governed by attention, but also engages the higher auditory system. The MMN test provides a physiological correlate to auditory discrimination without the subject attending to the task, and has been shown to be valuable for evaluating APD.

The ABR is generally normal in children with APD. However, cases where it is abnormal could be related to factors that could have an impact on auditory processing. In cases of auditory neuropathy, the ABR will be abnormal with normal otoacoustic emissions. Clearly deficits like these, though not effecting the CANS, will be devastating to auditory processing. An ABR may also be abnormal due to auditory deprivation related to such disorders as chronic otitis media or long standing hearing loss (Gunnerson and Finitzo 1991). Abnormal ABRs can result from disorders of the brainstem pathway and though rare, can have an impact on auditory processing ability (Musiek and Lee 1995).

The MLR has been shown to be abnormal in children with learning disabilities (Arehole, Augustine, and Simhadri 1995). More research with MLR needs to be done with APD and ADHD populations, because it would seem to have potential for learning more about differences in these populations.

The P300 along with the late potentials N1 and P2 have been shown to be of lower amplitude and greater latency in children with CAPD than matched controls (Jirsa and Clontz 1990). The mismatched negativity (MMN) has demonstrated (physiological) compromised auditory discrimination in APD. Again however, more work must be done to show the true value of the P300, late potentials, and MMN in not only defining APD but differentiating it from ADHD.

Evoked potential recording has become a useful functional diagnostic technique in the neurosciences. Latency prolongations provide objective evidence of clinical or subclinical disease. Short latency potentials are useful in studying fairly well-defined generators in the peripheral nervous system and the proximal central nervous system. Long latency potentials like the P300 are useful in studying cognitive and attentional functions. According to Picton (1992), if the P300 is abnormally small or delayed, there is probably some abnormality of cognitive processing. Latency is a much more reliable indicator than amplitude, since latency is difficult to alter with attention. Also, P300 amplitude may be reduced in some forms of ADHD, and may improve with treatment.

Sangal, Sangal, and Persky (1995) conducted a study to develop a classification of ADHD using P300 topography, and to find P300 topographic predictors of treatment response. They found no P300 differences between control and ADHD patients, and more treatment with pemoline produced no P300 changes. Using their paradigm, they concluded that P300 topography classifies ADHD into group 1 with normal P300 topography and good response to pemoline, and group 2 with small right frontal central auditory P300 amplitudes and poor response to pemoline.

Jonkman et al. (1999) studied ADHD and normal control children's (7 to13-years-old) performance in an auditory and visual modality on event related potential (ERP). In the auditory task, controls had more correct detections (hits), less false alarms, larger P3b amplitudes to nontarget stimuli, a larger central PN and larger early frontal positivity (100-250 milliseconds) to target stimuli than ADHD subjects. It was hypothesized that for children with ADHD, in both the auditory and the visual task, there is a deficit in the activation of the P3b process. Incorrect triggering of the P3b process might be caused by disturbances in other aspects of the attention process, preceding the P3b.

Kilpelainen et al. (1999) recorded event-related potentials of 9-year-old children with and without ADHD. The results suggest that increased distractibility may be associated with an abnormally strong cerebral orienting toward non-attended stimuli. A later negativity at around 300 milliseconds was significantly smaller in the children with ADHD than for the control group. For the authors, these findings demonstrate that event-related potential measures may be useful in helping to understand the information processing found in distractible children.

Kilpelainen, Partanen, and Karhu (1999) studied MMN in easily distractible ($n = 20$) and in non-distractible ($n = 20$) healthy 9-year-old children. The response was significantly reduced in amplitude in the distractible children. Their findings suggest that distractible children may have deficits in the frontally mediated aspects of auditory sensory memory.

Kilpelainen et al. (1999) used the P300 event-related potential (ERP) to study the auditory discrimination ability of 70 "normal" children. They investigated performance at the beginning, in the middle, and at the end of an auditory stimulus discrimination task. Easily distractible children showed frontally a short-latency P300 response to target stimuli throughout the task, whereas in the non-distractible children the corresponding response was distinctly smaller and also showed a tendency to decrease in size toward the end of the task. The short-latency frontal P300 response reflects activation of the brain's orienting networks, and it normally decreases in size when stimuli lose their "novelty value" with stimulus repetition. Persistent frontal P300 suggests that distractible children continued to show enhanced orienting to stimuli that should have already been well encoded and/or categorized.

It must be remembered that the P300 is probably generated by a number of neural processes, some of them auditory, and some of them not. It remains difficult to be sure which processes are reflecting the abnormality in the P300. However, in the use of the MLR, MMN or N1 and P2, the auditory link is strong and provides great influence to the result; however, again, even in these Eps, the auditory processes do not work alone.

Though clearly much more work must be done in differentiating APD from ADHD, there are some ways in which insights can be gained that may assist in the differentiation of these two disorders. By comparing behavioral profiles, as well as administering behavioral and electrophysiologic central auditory tests, the clinician may garner enough information to begin to untangle the APD ADHD mystery.

Finally, considerable studies need to focus on the concept of APD and ADHD disorders, and more studies must be done on the sensitivity and specificity of the instruments that are currently in use for the diagnosis of APD and ADHD.

REFERENCES

American Academy of Pediatrics 2000. Clinical practice guideline: Diagnosis and evaluation of the child with attention deficit hyperactivity disorder. *Pediatrics* 105(5):1158–70.

American Psychiatric Association 1994. *Diagnostic and Statistical Manual for Mental Disorders*, 4th ed. Washington, DC: American Psychiatric Association.

American Speech-Language-Hearing Association Task Force on Central Auditory Processing Consensus Development. 1996. Central auditory processing: Current status of research and implications for clinical practice. *American Journal of Audiology* 5:41–54.

Arehole, S., Augustine, L., and Simhadri, R. 1995. Middle latency response in children with learning disabilities: Preliminary findings. *Journal of Communications Disorders* 28:21–38.

Baker, L., and Cantwell, D. P. 1990. The association between emotional/behavior disorders and learning disorders in children with speech/language disorders. *Advances in Learning and Behavioral Disabilities* 6:27–46.

Barkley, R. A. 1990. *Attention Deficit Hyperactivity Disorder: A Handbook for Diagnosis and Treatment*. New York: Guilford Press.

Barkley, R. A. 1997. Behavioral inhibition, sustained attention and executive functions: Constructing a unifying theory for ADHD. *Psychological Bulletin* 121:65–94.

Benson, D. F. 1991. The role of frontal dysfunction in attention deficit hyperactivity disorder. *Journal of Child Neurology* 6:9–12.

Cantwell, D. P., and Baker, L. 1991. Association between attention deficit hyperactivity disorder and learning disorders. *Journal of Learning Disabilities* 24: 88–94.

Chermak, G. D., and Musiek, F. E. 1997. *Central Auditory Processing Disorders: New Perspectives*. San Diego: Singular Press.

Chermak, G. D., Somers, E. K., and Seikel, J. A. 1998. Behavioral signs of central auditory processing disorders and attention deficit hyperactivity disorder. *Journal of the American Academy of Audiology* 9:78–84.

Chermak, G. D., Hall III, J. W., and Musiek, F. E. 1999. Differential diagnosis and management of central auditory processing disorder and attention deficit hyperactivity disorder. *Journal of the American Academy of Audiology* 10:289–303.

Cook, J. R., Mausbach, T., Burd, L., Gascon, G. G., Slotnick, H. B., Patterson, B., Johnson, R. D., Hankey, B., and Reynolds, B. W. 1993. A preliminary study of the relationship between central auditory processing and attention deficit disorder. *Journal of Psychiatry Neuroscience* 18(3):130–7.

Fletcher, J. M., Morris, R. D., and Francis, D. J. 1991. Methodological issues in the classification of attention-related disorders. *Journal of Learning Disabilities* 24:72–7.

Galaburda, A., Sherman, G. F., Rosen, G. D., Aboitiz, F., and Geschwind, N. 1985. Developmental dyslexia: Four consecutive patients with cortical anomalies. *Annals of Neurology* 18:222–33.

Gordon, M. 1991. *ADHD / Hyperactivity: A Consumer's Guide* 1991. Dewitt, NY: GSI Publications.

Gunnerson, A., and Finitzo, T. 1991. Conductive hearing loss during infancy: Effects on later auditory brainstem electrophysiology. *Journal of Speech and Hearing Research* 34:1207–15.

Hynd, G. W., Semrud-Clickeman, M., Lorys, A. R., Novey, E. S., and Eliopulos, D. 1990. Brain morphology in developmental dyslexia and attention deficit disorder/hyperactivity. *Archives of Neurology* 47:919–26.

Hynd, G. W., Semrud-Clickeman, M., and Lyytinen, H. 1991. Brain imaging in learning disabilities. *Neuropsychological Foundations of Learning Disabilities* 18:475–511.

Jerger, S., Johnson, K., and Loiselle, L. 1988. Pediatric central auditory dysfunction: Comparison of children with a confirmed lesion versus suspected processing disorders. *American Journal of Otology* 9:63–71.

Jerger, J., and Musiek, F. 2000. Report of the consensus conference on the diagnosis of auditory processing disorders in school-aged children. *Journal of the American Academy of Audiology* 11:467–74.

Jirsa, R., and Clontz, K. 1990. A long latency auditory event-related potentials from children with auditory processing disorders. *Ear and Hearing* 11:222–32.

Jonkman, L. M., Kemner, C., Verbaten, M. N., Koelega, H. S., Camfferman, G., v d Gaag, R. J., Buitelaar, J. K., and van Engeland, H. 1999. Event-related potentials and performance of attention-deficit hyperactivity disorder: Children and normal controls in auditory and visual selective attention tasks. *Neuroreport* 10 (9):1869–74.

Kaufmann, W. E., and Galaburda, A. M. 1989. Cerebrocortical microdysgenesis in neurologically normal subjects: A Histopathic study. *Neurology* 39:238–44.

Keith, R. W., and Engineer, P. 1991. Effects of methylphenidate on the auditory processing abilities of children with attention deficit-hyperactivity disorder. *Journal of Learning Disabilities* 24:630–6.

Keller, W. D. 1992. Auditory processing disorder or attention deficit disorder. In *Central Auditory Processing: A Transdisciplinary View*, eds. J. Katz, N. Stecker, and D. Henderson. Chicago: Mosby Yearbook.

Kilpelainen, R., Partanen, J., and Karhu, J. 1999. Reduced mismatch negativity (MMN) suggests deficits in pre-attentive auditory processing in distractible children. *Neuroreport* 10(16):3341–5.

Kilpelainen, R., Luoma, L., Herrgard, E., Ypparila, H., Partanen, J., and Karhu, J. 1999. Persistent frontal P300 brain potential suggests abnormal processing of auditory information in distractible children. *Neuroreport* 10(16):3405–10.

Lazar, J. W., and Frank, Y. 1998. Frontal systems dysfunction in children with attention deficit/hyperactivity disorder and learning disabilities. *The Journal of Neuropsychiatry and Clinical Neurosciences* 10:160–7.

Lou, H. C., Henriksen, L., Bruhn, P., Borner, H., and Nielsen, J. B. 1989. Striatal dysfunction attention deficit and hyperkinetic disorder. *Archives of Neurology* 46:48–52.

Musiek, F. E., Kibbe, K., and Baran, J. A. 1984. Neuroaudiological results from split-brain patients. *Seminars in Hearing* 5:219–30.
Musiek, F. E., and Chermak, G. D. 1994. Three commonly asked questions about central auditory processing disorders: Assessment. *American Journal of Audiology 3:23–27.*
Musiek, F., and Lee, W. 1995. Auditory brainstem response in patients with brainstem or cochlear pathology. *Ear and Hearing* 16:631–6.
Phillips, D. 1990. Neural representation of sound amplitude in the auditory cortex: Effects of noise masking. *Behavioral Brain Research* 37:197–214.
Picton, T. W. 1992. The P300 wave of the human event related potential. *Journal of Clinical Neurophysiology* 9:456–79.
Pillsbury, H. C., Grose, J. H., Coleman, W. L., Conners, C. K., Hall, J. W. 1995. Binaural function in children with attention-deficit hyperactivity disorder. *Archives of Otolaryngology Head Neck Surgery* 121:1345–50.
Reid, R., Maag, J. W., and Vasa, S. F. 1993. Attention deficit hyperactivity disorder as a disability category: A critique. *Exceptional Child* 60:198–214.
Riccio, C. A., and Hynd, G. W. 1993. Developmental language disorders in children: Relationship with learning disabilities and attention deficit hyperactivity disorder. *School Psychology Review* 22:696–708.
Riccio, C. A., Hynd, G. W., Cohen, M. J., Hall, J., and Molt, L. 1994. Comorbidity of central auditory processing disorder and attention deficit hyperactivity disorder. *Journal of the American Academy of Child and Adolescent Psychiatry* 33:849–57.
Sangal, J. M., Sangal, R. B., and Persky, B. 1995. Abnormal auditory P300 topography in attention deficit disorder predicts poor response to Pemoline. *Clinical Electroencephalography* 26(4):204–13.
Swanson, J. M., Posner, M., Potkin, S., Bonforte, S., Youpa, D., Fiore, C., Cantwell, D., and Crinella, F. 1991. Activating tasks for the study of visual-spatial attention in ADHD children: A cognitive anatomic approach. *Journal of Child Neurology* 6:119–27.
Taylor, E. 2000. *The Overactive Child. Clinics in Development Medicine,* No. 97, Philadelphia: J. B. Lippincott.
Tillery, K. L., Katz, J., and Keller, W. D. 2000. Effects of Methylphenidate (Ritalin) on auditory performance in children with attention and auditory processing disorders. *Journal of Speech, Language, and Hearing Research* 43:893–901.

Section • III

Treatment and Outcome

Chapter • 9

Comprehensive Treatments for Children with ADHD

Anil Chacko, Gregory A. Fabiano, Andy Williams, and William E. Pelham, Jr.

Attention deficit/hyperactivity disorder (ADHD) is the most common mental health disorder of childhood; it affects 3% to 5% of the population. Approximately 90% of children in clinic samples are boys. It is a chronic disorder characterized by abnormally high levels of inattention, impulsivity, and overactivity. The symptoms of ADHD result in serious impairment in many domains of functioning for affected children, including school, family, and peer domains. These dysfunctions highlight the seriousness of ADHD as a childhood problem, and predict the development of even more serious problems and poor outcomes that occur for individuals with ADHD in adolescence and adulthood. Thus, effective treatment for childhood ADHD is a major concern for parents, educators, and primary medical and mental health workers.

Children with ADHD are referred to treatment through a number of avenues. Teachers are often the first people to recognize the behavioral excesses of children with ADHD, perhaps because they are better able than parents to compare the child's behavior to a normative group of classmates, and the demands in school are greater than at home (e.g., sitting at a desk for the day or completing tasks that require sustained mental effort). The Individuals with Disabilities Act (IDEA) is a federal law that mandates that all schools actively identify and provide special education services to children with disabilities that impair academic progress, and many children are identified with

ADHD and receive services through this process. Once identified by the school, the most common referral is to primary health care professionals for further evaluation.

ASSESSMENT

Diagnosis of ADHD should be based on DSM-IV criteria (APA; American Psychiatric Association 1994). Children must exhibit symptoms of inattention and/or hyperactivity/impulsivity for at least six months to meet criteria for ADHD. In addition, there must be clear evidence that these symptoms cause impairment in daily life functioning and that this impairment is present in two or more settings (e.g., home, school, recreational activities). Clinicians must also determine that the symptoms are chronic in nature, and that some symptoms must have caused impairment before the age of seven. The American Academy of Pediatrics (AAP, 2000) recently published clinical practice guidelines for the diagnosis and evaluation of ADHD in children. Our recommendations below closely adhere to those found in these practice guidelines in several ways, including the use of parent and teacher ratings of the child's behavior for diagnosis, the importance of functional impairment in diagnosis and treatment, the evaluation of comorbid disorders in a comprehensive assessment, and the lack of evidence for the use of office-based tests with the child to establish the diagnosis of ADHD. These recommendations and several others are detailed below.

How should a diagnosis be made in clinical practice? Diagnostic information should be gathered from adults in the natural environment regarding (1) the degree to which the child displays developmentally inappropriate levels of the core symptoms (inattention, impulsivity, hyperactivity) and (2) associated impairment in daily life functioning. This information is typically gathered in several ways. Informed, clinical interviews with parents and teachers in which information is gathered regarding presenting problems and symptomatology. Clinicians with an eye on subsequent treatment will additionally ask about the associated environmental settings, events, and responses that might be useful in conceptualizing the targets of and nature of behavioral treatments. Alternately, especially in research settings, systematic structured interviews are used (i.e., K-SADS; Orvaschel and Puig-Antich 1995; Diagnostic Interview Schedule for Children; Shaffer et al. 1996). Such interviews ask about DSM symptoms of ADHD; they are designed to yield a DSM diagnosis. Their high degree of structure makes them very reliable, but impractical for clinical practice. Because children tend to be poor/inaccurate raters of their externalizing behavior problems, interviewing the child has little utility for diagnosing ADHD, and therefore interviewing the child is not recommended.

In addition to a structured interview, rating scales should be administered to the parent and teacher to obtain information on symptoms of ADHD as well as associated problems and functional impairment (e.g., Swanson, Nolan, and Pelham [SNAP] rating scale; Atkins, Pelham, and Licht 1984; Disruptive Behavior Disorder Scale [DBD]; Pelham, Gnagy, Greenslade, and Milich 1992; ADHD Rating Scale; DuPual et al. 1998; Conners Rating Scale; Goyette, Conners, and Ulrich 1978; Pelham, Milich, Murphy, and Murphy 1989; Child Behavior Checklist [CBCL]; Achenbach 1978; Achenbach and Edelbrock 1981). Some standardized rating scales ask about DSM symptoms of ADHD and disruptive behavior disorders (e.g., SNAP, DBD, ADHD rating scale), although others ask about a broad range of behaviors in addition to ADHD symptoms (e.g., Conners Rating Scale, CBCL). An advantage of using such rating scales is that they are less costly than interviews, yet they provide comparable data regarding the child's symptoms. It is important to note, however, that interpretation of rating scales without an accompanying discussion with the parent might result in the parent's inadvertently exaggerating the nature of the child's difficulties, whereas some teachers may minimize the child's difficulties. The correlations between parent and teacher ratings are typically on the order of .4 to .6 (Achenbach, McConaughy and Howell 1987). As is often the case, discrepancies occur in ratings because of differences in adult perceptions and tolerance of problematic behavior. Also, a child's behavior may vary across settings and with different adults, and differences in ratings reflect these differences in behavior. When parent and teacher ratings are discrepant, it is important to place more weight on the teacher's report of the child's problems. Teachers have more knowledge than parents regarding normative behavior and therefore are better able to compare the child's behavior to his or her peers. In addition, when confronted with discrepancies, it is useful to gather information from multiple sources (e.g., father, other teachers), thereby obtaining a more complete picture of the child's impairment across settings and raters.

As the AAP diagnostic guidelines (2000) make clear, it is important to note that no medical (e.g., neurological exam, MRI, EEG) or psychological (e.g., intelligence and achievement testing, continuous performance tasks, neuropsychological testing) tests are useful for diagnosing ADHD. Although some advocate, for example, neuropsychological tests, reviews have shown such tests to be lacking in their ability to accurately diagnose ADHD (Barkley 1992). Despite the fact that traditional testing is not useful in diagnosing ADHD, some tests may be useful for ruling other disorders in or out. For example, learning disabilities are often comorbid with ADHD, and standardized intelligence and achievement testing is necessary for identifying the presence of comorbid learning disabilities. The *absence* of symptoms during an office visit, one-to-one testing session, or while watching television/playing video games is also usually not informative. Physicians who base their diagnoses of ADHD on children's behavior during office visits miss a large portion of true ADHD cases (Sleator 1982) and ADHD children can watch television with little difficulties under most circumstances (Milich and Lorch 1994).

A major point regarding assessment for ADHD concerns what are the appropriate foci of assessment and targets of treatment. Over the past 20 years, most researchers and clinicians in the psychiatric community have strongly emphasized the importance of making an accurate DSM diagnosis for ADHD and using DSM symptoms of ADHD as targets in treatment and measures of treatment outcome. We have contributed to this approach through our development of parent and teacher rating scales that enabled DSM symptomatology to be relatively easily measured (e.g., the SNAP rating scale, DBD rating scale). We have recently become increasingly aware of the incompatibility between our routine clinical practice and this emphasis on diagnosis and symptoms. Specifically, we have always focused our initial assessment and our behavioral treatments, as well as our evaluation of pharmacological interventions, on the child's problems in daily functioning in the home, school, and peer settings. These problems in daily functioning (e.g., peer relationships, adult relationships, academic achievement, self-esteem, family functioning) are codified in DSM-IV as *impairment*, and clinically significant and cross-situational impairment must be demonstrated for a diagnosis to be made (APA 1994; Lahey et al. 1998). Such functional outcomes also constitute the goals and measures of treatment response. Practitioners of behavior modification have always known this and have therefore focused initial assessment and subsequent interventions on socially valid problems in daily functioning—typically called "target behaviors"—rather than focusing on DSM symptoms (Mash and Terdal 1997).

For example, our clinical work always begins with a detailed, functional analysis of a child's referring problems. This is accomplished by obtaining information from parents, teachers, and other sources about the child's functioning in multiple domains (e.g., academic, peer) and contexts (home, school, and recreational settings). Parents do not bring children for treatment complaining about DSM symptoms. Rarely do presenting problems include the DSM symptoms of ADHD (e.g., "fidgeting" or "often does not seem to listen when spoken to directly"). Instead, referring problems typically include peer-rejection, noncompliance with adult requests, not completing school assignments in a timely fashion, failure to follow school and home rules, and disruptive classroom behavior.

Although the DSM system is useful for screening for ADHD and identifying the presence of symptoms of the disorder, its utility is limited because a DSM diagnosis does not provide any useful treatment information, and it does not provide targets for intervention, or information regarding treatment outcomes (Scotti et al. 1996). Instead of DSM symptoms the clinician should identify socially relevant and individually meaningful target behaviors, the environmental and interpersonal antecedents and consequences, and the setting events that are associated with these behaviors and used in treatment. This may only be achieved through a comprehensive functional analysis. A functional analytic approach includes an A-B-C analysis; an analysis that describes the functional relationship between the antecedents of the behavior (A; i.e., settings, people, time of day), the behavior itself (B), and the consequences of the behavior (C; i.e., what does the child obtain from the behavior—attention, removal of demands). (See Mash and Terdal 1997, for an expanded discussion of how to conduct a functional analysis in the initial stages of treatment planning.) It is important to note that assessment and treatment conceptualization is an ongoing process because the child's presenting problems change over time and require ongoing monitoring and modification.

TREATMENT APPROACHES

There are two effective short-term approaches to treatment for ADHD: medication with a central nervous stimulant, and behavior modification. Pharmacotherapy has been widely reviewed (Swanson et al. 1995); we shall focus here on behavioral treatment and the combination of behavioral and pharmacological treatment. Because attention deficit hyperactivity disorder is a chronic disorder that manifests itself throughout the life of an individual, treatment must be sustained throughout development. A number of reviews on the treatment literature have been recently completed on ADHD. Pelham, Wheeler, and Chronis (1998) determined that behavioral parent training and behavioral classroom interventions (e.g., daily home notes, time out, reward programs), but not cognitive-behavioral interventions, met criteria for well-established, evidence-based treatments in a review by the Task Force of the American Psychological Association (Lonigan, Elbert, and Johnson 1998). Similarly, DuPaul and Eckert (1997) recently reviewed school-based interventions used to treat ADHD, and they also concluded that contingency management strategies were effective treatments for ADHD in the schools. Fabiano et al. (2000) recently presented a meta-analysis of behavioral and combined behavioral and pharmacological treatments that indicated significant effects of both treatment modalities. In total, more than 70 studies were reviewed with more than 2000 participants.

Based on the available evidence, both behavior modification, and the combination of behavioral and pharmacological treatment for ADHD have demonstrated short-term effectiveness for reducing both impairment and symptoms in a number of studies, a conclusion also reached by representatives of the American Medical Association (Goldman et al. 1998), a National Institutes of Health Consensus Conference Statement (1998), and the American Academy of Child and Adolescent Psychiatry (1998).

Behavior Modification

The implementation of behavioral interventions in the treatment for children with ADHD has a history dating back more than 25 years (O'Leary et al. 1976), and has been used for more than 30 years to treat children described as being disruptive, aggressive, or conduct disordered (e.g., O'Leary and Becker 1967). It is important to note that many of the children in studies of behavioral treatment in the 60s and 70s would have met criteria for ADHD if DSM criteria had been used (e.g., Walker, Hops, and Johnson 1976; O'Leary and Becker 1967; Patterson 1974). Thus, there is an extensive literature with a long history on the implementation and efficacy of behavior modification as a treatment option for children with ADHD that even predates the widespread use of the ADHD diagnosis.

Applications of traditional, outpatient-based clinical behavior therapy have typically involved training either parents or teachers, or both, to implement contingency management programs with their children (e.g., Anastopoulos et al. 1993; Horn et al. 1987; MTA Cooperative Group 1999; O'Leary and Pelham 1978; Pelham et al. 1988; Pisterman et al. 1989). Typical clinical parent training programs consist of a series of 8 to 16 weekly sessions wherein parents are given assigned readings and are taught standard behavioral techniques (Barkley 1987; Barkley 1995; Cunningham, Bremner, and Secord-Gilbert 1994; Forehand and Long 1996; Webster-Stratton 1992). Table I lists the components of a typical sequence of parent training sessions.

These programs typically use manuals as guides for a clinician to follow when conducting treatment and teach the fundamentals of social learning theory, as well as basic information about ADHD. Parent training is usually accomplished in groups, although some programs include individual sessions, with homework assignments given for parents to track behavior and practice techniques with their children. In a chronic disease model, treatment may change form but it does not stop. Thus, there should be continued support and contact with the family for as long as necessary, sometimes over a period of years and/or periodically when deterioration of behavior occurs for the child.

Table I. Typical Sequence of Sessions for Parent Training and Teacher Consultation in a Clinical Behavioral Intervention.

Parent Training	
1.	Introduction to ADHD, rationale for treatment, overview of Social Learning and Behavior Management Principles
2.	Home/school daily report card, home-based reward menu
3.	Giving effective commands and reprimands
4.	Time out
5.	Attending, rewarding and ignoring skills
6.	Establishing and enforcing rules/when—then contingencies
7.	Home point system-reward and response cost
8.	Planned activities and setting generalization outside of the home
9.	Level systems and fading procedures
10.	Maintenance of program after contact ends
Teacher Consultation	
1.	Introduction to ADHD, rationale for, and overview of treatment; obtain teacher/school commitment to implement intervention, introduce social learning theory and behavioral classroom management procedures, assess teacher knowledge and use of behavioral procedures, and design content of subsequent sessions accordingly.
2.	Establish and post operationalized classroom rules
3.	Home/school daily report card (always done)
4.	Structure/instructional modifications for an individual child
5.	Attending, praising, rewarding, skills
6.	Giving effective commands and reprimands, enforcing rules and when—then contingencies
7.	Class-wide interventions
8.	Group contingencies
9.	Response cost/reward point or token system for the target child
10.	Time out (classroom, office, and systematic exclusion)

Note: Every consultation contact includes a functional assessment of child's current progress toward treatment goals, and these goals/treatment strategies are continually added, deleted, and modified based on the effectiveness of current treatment and the child's current functional impairment.

Programs for maintenance and relapse prevention are also components of effective treatment for intervening in issues such as the development of plans that deal with other related family problems— maternal depression, parental substance abuse, and divorce. Given a chronic disease model and the developmental changes that occur in ADHD (i.e., puberty, changes in school, parent-child relationships) it will also be necessary to re-establish contact with the family for major developmental transitions such as adolescence, when the problems of ADHD children often worsen at the same time they become most reluctant to take mediation. This speaks to the need for consistent monitoring and contact on the part of the primary care physician with these families.

Regarding school interventions, therapists or within-district school consultants (e.g., school psychologists) often work with the teachers in a consultation model to teach the same kinds of behavioral strategies (see table I) that are taught to parents, including daily report cards (DRCs) and other classroom management strategies that can be implemented by the teacher with the target child or the entire class, such as immediate feedback following target behaviors, reward or response cost point systems (that is earning and losing points toward a reward), group contingencies, and time out (Abramowitz et al. 1992; Atkins, Pelham, and White 1989; Carlson et al. 1992; Hoza et al. 1992; Kelley and McCain 1995; Pelham et al. 1993; Rapport, Murphy, and Bailey 1982).

The development of the Daily Report Card (DRC) is an essential and first-line behavioral strategy in a school-based treatment of ADHD. There are several advantages of implementing a DRC. The DRC is an effective, inexpensive, method of identifying, monitoring, and changing the child's classroom problems. It provides an avenue of regular communication between the parents and the teacher, is highly motivating to the child if the parents have selected the right rewards at home, and can be used to titrate medication dosages. Figure 1 depicts a typical DRC for a child with ADHD.

Child's Name: ______________________ Date: __________

	Special	LA	Math	Reading	SS/ Science
Follows class rules with no more than 3 rule violations per period.	Y N	Y N	Y N	Y N	Y N
Completes assignments within the designated time.	Y N	Y N	Y N	Y N	Y N
Completes assignments at 80% accuracy.	Y N	Y N	Y N	Y N	Y N
Complies with teacher requests. (no more than 3 instances of noncompliance per period)	Y N	Y N	Y N	Y N	Y N
No more than 3 instances of talking back to adults per period	Y N	Y N	Y N	Y N	Y N
OTHER					
Follows bus rules.	Y N				
Follows recess rules.	Y N				
Total Number of Yeses	________				
Teacher's Initials					

Comments: ______________________________

Figure 1. Sample Daily Report Card (DRC).

To establish a DRC, the therapist meets with the teachers and other school staff involved with the child to assess the child's impairment in a variety of domains in the manner previously described. The purpose of this assessment is to identify general target functional goals (e.g., improving academic performance). These general goals are then defined in terms of operationally defined, specific target behaviors that can be changed to accomplish the defined goal (e.g., following classroom rules, not disturbing other children, and completing seatwork with accuracy). The therapist, teacher and school staff should then list approximately three to six target behaviors and decide upon what criteria a child must meet in order to earn a reward for attaining the DRC. The criteria for meeting the DRC criteria should be attainable for the child so that the child has initial success with the DRC, and then gradually changed over time in order to shape the child's behavior to the desired goal. For example, a behavior that may be targeted for a student can be following classroom rules. In the sample DRC in figure 1, the child's typical level of rule violations was four per period, and the teacher felt that a reduction of one per period was reachable for this child.

After meeting with the school staff and setting appropriate goals, the therapist meets with the parents to help them establish appropriate home-based rewards contingent upon the child's daily school performance. The menu of possible rewards should incorporate the child's suggestions in order to include items that are reinforcing to the child. The menu should be developed to provide reinforcement for partial success by having the menu broken down into several units or levels. As depicted in table II, the child has the opportunity to earn a variety of rewards, depending upon the percentage attained on the DRC for that day. If the child has an extremely good day, he or she has the opportunity to earn his or her most reinforcing daily reward (e.g., earning a day off from chores).

Some teachers establish goals for children at school but refrain from providing rewards for successful behavior either at school or at home. Such programs are unlikely to have a beneficial impact on the child. Rewards, contingent upon the child's behavior, must be used in order to motivate the child to change his or her behavior. We also recommend that parents implement weekly and longer-term reinforcers so that the child is motivated toward long-term goals (e.g., saving points for a weekend movie) along with the daily reinforcers. Such long-term rewards may aid the child in developing the ability to delay gratification, a suggested deficit that is specific to externalizing disorders of childhood (Krueger et al. 1996).

The DRC is an effective method of monitoring and changing difficult behavior within the classroom, at the same time providing a

Table II. Reward Menu List

Possible Reward List

Level I (Attains 95% or greater on DRC)
- Visiting a friends house
- Games on computer
- Earning a day off from chores
- 30 minutes of T.V.

Level II (Attains 85%- 94% on DRC)
- Having story read to
- Making popcorn
- 15 minutes of video game time

Level III (Attains 75%-84% on DRC)
- Talking on phone
- Listening to radio/stereo
- Playing outside
- Extra bathtub time

Weekly Rewards
- Going to a park
- Having friend over to spend the night
- Going to see a movie
- Renting a movie
- Going to fast-food restaurant with parent/family
- Going fishing

Note: Older children could save over weeks to get a monthly (or longer) reward as long as visual displays (e.g., having pieces of a puzzle that, when combined, depicts the activity the child has chosen) are used; camping trip with parent, trip to baseball game, purchase of a video game cartridge

means of daily communication between the school and the child's parents. However, it is extremely important to remember that the implementation of behavioral interventions can be complicated; consistency, and ongoing monitoring and modification are the rule. Research has indicated that brief behavioral consultations, in which teachers have one or two consultations and then are left to implement behavioral interventions on their own, are ineffective (Fuchs and Fuchs 1989). Given the chronic nature of this disorder, continuous monitoring and adjustment of treatment goals must occur within and across school years.

The efficacy of clinical behavior therapy approaches have been evaluated in a number of studies (Klein and Abikoff 1997; Pelham et al. 1988; MTA Cooperative Group 1999). In general, the behavior therapy techniques examined in these studies consistently revealed considerable improvement relative to control conditions, in both classroom and home settings, results similar to those reported in numerous studies of behavioral treatments of aggressive (e.g., CD, ODD) children (Brestan and Eyberg 1998), many of whom also have comorbid ADHD. Additionally, some studies examined a broad array of measures of parental functioning and reported improvement in those domains, though they were not specifically targeted (Anastopoulos et al. 1993; Pisterman et al. 1992; Wells et al. 2000). Although not as dramatic, not as large in magnitude, and requiring more time and effort than pharmacological interventions, the changes brought about by behavioral interventions are typically substantial, reflected in clinically significant improvement in adaptive functioning at home and at school (MTA Cooperative Group 1999). Further, parents and teachers are much less likely to drop out of treatment and much more satisfied with behavioral treatment compared to medication (Pelham, Gnagy, and Greiner 2000). For many children with ADHD, behavioral treatment consisting of parent training and DRCs at school are a sufficient treatment as long as they are maintained over time. For others, additional interventions, either more intensive behavioral treatment or adjunctive pharmacological treatments are required. Which of these two alternatives—more intensive behavioral treatments or medication—is used, depends on parent and teacher preferences and family and school resources. Some single-subject studies using potent behavior modification procedures (Hoza et al. 1992; Hupp and Reitman 1999; Northup et al. 1999; Rapport et al. 1982) demonstrate equivalent, or even superior, effects of behavior modification compared to medication in classroom and play settings, demonstrating a "dosage" effect of behavior modification comparable to dose effects with CNS stimulants. For parents who have the skills and resources, relatively more time- and energy-intensive interventions, such as response cost procedures or time out, may be equivalent treatment alternatives for stimulant medication.

Over the past decade, there has been a significant development in the area of intensive behavioral treatment programs, including the Children's Summer Treatment Program (STP; MTA Cooperative Group 1999; Pelham and Hoza 1996, Pelham et al. 2000). The STP combines an intensive treatment program, which includes home-, school-, and child-based behavioral modification techniques with built-in maintenance treatment, and an outpatient follow-up program to provide maximally effective psychosocial interventions. The STP runs for nine hours on weekdays for eight weeks. In the context of a summer-camp/summer-school-like program with a broad treatment focus, children are placed in age-matched groups of 12 that stay together throughout the day, so that the children receive intensive experience in functioning as a group and in developing peer-relationships. Each group spends 2 hours daily in classrooms in which paper and pencil, peer tutoring, and computer-assisted instruction is provided. The remainder of the day consists of recreational group activities. During these classes and recreational activities, a set of evidence-based treatment components is implemented.

The STP has been shown to result in dramatic improvements in many areas of functioning including parent, teacher, and staff ratings of improvement; standardized parent ratings of disruptive behavior, direct observations of social and academic behaviors, self-esteem, parental satisfaction, and measures of social validity (Pelham and Hoza 1996). For example, 96% of the parents rated the children as improved and 93% said that they would recommend the program to other parents. Notably, these positive treatment effects were equivalent for children in areas that routinely predict poor treatment response; children with comorbid aggression, children from single-parent households, and for children from low-income families, with a low (3%) dropout rate from treatment. This suggests that the STP effects are potent enough to overcome these variables and the context of the STP may prove to be a useful one for children who are resistant to other behavioral interventions. A recent study showed that when children in the multisite treatment study for ADHD (MTA Cooperative Group 1999) were in the STP, the most intensive phase of the behavioral treatment, the STP behavioral treatment was as effective as stimulant medication in changing outcomes and normalizing ADHD children on most measures (Pelham et al. 2000).

Adjunctive Psychostimulant Medication

If parents whose children are not sufficiently responding to behavioral treatment decide to turn to adjunctive medication treatment, rather then more potent behavioral treatments, central nervous system stimulants are the well-validated choice. In addition to psychosocial treatments, the short-term efficacy of central nervous system stimulants is well documented in the treatment of ADHD (Spencer et al. 1996; Swanson et al. 1995), having been very widely used and recommended for the past 30 years. Although our focus on medication is how to combine it with behavioral treatments, we shall discuss several aspects of medication that are relevant.

First, approximately two-thirds of ADHD children show beneficial short-term responses to stimulant medication, with the other third showing no response or an adverse response. Improvements resulting from stimulant medication have been found on teacher ratings of classroom behavior, parent-child interactions, peer interactions (e.g., aggression), and daily classroom seat work productivity. However, there are large individual differences among children who respond positively to medication, both in terms of the effects of medication on different domains of functioning and the specific medication and dosage needed to bring about beneficial effects (Pelham and Smith 2000). Thus, stimulant effects in the natural environment cannot be predicted either from a placebo-controlled, single-dose test on a laboratory/office task, or from some other variable that can be measured prior to medicating children (Pelham and Milich 1991). The only way to determine whether stimulant medications are beneficial for a child with ADHD is to measure drug effects on that child's domains of impairment in the setting of interest (e.g., school and home) and to base titration and dosing decisions on those measures. We discuss below an efficient way for the physician to gather information from parents and teachers.

Methylphenidate (Ritalin; MPH) is the most commonly prescribed of the stimulants. Behavioral effects of methylphenidate are typically observed within thirty minutes, peak approximately two hours after ingestion, and disappear two hours later. Therefore, most children with ADHD who are medicated with Ritalin must take two or three doses of medication (e.g., morning, noon, and late afternoon) to ensure that they are effectively medicated throughout an entire day. Although stimulants tend to be somewhat less effective for preschoolers, adolescents, and adults than they are with elementary-aged children, positive results have been reported with these age groups (Smith et al. 1998, Evans et al. in press). With adolescents, the utility of medication may depend largely upon compliance, an understudied issue.

Children with ADHD do not all respond similarly to all stimulants. A number of studies have shown that some children responded best to a d-amphetamine-based stimulant; others respond best to a MPH-based drug, while still others respond equally to the two different drugs (Pelham et al. 1999a, b). The implication of these studies is that children should be routinely tried on both forms of stimulants prior to selecting a drug for the child's long-term regimen. This argument does not extend to nonstimulants, however. The U.S. Food and Drug Administration (FDA) has not approved other drugs (e.g., antianxiety agents, antidepressants, major tranquilizers) either alone or in combination with stimulants for the treatment of ADHD, and evidence for the efficacy and safety of these agents in ADHD is sorely lacking. What evidence is available suggests that these second line agents are not very effective in treating ADHD. Therefore, it is the responsibility of physicians to inform parents that there is no proven efficacy of these medications in children, and the risks are unknown when prescribing them for children with ADHD.

Issues with compliance and the short-term effects (i.e., 3–4 hours) of immediate release MPH have been partially responsible for recent and increasing interest in long-lasting formulations of stimulants. Pelham et al. (1990) reported that Dexedrine Spansules are an effective alternative to immediate release MPH, but that Slow Release Ritalin was not (Pelham et al. 1987, 1990). Recent studies have shown that some dosage strengths of Adderall (e.g., 10 mg or .3 mg/kg), can be effectively administered once in the morning to last throughout a typical school day, while the same dose of MPH must be administered both morning and noon (Manos, Short, and Findling 2000; Pliszka, Browne, Olvera, and Wyne 2000; Swanson, et al. 1998; Pelham et al. 1999b). Thus both Dexedrine Spansules and Adderall provide effective coverage throughout a school day with a single morning dose. For children whose impairment requires medication in the evening hours, a t.i.d. regimen of immediate release MPH is useful, as is a small late afternoon booster dose of Adderall (Pelham et al. 1999b; Stein et al. 1996).

Alternatively, there is a new long-acting preparation of methylphenidate, Concerta, which is as effective as t.i.d. dosing of immediate release methylphenidate across multiple domains (e.g., disruptive behavior, attention, seat work completion and accuracy) and settings (laboratory recreation and classroom, home, regular classroom) (Pelham et al., under review). Thus, Adderall, Concerta, and Dexedrine Spansules are viable alternatives to multiple dosing regimens of methylphenidate and offer families with medication compliance issues an effective means of ensuring that their children are dosed in crucial impaired domains and settings with once daily dosing.

A final issue regarding medication is how often children should be medicated. Some experts recommend that all children be treated t.i.d., 7 days a week, 52 weeks per year. We disagree with this approach. Just as with any other treatment, stimulants are used to reduce impairment and improve functioning in target domains. Therefore, medication regimens should be based firmly on impairment. A child should be medicated only in settings and during times when impairment is experienced and other treatments do not alleviate it. For some children, this may mean school time only, while for others it may mean medicating for coverage at home in the evenings and on weekends. All things considered, minimizing a child's lifetime dose of medication is an important goal. By medicating for impairment rather than across the board regardless of need, this goal can be accomplished.

Much evidence supports the use of stimulants in the treatment of ADHD. However, the use of stimulants and other pharmacological interventions as viable treatments for ADHD must be tempered by their limitations (Swanson et al. 1995).

Parents need to be clearly informed regarding these limitations. Notably, despite many studies documenting the short-term efficacy of stimulant treatment, there *are no studies documenting long-term stimulant efficacy in improving any area of impairment or outcome.* For example, long-term stimulant therapy does not produce gains in academic achievement (MTA Cooperative Group 1999).

Second, disturbances in parent-child relationships are often left untreated by stimulants. The parenting skills that are critical to ensuring positive long-term outcomes for children such as those with ADHD are not produced by medicating ADHD children. They must be taught to parents (Chamberlain and Patterson 1995). This is particularly important considering that children often exhibit a wide range of behavioral difficulties that are not amenable to stimulant medication. Medication side effects, such as decreased appetite and trouble sleeping, necessarily prohibit medicating a child 24 hours a day, 7 days a week. Notably, medication is typically not active when a child wakes up in the morning, or right before bedtime, two times frequently noted as problematic by many parents of ADHD children. During these times parenting skills are vital. Although veridical causal pathways to ADHD do not exist, it is clear that parent-child interactions influence the degree and range of an ADHD child's problems (Patterson 1982). To the extent that poor parenting practices do contribute to child maladjustment, treating children solely with medication ignores a critical variable that is very likely to maintain the child's disruptive behavior in the long term, despite the acute benefit of medication.

Third, medication effects are not uniform across children, with a third of children being nonresponsive to stimulants.

Fourth, medication compliance is often problematic, especially as ADHD children approach adolescence. The vast majority of children with ADHD take stimulant medication for only a few months (Sherman and Hertzig 1991) and most stop taking medication in adolescence. A recent clinical trial revealed that parents are considerably less satisfied with stimulant therapy and their child's response to it then they are with behavioral and combined treatments (Pelham et al. 2000). Only a third of the parents of medicated children in the MTA were strongly satisfied with their child's treatment compared to 15% who dropped out or were dissatisfied. Only 22% of parents viewed "the problem that prompted me to begin the child's treatment" as much improved—nearly as large as the percentage who dropped out, or rated their child as worse on medication— 18%. Thus, despite its clear benefit in improving symptoms of ADHD when used as the sole form of treatment, stimulant medication is not viewed by parents as a sufficient or satisfying intervention for their child. It is then not surprising that so few medicated children take stimulants for long periods of time. This may turn out to be the major reason that studies have not proven to be a long-term benefit—they simply cease being taken by the vast majority of ADHD children and adolescents.

Fifth, administering medication as the initial treatment may reduce the likelihood that parents and teachers will initiate or continue psychosocial treatments. Relying solely on medication to treat children with ADHD may leave untreated significant areas of impairment and skill deficits not typically amenable to stimulant medication. A few examples common to ADHD children include poor problem-solving strategies, lack of knowledge and proficiency in sports, weakness in specific academic skills (e.g., note taking), and in specific social skills. In addition, common comorbid problems such as specific learning disabilities, anxiety, depression, and enuresis are not benefitted by stimulant medication. It may also be the case that parents and teachers will encounter behavioral difficulties with siblings, neighborhood children, and classmates, who may or may not be candidates for medication. Therefore, teaching parents and teachers fundamental behavioral management skills enables them to use these skills with other children (Danforth 1999; Resick, Forehand, and McWhorter 1976). Notably, teachers of children in the MTA study were likely to say they were better prepared to deal with ADHD in the classroom if the intervention included behavioral components versus medication alone (Pelham et al. 2000).

Combined treatments

There are many reasons to believe that a combined treatment approach provides incremental benefit over either unimodal treatment alone (Pelham and Waschbusch 1999). First, it is clear that either unimodal treatment alone has clear limitations, notably that neither provides any proven long-term gain and both, alone, often fail to improve functioning into the normative range. Second, combined treatment typically produces additive or interactive effects in many domains, which bring the child closer to normative functioning. For example, in the only adequate study of treatment effects on academic achievement, 14 months of combined treatment produced significant benefit on academic achievement in contrast to behavioral and medication treatment alone (MTA Cooperative Group 1999). Third, maximal improvement may be reached in school both with a less complex and less restrictive behavioral intervention (e.g., special class placement can often be avoided) and with a lower dose of medication (half of what would be needed without a behavioral intervention). Because behavioral interventions in a combined treatment are easier for parents and teachers to implement, and compliance with lower doses of medication may be better because side effects are less severe, combined interventions may be more likely to yield maintenance over time than the unimodal interventions. The relatively unfavorable ratings that parents gave to the medication treatment arm of the MTA were substantially different if behavioral treatments were combined with medication, reducing dropouts and negative evaluations by more than half and more than doubling ratings of strong satisfaction and improvement. These findings imply that one dramatic benefit of adding behavioral treatments to medication is that parents will find the treatment more palatable and will stick with it for a longer time. Also, because the concurrent medication enables a less intensive behavioral intervention to be implemented, a combined intervention is considerably more cost effective than the use of an intensive behavioral intervention alone. Perhaps owing to these reasons, the effect of combined treatment is typically larger than either unimodal treatment alone (Fabiano et. al. 2000).

A robust finding in the treatment literature is that combined treatments enable lower doses of medication to be efficacious. Pelham et al. (1980) found that .25 mg/kg of methylphenidate (MPH), plus a typical clinical behavioral intervention produced the same effects as .75 mg/kg MPH alone. Likewise, Carlson et al. (1992) and Pelham et al. (1993) found that .3 mg/kg MPH when combined with a behavioral intervention, was equivalent to a .6 mg/kg MPH alone. Importantly, by combining treatments, the child's daily, and therefore lifetime, intake of medication may be reduced by half. The cited studies were short-term evaluations. When the rate of increase of medication dose in a long-term study is evaluated, it is found that dose increases at a four to five times higher rate in a medication alone condition versus a combined behavioral and medication treatment (MTA Cooperative Group 1999). Finally, given that the long-term risks of stimulant medication are unknown, keeping a child's dose as low as possible is an important outcome.

The recently completed MTA study (MTA Cooperative Group 1999; Wells et al. 2000; Pelham et al. 2000; Conners in press; Swanson et al. in press) compared combined treatment, behavioral treatment alone, medication treatment alone, and a community treatment group, most of whom received medication from their own physicians. The results showed that combined treatment, relative to unimodal treatment, produced more improvement in important domains of impairment, greater normalization effects, better effects on academic achievement, more improvement in parent-child functioning, and dramatically greater parent satisfaction—all with 20% lower doses of medication. These results are consistent with the previous literature supporting the advantage of combined treatment for children with ADHD. Finally, we would like to emphasize that another advantage of combined treatment over medication alone is that if the child stops taking medication, then the effects of behavioral treatment remain and continue (Klein and Abikoff 1997; Pelham et al. 1988). When medication is terminated for a child who is not receiving a concurrent behavioral treatment, all of the beneficial effects disappear.

Procedures for School-based Medication Assessment

If the premise is accepted that combined treatments should be employed rather than medication alone, then an important question is what approach should be used first. For two reasons we argue that intervention should begin with the behavioral component. First, if a child responds well to a stimulant and is medicated daytime and evenings every day of the week, there may be few or no target behaviors on which parents and teachers can work. In that case, parent and teacher motivation and ability to implement behavioral treatments would be diminished. Second, if behavioral treatments are implemented first, children improve—some so much that medication is not needed—others need medication, but lower doses than if medication had been begun before the behavioral treatment. We have long argued that the optimal way to determine the need for medication and the best therapeutic dose for a child is through a randomized, double-blind, placebo-controlled, medication assessment (Pelham 1993). A medication assessment systematically evaluates the efficacy of selected doses relative to no medication or to placebo over time. The main benefits of such an assessment are that parents, teachers, and physicians can be confident that the child responds well to the medication and that the child receives the lowest effective dose of medication—that is the lowest dose that successfully treats the impairment with minimal side effects.

As we have argued, medication should not be used until a comprehensive behavioral intervention, such as the DRC, has been established, modified, stabilized, and shown to be insufficient. Thus, a DRC should always be in place when a decision about medication needs to be made for a child. At that point, a medication assessment should be conducted, using the child's degree of success on his DRC targets as the measure of medication effectiveness. Because the behavior targets on the DRC are the most impairing problems the child exhibits in school and his or her major goals for improved functional outcomes, the goal of an assessment is to select the dose of medication that maximizes the child's success on his or her DRC without accompanying elevations in side effects. Indeed, DRC targets have been shown to be sensitive indices of medication response (Pelham et al. 1999b, Pelham et al. under review).

A medication assessment is a simple procedure for primary care physicians in that their main responsibilities are to conduct a physical examination and history to rule out conditions that might preclude an assessment with stimulant medication, to prescribe the type and doses of medication that will be assessed, and to review the results of the assessment. The majority of the organization and the administration of the assessment can be conducted by a physician assistant, office nurse, school coordinator, a psychologist, or the child's parents (see table III).

Before a medication regimen begins, of course the physician will perform a physical examination and take a history to rule out any conditions that might preclude an assessment with stimulant drugs. The physician should select the type, dosages, and regimen of stimulant medication that will be evaluated based upon the child's impairment across settings and times, the child's weight and height, and the feasibility of dosing in the school setting. A typical protocol might include a placebo or a no-pill condition, two doses of immediate release methylphenidate (e.g., .3 mg/kg per dose, .6 mg/kg per dose) a comparable single morning dose of Adderall or Dexedrine Spansule (e.g., .3 mg/kg) and a comparable dose of a long-acting MPH preparation such as Concerta. This combination of medications will enable the physician to determine (1) whether a relatively low or high dose of stimulant medication (the two immediate release MPH conditions) will be sufficient; (2) whether a d-amphetamine based compound would yield a better response; and (3) whether evening medication is needed (the Concerta condition). Once the doses are determined, an office nurse, school coordinator, or parent can coordinate the assessment with the pertinent professionals involved. The coordinator can establish a random, medication schedule in which conditions are changed daily. This is our strong preferential design because it yields

Table III. Medication Assessment Checklist

Physician

1. Conduct physical examination and history
2. Select type and dose of medication for assessment
3. Meet with all pertinent individuals to discuss the results of the assessment at the end of the assessment period.

Staff Nurse/ School Coordinator/ Parents

1. Establish a random, daily medication schedule
2. Coordinate with pharmacist to package medication and placebo dose in opaque capsules in dated, individual pill reminders according to the random order
3. Graph daily data and compute means and standard deviations for the dependent measures (i.e., DRC target behaviors)

the most interpretable information for the individual. Alternatively, conditions can be changed weekly as long as in the interpretation stage, attention is given to ruling out confounds over time. Each medication dose and placebo should be packaged in an opaque capsule in dated, individual pill reminders according to the random order. Finally, everyone, including the child, should know that the assessment is occurring. It is important to emphasize the importance of the placebo or no-pill condition to ensure that adult expectancy effects do not bias the results as well as to provide baseline for interpreting results. A placebo is not necessary to control for child expectancy effects (Pelham et al. 1997; Pelham et al. 2000), so if objective measures of response are used (e.g., DRC targets), simply withholding medication on some days is as good as a placebo condition.

The primary measure used to evaluate the effects of medication is the DRC, because it is a very specific index of the child's most salient areas of impairment, and it, therefore, will provide the most clinically meaningful data on response to the stimulants. Because the teacher has established target goals that the child is capable of reaching, medication response is reflected simply in the number of "yeses" that the child obtains on his DRC. A supplemental measure of medication response could include one of the standardized teacher and parent rating scales such as the IOWA Conners rating Scale (Pelham 1993). In addition, parents and teachers should complete the Pittsburgh Side Effects Scale (Pelham et al. 1993).

After the assessment has been completed, the assessment coordinator should graph the percentage or number of "yeses" for each medication condition and if desired, means and standard deviations can be easily computed in one of the common spreadsheet software programs (e.g., Microsoft Excel). Then, the assessment coordinator can review the data with the other collaborators and summarize feedback for the physician and parent. The question to address is whether there was clinically significant improvement in behavior relative to no medication in the areas most problematic to the child and what is the lowest dose that produces the desired level of functioning with minimum or no side effects. Figure 2 shows a plot of the percentage of daily yeses achieved by a child (i.e., "proportion positive") on one of his DRC goals (i.e., "completes assignments accurately") as a function of different medication conditions (placebo, .3 mg/kg, .6 mg/kg MPH).

Conclusions about the incremental benefit of medication for this child are clear. First, there is a low proportion positive on placebo days. Second, there is some, but not consistent, sufficient improvement with .3 mg/kg dose—he is good on some days, but not on others. Third, there was a consistently higher proportion positive on .6 mg/kg days, clearly demonstrating that this child benefitted from the

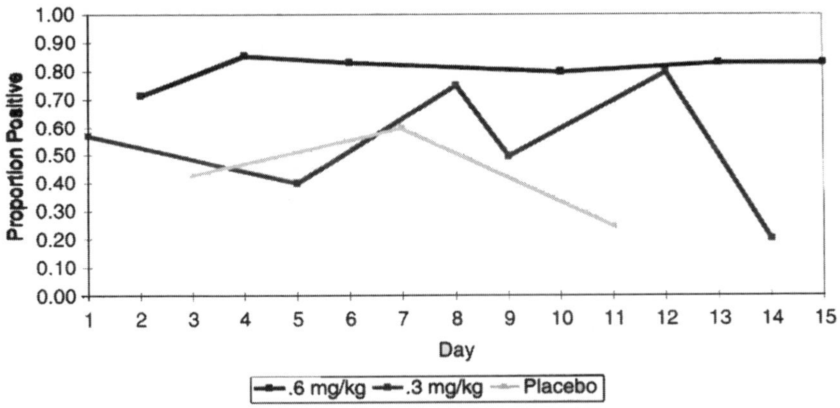

Figure 2. Sample results of daily report card-based medication assessment

addition of the .6 mg/kg dose on this target behavior. If the pattern across all of his target behaviors were similar, that dose would be recommended for this child.

It is important to state that an increase in dose does not necessarily always lead to an increase in effectiveness. In fact, a very consistent finding across a large number of studies is that the degree of improvement yielded by stimulant medication begins to level off at doses of about .3 mg/kg or 10 mg per dose (see Smith et al. 1998, for a discussion). That this child needed the higher of two doses of MPH, when most children do not, illustrates the individual differences in response to combined treatment. This point is important to keep in mind when analyzing the results of a medication assessment—effectiveness can be maximized and side effects can be minimized at the lowest possible dose for each individual child.

CONCLUSIONS

Attention deficit hyperactivity disorder is a chronic disorder that impairs an individual's ability throughout life. Therefore, a chronic treatment approach is necessary. A great deal of progress has been made in the identification and the validation of treatments for children with ADHD. The next, and vital step, is to increase the utilization of these treatments for ADHD in the community. Primary care physicians are often the initial professionals requested to diagnose and provide treatment for children with ADHD, and they thus play an increasingly important role in coordinating comprehensive treatment programs for their ADHD patients. Along with stimulant medication, behavioral treatment and combined behavioral and pharmacological treatment for ADHD are well-validated treatments. Behavioral treatment represents a viable alternative for parents who do not want to use medication with their children or with the 25% of ADHD children who are nonresponders to stimulant medication. Major advantages of behavioral and combined treatments include that they produce incremental improvement beyond unimodal approaches for many children, and that they have more lasting effects of treatment relative to medication, the effects of which disappear as soon as medication is discontinued. Parental satisfaction with treatment in the MTA study (Pelham et al. 2000) indicated that parents greatly prefer behavioral and combined treatments to medication treatment alone. These results are of particular importance considering that long term compliance to treatment is a critical factor in the long-term outcome of children with ADHD: the more satisfied one is with treatment, the greater the likelihood of long-term adherence and compliance. By focusing on functional outcomes or impairment rather than DSM symptoms of ADHD and constantly monitoring functioning in response to treatment, the treating physician can adjust the child's treatment package as needed to maximize the child's adaptive functioning. This requires staying in regular contact with the family, and that is what should be expected with a chronic disease in primary care.

REFERENCES

Abramowitz, A. J., Eckstrand, D., O'Leary, S. G., and Dulcan, M. K. 1992. ADHD children's responses to stimulant medication and two intensities of a behavioral intervention. *Behavior Modification* 16:193–203.

Achenbach, T. M., McConaughy, S. H., and Howell, C. T. 1987. Child/adolescent behavioral and emotional problems: Implications of cross-informant correlations for situational specificity. *Psychological Bulletin* 101:213–32.

Achenbach, T. M. 1978. The child behavior profile: I. Boys aged 6–11. Journal of Consulting and Clinical Psychology 46:478–88.

Achenbach, T. M., and Edelbrock, C. S. 1981. Behavioral problems and competencies reported by parents of normal and disturbed children aged four through sixteen. *Monographs of the Society for Research in Child Development* 46.

American Academy of Child and Adolescent Psychiatry. 1998. Practice Parameters for the assessment and treatment of children, adolescents, and adults with attention deficit/ hyperactivity disorder. *Journal of the American Academy of Child and Adolescent Psychiatry* 36:(supplemental).

American Academy of Pediatrics. 2000. Clinical practice guideline: Diagnosis and evaluation of the child with attention-deficit/hyperactivity disorder. *Pediatrics* 105:1158–70.

American Psychiatric Association. 1994. Diagnostic and Statistical Manual of Mental Disorders, Fourth Edition. Washington, D.C.: *American Psychiatric Association.*

Anastopoulous, A. D., Shelton, T. L., DuPaul, G. J., and Guevremont, D. C. 1993. Parent training for Attention-deficit hyperactivity disorder: Its impact on parent functioning. *Journal of Abnormal Child Psychology* 21:581–96.

Atkins, M. S., Pelham, W. E., and Licht, M. H. 1984. Behavioral correlates of teacher ratings of attention deficit disorder. Paper presented at the annual meeting of the Association for the Advancement of Behavior Therapy, Philadelphia, November.

Atkins, M. S., Pelham, W. E., and White, .K. J. 1989. Hyperactivity and attention deficit disorders. In *Psychological Aspects of Developments and Physical Disabilities: A Casebook*, ed. M. Hersen. California: Sage Publications.

Barkley, R. A. 1987. *Defiant Children: A Clinician's Manual for Parent Training.* New York: The Guilford Press.

Barkley, R. A. 1995. *Taking Charge of ADHD: The Complete, Authoritative Guide for Parents.* New York, NY: Guilford Press.

Brestan, E. V., and Eyberg, S. M. 1998. Effective psychosocial treatments of conduct-disordered children and adolescents: 29 years, 82 studies, and 5272 kids. *Journal of Clinical Child Psychology* 27:180–89.

Carlson, C. L., Pelham, W. E., Milich, R., and Dixon, J. 1992. Single and combined effects of methylphenidate and behavior therapy on the classroom performance of children with ADHD. *Journal of Abnormal Child Psychology* 20:213–32.

Chamberlain, P., and Patterson, G. R. 1995. Discipline and child compliance in parenting. In *Handbook of Parenting: Applied and Practical Parenting* Vol. 4, ed. M. H. Bornstein. New Jersey: Lawrence Erlbaum Associates.

Chambers, W. J., Puig-Antich, J., Hirsh, M., Paez, P., Ambrosini, P. J., Tabrizi, M. A., and Davies, M. 1985. Test-retest reliability of the schedule for affective disorders and schizophrenia for school-age children, present episode version. *Archives of General Psychiatry* 42:696–702.

Conners, C. K., MTA Cooperative Group (in press). Multimodal treatment of ADHD (MTA): An alternative outcome analysis. *Journal of the Academy of Child and Adolescent Psychiatry*

Cunningham, C. E., Bremner, R., and Secord-Gilbert, M. 1995. The Community Parent Education Program: A School Based Family Systems Oriented Workshop for Parents of Children with Disruptive Behavior Disorders. Unpublished manuscript.

Danforth, J. S. 1999. The outcome of parent training using the behavior management flow chart with a mother and her twin boys with oppositional defiant disorder and attention-deficit hyperactivity disorder. *Child and Family Behavior Therapy* 21:59–80.

DuPaul, G. J., and Eckert, T. L. 1997. The effects of school-based interventions for attention deficit hyperactivity disorder: A meta-analysis. *School Psychology Review* 26:5–27.

DuPaul, G. J., Power, T. J., McGoey, K. E., Ikeda, M. J., and Anastopoulos, A. D. 1998. Reliability and validity of parent and teacher ratings of attention-deficit/hyperactivity disorder symptoms. *Journal of Psychoeducational Assessment* 16:55–68.

Evans, S. W., Pelham, W. E., Smith, B. H., Bukstein, O., Gnagy, E. M., Greiner, A. R., Altenderfer, L., and Baron-Myak, C. 2001. Dose-response effects of methylphenidate on ecologically-valid measures of academic performance and classroom behavior in adolescents with ADHD. *Experimental and Clinical Psychopharmacology* 9:163–175.

Fabiano, G. A., Pelham, W. E., Gnagy, E. M., Coles, E. K., and Wheeler, T. 2000. A meta-analysis of behavioral and combined treatments for ADHD.

Paper presented at the annual meeting of the American Psychological Association, Washington, D.C., August.

Forehand, R., and Long, N. 1996. *Parenting the Strong—willed Child: The Clinically Proven Five-week Program for Parents of Two- to Six-Year-Olds* Lincolnwood, IL: Contemporary Books.

Fuchs, D., and Fuchs, L. S. 1989. Exploring effective and efficient prereferral interventions: A component analysis of behavioral consultation. *School Psychology Review* 18:260–79.

Goldman, L. S., Genel, M., Bezmen, R. J., and Slanetz, P. J. 1998. Diagnosis and treatment of attention-deficit/hyperactivity disorder in children and adolescents. *JAMA* 279:1100–07.

Goyette, C., Conners, C., and Ulrich, R. 1978. Normative data on revised Conners parent and teacher rating scale. *Journal of Abnormal Child Psychology* 6:221–36.

Horn, W. F., Ialongo, S., Popovich, S., and Peradotto, D. 1987. Behavioral parent training and cognitive behavioral self-control therapy with ADD-H children: Comparative and combined effects. *Journal of Clinical Child Psychology* 16:57–68.

Hoza, B., Pelham, W. E., Sams, S. E., and Carlson, C. 1992. An examination of the "dosage" effects of both behavior therapy and methylphenidate on the classroom performance of two ADHD children. *Behavior Modification* 16:164–92.

Hupp, S. D., and Reitman, D. 1999. Improving sports skill and sportmanship in children diagnosed with attention-deficit/hyperactivity disorder. *Child & Family Behavior Therapy* 23:35–51.

Hupp, S. D. A., Reitman, D., O'Callaghan, P., Gulley, V., and Northup, J. (in press) The influence of a token economy and methylphenidate on attention during sports with children diagnosed with ADHD. *Behavior Therapy*

Kelley, M. L., and McCain, A. P. 1995. Promoting academic performance in inattentive children. *Behavior Modification* 19:357–75.

Klein, R. G., and Abikoff, H. 1997. Behavior therapy and methylphenidate in the treatment of children with ADHD. *Journal of Attention Disorders* 2:89–114.

Krueger, R. F., Caspi, A., Moffitt, T. E., White, J., and Stouthamer-Loeber, M. 1996. Delay of gratification, psychopathology, and personality: Is low self-control specific to externalizing problems. *Journal of Personality* 64:107–129.

Lahey, B. B., Pelham, W. E., Stein, M. A., Loney, J., Trapani, C., Nugent, K., Kipp, H., Schmidt, E., Lee, S., Cale, M., Gold, E., Hartung, C. M., Wilcutt, E., and Baumann, B. 1998. Validity of DSM-IV attention-deficit/hyperactivity disorder for younger children. *Journal of the American Academy of Child and Adolescent Psychiatry* 37:695–702.

Lonigan, C. J., Elbert, J. C., and Johnson, S. B. 1998. Empirically supported psychosocial interventions for children: An overview. *Journal of Clinical Child Psychology*. 27:138–45

Manos, M. J., Short, E. J., and Findling, R. L. 1999. Differential effectiveness of methylphenidate and Adderall in school-age youths with attention deficit/hyperactivity disorder. *Journal of the American Academy of Child and Adolescent Psychiatry* 38:813–819.

Mash, E. J., and Terdal, L. G. 1997. Assessment of child and family disturbance: A behavioral systems approach. In *Assessment of Childhood Disorders*. Vol. 3, eds. E. J. Mash and L. G. Terdal. New York: Guilford Press.

Milich, R., Lorch, E. P. 1994. Television viewing methodology to understand cognitive processing of ADHD children. In *Advances in Clinical Child*

Psychology Vol. 16 eds. T. H. Ollendick and R. J. Prinz New York: Plenum Press.

MTA Cooperative Group. 1999. 14-month randomized clinical trial of treatment strategies for attention deficit hyperactivity disorder. *Archives of General Psychiatry* 56:1073–86.

NIH Consensus Statement. 1998. Diagnosis and treatment of attention deficit hyperactivity disorder (ADHD) Vol. 16. Washington, D.C.: National Institutes of Health

Northup, J., Fusilier, I., Swanson, V., Huete, J., Bruce, T., Freeland, J., Gulley, V., and Edwards, S. 1999. Further analysis of the separate and interactive effects of methylphenidate and common classroom contingencies. *Journal of Applied Behavior Analysis* 32:35–50.

O'Leary, K. D., and Becker, W. C. 1967. Behavior modification of an adjustment class: A token reinforcement program. *Exceptional Children* 33:637–42.

O'Leary, K. D., Pelham, W. E., Rosenbaum, A., and Price, G. 1976. Behavioral treatment of hyperkinetic children: An experimental evaluation of its usefulness. *Clinical Pediatrics* 15:510–14.

O'Leary, S. G., and Pelham, W. E. 1978. Behavior therapy and withdrawal of stimulant medication in hyperactive children. *Pediatrics* 61:211–17.

Patterson, G. R. 1974. Intervention for boys with conduct problems: Multiple settings, treatment and criteria. *Journal of Consulting and Clinical Psychology* 42:471–81.

Patterson, G. R. 1982. *A Social Learning Approach: III. Coercive Family Processes.* Eugene, OR: Castalia.

Pelham, W. E. 1993. Pharmacotherapy for children with attention-deficit hyperactivity disorders. Introduction to minisiries. *School Psychology Review* 22:199–227.

Pelham, W. E., Aronoff, H. R., Midlam, J. K., Shapiro, C. J., Gnagy, E. M., Chronis, A. M., Onyango, A. N., Forehand, G., Nguyen, A., Steiner, R., and Waxmonsky, J. 1999a. A comparison of Ritalin and Adderall: Efficacy and time-course in children with ADHD. Pediatrics 103: (4). {online}. Available: http://www.pediatric.orglegi/content/full/10314/e43.

Pelham W. E., Carlson C., Sams S. E., Vallano, G., Dixon, J., and Hoza, B. 1993. Separate and combined effects of methylphenidate and behavior modification on boys with ADHD in the classroom. *Journal of Consulting and Clinical Psychology* 61:506–15.

Pelham, W. E., Gnagy, E. M., Chronis, A. M., Burrows-MacLean, L., Fabiano, G. A., Onyango, A. N., Meichenbaum, D. L., Williams, A., Aronoff, H. R., and Steiner, R. L. 1999b. A comparison of morning-only and morning/late afternoon Adderall with morning-only, twice daily and three-times daily methylphenidate in children with attention-deficit/hyperactivity disorder. *Pediatrics* 104(6):1300–1311

Pelham, W. E., Gnagy, E. M., Greenslade, K. E., and Milich, R. 1992. Teacher ratings of DSM-III-R symptoms for the disruptive behavior disorders. *Journal of the American Academy of Child and Adolescent Psychiatry* 31:210–218.

Pelham, W. E., Gnagy, E. M., Greiner, A. R., for the MTA Cooperative Group. 2000. Parent and teacher satisfaction with treatment and evaluation of effectiveness. Poster presented at the annual meeting of the Association for the Advancement of Behavior Therapy, New Orleans, November.

Pelham, W. E., Gnagy, E. M., Greiner, A. R., Hoza, B., Hinshaw, S. P., Swanson, J. M., Simpson, S., Shapiro, C., Bukstein, O., and Baron-Myak.

2000. Behavioral vs. behavioral and pharmacological treatmnet in ADHD children attending a summer treatment program. *Journal of Abnormal Child Psychology* 28:507–526.

Pelham, W. E., Greenslade, K. E., Vodde-Hamilton, M. A., Murphy, D. A., Greenstein, J. J., Gnagy, E. M., Guthrie, K. J., Hoover, M. D., and Dahl, R. E. 1990. Relative efficacy of long-acting stimulants on children with attention deficit-hyperactivity disorder: A comparison of standard methlyphenidate, sustained-release methylphenidate, sustained-release dextroamphetamine, and pemoline. *Pediatrics* 86:226–237.

Pelham, W. E., and Hoza, B. 1996. Intensive treatment: A summer treatment program for children with ADHD. In *Psychosocial Treatments for Child and Adolescent Disorders: Empirically Based Strategies for Clinical Practice,* eds. E. Hibbs and P. Jensen. New York: APA Press.

Pelham, W. E., Hoza, B., Kipp, H. L., Gnagy, E. M., and Trane, S. T. 1997. Effects of methylphenidate and expectance on ADHD children's performance, self evaluations, persistence, and attributions on a cognitive task. *Experimental and Clinical Psychopharmacology* 5:3–13.

Pelham, W. E., Milich, R., Murphy, D. A., and Murphy, H. A. 1989. Normative data on the IOWA Conners teacher rating scale. *Journal of Child Clinical Psychology*. 18:259–62.

Pelham, W. E., and Milich, R. 1991. Individual differences in response to Ritalin in classwork and social behavior. In *Ritalin: Theory and Patient Management,* eds. L Greenhill and B. P. Osman. New York, NY: MaryAnn Liebert, Inc.

Pelham, W. E., Schendler, R. W., Bender, M. E., Nilsson, D. E., Miller, J., Budrow, M. S., Ronnei, M., Paluchowski, C., and Marks, D. A. 1988. The combination of behavior therapy and methylphenidate in the treatment of attention deficit disorders: A therapy outcome study. In *Attention Deficit Disorders III: New Research in Attention, Treatment, and Psychopharmacology,* ed. L. Bloomingdale. London: Pergamon Press.

Pelham, W. E., Schnedler, R., Bologna, N., and Contreras, A. 1980. Behavioral and stimulant treatmnet of hyperactive children: A therapy study with methylphenidate probes in a within-subject design. *Journal of Applied Behavior Analysis* 13:221–236.

Pelham, W. E., and Smith, B. H. 2000. Prediction and measurement of individual responses to Ritalin by children with attention deficit hyperactivity disorder. In *Ritalin: Theory and Practice,* eds. L. L. Greenhill and B. O. Osman. New York: MaryAnn Liebert Inc.

Pelham, W. E., Sturges, J., Hoza, J., Schmidt, C., Bijlsma, J., Milich, R., and Moorer, S. 1987. Sustained release and standard methylphenidate effects on cognitive and social behavior in children with attention deficit disorder. *Pediatrics* 80:491–501.

Pelham, W. E., and Waschbusch, D. 1999. Behavioral intervention in attention-deficit/hyperactivity disorder. In *Handbook of Disruptive Behavior Disorders,* eds. H. Quay and A. Quay. New York, NY: Plenum Press.

Pelham, W. E., Wheeler, T., and Chronis, A. 1998. Empirically supported psychosocial treatments for attention deficit hyperactivity disorder. *Journal of Clinical Child Psychology*. 27:190–205.

Pisterman, S., Firestone, P., McGrath, P., Goodman, J. T., Webster, I., Mallory, R., and Goffin, B. 1992. The effects of parent training on parenting stress and sense of competence. *Canadian Journal of Behavioural Science* 24:41–58.

Pisterman, S., McGrath, P., Firestone, P., Goodman, J. T., Webster I., and Mallory, R. 1989. Outcome of parent-medicated treatment with preschoolers with attention deficit disorder with hyperactivity. *Journal of Consulting and Clinical Psychology* 57:628–35.

Pliszka, S. R., Browne, R. G., Olvera, R. L., and Wyne S. K. 2000. A double-blind, placebo controlled study of Adderall and methylphenidate in the treatmnet of attention-deficit /hyperactivity disorder. *Journal of the American Academy of Child and Adolescent Psychiatry* 39:619–26.

Rapport, M. D., Murphy, H. A., and Bailey, J. S. 1982. Ritalin vs. response cost in the control of hyperactive children: A within-subject comparison. *Journal of Applied Behavior Analysis* 15:205–16.

Resick, P. A., Forehand, R., and McWhorter, A. Q. 1976. The effect of parental treatmnet with one child on an untreated sibling. *Behavior Therapy* 7:544–48.

Scotti, J. R., Morris, T. L., McNeil, C. B. and Hawkins, R. P. 1996. DSM-IV and disorders of childhood and adolescence: Can structural criteria be functional? *Journal of Consulting and Clinical Psychology*. 64:1177–91.

Shaffer, D., Fisher, P., Dulcan, M., Davies, M., Piacentini, J., Schwab-Stone, M., Lahey, B. B., Bourdon, K., Jensen, P., Bird, H., Canino, G., and Regier, D. 1996. The NIMH Diagnostic Interview Schedule for Children (DISC 2.3): Description, acceptability, prevalences, and performance in the MECA study. *Journal of the American Academy of Child and Adolescent Psychiatry*. 35:865–77.

Sherman, M., and Hertzig, M. E. 1991. Prescribing practices of Ritalin: The Suffolf County, New York study. In *Ritalin: Theory and Patient Management*, eds. L. Greenhill, B. Osman. New York, NY: MaryAnn Liebert.

Sleator, E. K. 1982. Office diagnosis of hyperactivity by the physician. *Advances in Learning & Behavioral Disabilities* 1:341–64.

Smith, B. H., Pelham, W. E., Evans, S., Molina, B., Gnagy, E. M., Greiner, A., Bukstein, O., Myak, C., Presnell, M., and Willoughby, M. 1998. Dosage effects of methylphenidate on the social behavior of adolescents diagnosed with attention deficit hyperactivity disorder. *Experimental and Clinical Psychopharmacology* 6:1–18.

Spencer, T., Beiderman, J., Wilens, T., Harding, M., O'Donnell, D., and Griffin, S. 1996. Pharmacotherapy of attention-deficit hyperactivity disorder across the life cycle. *Journal of the American Academy of Child and Adolescent Psychiatry* 35:409–32.

Stein, M. A., Blondis, T. A., Schnitzler, E. R., O'Brien, T., Fishkin, J., Blackwell, B., Szumowski, E., and Roizen, N. J. 1996. Methylphenidate dosing: Twice versus three times daily. *Pediatrics* 98(4):748–56.

Swanson, J. M., Kraemer, H. C., Hinshaw, S. P., Arnold, L. E., Conners, C. K., Abikoff, H. B., Clevengert, W., Davies, M., Elliot, G., Greenhill, L. L., Hechtman, L., Hoza, B., Jensen, P. S., March, J. S., Simpson, S., Vitiello, B., Wells, K. C., Wigal, T., and Wu, M. (in press). Clinical relevance of the primary findings of the MTA: Success rates based on severity of ADHD and ODD symptoms at the end of treatment. *Journal of the American Academy of Child and Adolescent Psychiatry*

Swanson, J. M., McBurnett, K., Christian, D. L., and Wigal, T. 1995. Stimulant medication and treatment of children with ADHD. In *Advances in Clinical Child Psychology* Vol. 17, eds. T. H. Ollendick and R. J. Prinz. New York: Plenum.

Swanson, J. M., Wigal, S., Greenhill, L. L., Browne, R., Waslik, B., Lerner, M., Williams, L., Flynn, D., Agler, D., Crowley, K., Fineberg, E., Baren, M., and Cantwell, D. P. 1998. Analog classroom assessment of Adderall in children with ADHD. *Journal of the American Academy of Child and Adolescent Psychiatry* 37(5):519–526.

Walker, H. M., Hops, H., and Johnson, S. M. 1975. Generalization and maintenance of classroom treatment effects. *Behavior Therapy*. 6:188–200.
Webster-Stratton, C. 1992. *The Incredible Years: A Trouble-Shooting Guide for Parents of Children Aged 3–8*. Toronto: Umbrella Press.
Wells, K. C., Epstein, J. N., Hinshaw, S. P., Conners, C. K., Klaric, J., Abikoff, H. B., Abramowitz, A., Arnold, L. E., Elliott, G., Greenhill, L. L., Hechtman, L., Hoza, B., Jensen, P. S., March, J. S., Pelham, W. E., Pfiffner, L., Severe, J., Swanson, J. M., and Vitiello, B. 2000. Parenting and family stress treatment outcomes in attention deficit hyperactivity disorder (ADHD): An empirical analysis in the MTA study. *Journal of Abnormal Child Psychology* 28:543–53.

Chapter • 10

Non-Stimulant Medication Alternatives for Children and Adolescents with ADHD

Chrystyna Nebesh-Jatsyshyn, Barbara L. Gracious, and Robert L. Findling

Attention-deficit/hyperactivity disorder (ADHD) is a common condition affecting 5% to 10% of school-age children (AACAP 1997), with symptoms persisting in 10% to 60% of adolescents and adults diagnosed in childhood (Spencer et al. 1996). Because ADHD can be a debilitating disorder, safe and effective treatments are necessary for young people affected with this condition. Data from research cohorts suggest that the vast majority of young people with ADHD respond adequately to treatment with a psychostimulant (Elia et al. 1991; The MTA Cooperative Group 1999). In addition, since there are more safety and efficacy data available about the psychostimulants than any other class of medicine, these drugs remain the "gold standards" of pharmacotherapy for children and adolescents with ADHD.

However, it has been suggested that approximately 20% to 30% of patients with ADHD who are seen in clinical settings either do not experience adequate symptom reduction or do not tolerate treatment with psychostimulants (Spencer et al. 1996). In addition, the utility of psychostimulants may also be limited for some patients who suffer from co-morbid neuropsychiatric conditions. These include illnesses such as major depression, bipolar affective disorder, anxiety disorders, psychosis, substance abuse, or tic disorders. For these reasons, clinical investigators continue to examine the roles that non-stimulant medications may have in the treatment of patients with ADHD. At present, quite a few non-stimulant psychotropic agents have been reported to show promise as treatments for children and adolescents with ADHD. These are listed in table I.

ANTIDEPRESSANTS

Tricyclic and related antidepressants

Members of the tricyclic antidepressant (TCA) class of drugs are the non-stimulant agents that have received the most extensive study as treatment alternatives for children and adolescents with ADHD. Data from numerous open studies as well as double-blind trials have demonstrated that several TCAs have efficacy for the treatment of ADHD. These include the secondary amines desipramine and nortriptyline, and the tertiary amines amitriptyline and imipramine. TCAs modulate central nervous system neurotransmission by blocking the pre-synaptic reuptake of norepinephrine and serotonin. The secondary amines are more selective for norepinephrine.

Table I. Non-stimulant medications of putative benefit for Children and Adolescents with Attention-Deficit/Hyperactivity Disorder (ADHD)

Tricyclic and related antidepressants
Amitriptyline
Clomipramine
Desipramine
Imipramine
Nortriptyline
Monoamine Oxidase Inhibitors (MAOIs)
Clorgyline
Moclobemide
Selegiline
Tranylcypromine sulfate
Novel Antidepressants and Related Compounds
Bupropion
Venlafaxine
GW 320659*
Atomoxetine*
Alpha-2 Adrenergic Agonists
Clonidine
Guanfacine
Anxiolytic agent
Buspirone
Cholinergic agents
Donepezil
ABT-418*

*not yet available

The TCAs that have been most thoroughly examined in double-blind placebo-controlled studies include imipramine, amitriptyline, and desipramine (see review by Spencer et al. 1996). There has also been a single placebo-controlled study that has examined the efficacy of clomipramine (Garfinkel et al. 1983). Other reports have suggested that nortriptyline also may be effective for young patients with ADHD (Prince et al. 2000; Spencer et al. 1993; Wilens et al. 1993). However, a study of protriptyline in children and teenagers with ADHD did not support its clinical utility (Wilens et al. 1996). An overview of the results of the TCA trials that have been performed in children and adolescents with ADHD is summarized in tables II through IV.

Table II. Selected Studies of Imipramine (IMI) in Children with ADHD

First Author/ Year	Study Type	Number/ Description of Subjects	Outcome
Rapoport 1974	Double-blind, Placebo-Controlled comparison with MPH	76 Males	IMI > placebo MPH > placebo MPH > IMI
Quinn 1975	Open 1year follow-up	76 Males	IMI = MPH
Werry 1980	Double-blind placebo controlled crossover comparison with MPH	30	IMI > MPH
Winsberg 1980	Placebo controlled crossover	10 (MPH unresponsive)	IMI = placebo
Cox 1982	Open	14 males w/ ADHD and Separation Anxiety Disorder	Improvements noted
Pozzi 1984	Randomized, controlled	32 (treated with IMI or MPH)	Improved memory
Gualtieri 1988	Double-blind placebo controlled with low, medium & high doses	9	Improved hyperactivity but negative dose response effects on motor speed and pursuit
Sangal 1996	Open	17 (Unresponsive to pemoline)	Poor IMI responders had longer visual & auditory p300 latencies and small auditory p300 amplitudes

ADHD = attention-deficit/hyperactivity disorder, MPH = methylphenidate

Table III. Selected Desipramine (DMI) Studies in Children and Adolescents with ADHD

First Author/ Year	Study Type	Number/ Description of Subjects	Outcome
Garfinkel 1983	Double-blind placebo controlled crossover comparison w/ MPH and CMI	12 males	MPH > DMI, CMI, and placebo
Gastfriend 1984	Open	12 adolescents	11/12 improved w/ 8/12 much or very much improved
Biederman 1986	Prospective open trial	18 children and adolescents	Significant improvement
Donnelly 1986	Double-blind, placebo controlled	29 males	DMI > placebo
Riddle 1988	Open	7 children w/ ADHD and various tic disorders	4 improved "remarkably," 1 moderately, 2 non-responsive; 6/7 no change in tic status or severity
Biederman 1989	Double-blind placebo controlled randomized parallel groups	62 w/ ADD (42 children and 20 adolescents)	DMI > placebo
Gualtieri 1991	Randomized controlled	12 children w/ ADHD	Improved clinically. Small but significant decline in motor performance
Rapport 1993	Randomized double-blind placebo controlled crossover comparison w/ MPH, placebo and combined DMI + MPH	16 child inpatients w/ ADHD and MDD	MPH > DMI for vigilance; both independently improved short- term memory and visual problem solving. Combined DMI + MPH improved higher order relationships.
Spencer 1993	Retrospective	33 children and adolescents w/ Tourette's syndrome, ADHD or chronic tic	Significant improvement in ADHD in 80 %.
Singer 1995	Double-blind placebo controlled comparison w/ clonidine	34 children and adolescents w/ ADHD and Tourette's syndrome	DMI > clonidine > placebo

ADHD = Attention-deficit/hyperactivity disorder, MPH = methylphenidate, CMI = clomipramine

Table IV. Selected Amitriptyline (AMI), Nortriptyline (NORT), Clomipramine (CMI), and Protriptyline (PRO) Studies in Children and Adolescents with Attention-Deficit/Hyperactivity Disorder (ADHD)

First Author/ Year	Study Type	Number of Subjects	Outcome
Krakowski 1965	Double-blind controlled randomized AMI	50 children w/ hyperkinesis and various diagnoses	AMI > placebo
Kupietz 1976	Placebo-controlled randomized comparison of AMI w/ MPH	20 hyperactive aggressive children	AMI and MPH > placebo for vigilance
Yepes 1977	Placebo controlled randomized comparison of AMI w/ MPH	50 children	AMI = MPH in decreasing hyperactivity and aggression in home and school. Severe sedation often associated w/ effective AMI doses.
Saul 1985	Open NORT	60 children and adolescents	90% improved
Spencer 1993	Retrospective NORT	12 children and teens with ADHD and movement disorders	92% much or very much improved
Wilens 1993	Retrospective NORT	58 children and adolescents with ADHD and co-morbid conditions	76% moderate to marked improvement
Prince 2000	Open NORT with double-blind discontinuation phase	35 children and adolescents	Significant improvements with NORT
Garfinkel 1983	Double-blind, placebo-controlled crossover comparison of CMI with MPH and DMI	12 males	MPH>CMI, DMI or placebo for overall function
Wilens 1996	Retrospective PRO review	13 children and teenagers who had failed 1 or more prior medication trials	45% were considered responders. 38% discontinued due to adverse events.

MPH = Methylphenidate, DMI = Desipramine

Studies that have compared TCAs to the psychostimulants have provided mixed results. Some studies have reported the psychostimulants have similar efficacy to TCAs (Kupietz and Balka 1976; Quinn and Rapoport 1975; Yepes, Balka, and Winsberg 1977). Other data suggest that the TCAs have superior salutary effects when compared to the stimulants (Hilton et al. 1991; Werry, Aman, and Diamond 1980). Conversely, other reports note that the TCAs are not as effective as psychostimulants for treating patients with ADHD (Garfinkel et al. 1983; Rapport et al. 1993; Rapoport et al. 1974). Overall, it appears that TCAs have more robust effects on hyperactivity and impulsivity, and more modest effects on inattention (Gualtieri and Evans 1988; Rapport et al. 1993; Werry et al. 1980).

Despite the numerous studies reporting that the TCAs may be safe and effective for young people with ADHD, recent concerns about the potential for cardiotoxic side effects have limited their use. Since 1990, there have been several reported cases of sudden death in children and adolescents prescribed desipramine. Of particular concern is that there was no evidence of overdose or other acute medical illness in the first six patients who died while taking desipramine (Popper 2000). Although no evidence of a causal relationship between the TCAs and these tragic deaths has been established, these inexplicable sudden deaths raise justifiable concern about the use of TCAs in children and adolescents.

It also should be noted that TCAs have known effects on cardiovascular functioning. They can cause slowing of intracardiac conduction, sinus tachycardia, and changes in blood pressure in children and adolescents (Leonard et al. 1995). Other potentially adverse effects that can occur during TCA treatment include central and peripheral anticholinergic effects.

In short, TCAs are the most extensively studied non-stimulant treatment alternatives for children and adolescents with ADHD. Despite their demonstrated efficacy, TCA use is no longer as widespread as it once was due to the cardiovascular side effects and rare cases of inexplicable sudden death.

Monoamine Oxidase Inhibitors

Monoamine oxidase inhibitors (MAOIs) inhibit the intracellular catabolic enzyme monoamine oxidase. Treatment with irreversible MAOIs such as clorgyline and tranylcypromine can be associated with the development of hypertensive crises after the ingestion of tyramine-containing foods.

Several studies have examined the use of MAOIs in children and adolescents with ADHD (table V). The results of one controlled study of 14 boys has suggested that the irreversible MAOIs clorgyline and tranylcypromine may have efficacy in the treatment of children with ADHD (Zametkin et al. 1985). Moclobemide, which has not been commercially released in the United States, has been reported to be effec-

Table V. Selected Monoamine Oxidase Inhibitor (MAOI) Studies in children and adolescents with ADHD

Drug	First Author/ Year	Study Type	Number of Subjects	Outcome
CGL or TCM	Zametkin 1985	Double-blind crossover comparison of MAOI and DATM	14 children	CGL = TCM= DA = TM All had clinically significant effects.
Selegiline	Jankovic 1993	Open	29 children and adolescents with co-morbid Tourette's disorder	90% clinical improvement in ADHD symptoms. 2 had exacerbation of tics.
Selegiline	Feigin 1996	Double-blind placebo controlled crossover disorder.	24 children and adolescents with co-morbid Tourette's	No statistically sig. benefit on primary analysis. Post-hoc analysis showed effect in first few weeks was substantial.
Moclobemide	Trott 1992	Open	12 children who were unable to tolerate MPH	
Moclobemide	Antkowiak 1998	Open	15 children	Found to be effective in 13/15 patients

ADHD = Attention-deficit/hyperactivity disorder, DATM = dextroamphetamine, CGL = clorgyline, TCM = tranylcypromine, MPH = methylphenidate

tive in open trials of patients with ADHD (Trott et al. 1992; Antkowiak and Rajewski1998). Selegiline, another MAOI, was reported to improve ADHD symptoms in youths in a double-blind placebo controlled crossover study (Feigin et al. 1996) and in an open trial (Jankovic 1993). Since selegiline is a selective inhibitor of MAOI-B and moclobemide is a reversible inhibitor of MAOI-A, it appears that the dietary restrictions that are necessary during treatment with some MAOIs are not needed. Although both agents appear to be potentially viable treatment options for pediatric patients, the limited available data suggests that they should not be used routinely.

Novel Antidepressants and Related Compounds

The use of novel antidepressants such as bupropion (Wellbutrin®) and venlafaxine (Effexor®) in the treatment of children and adolescents with ADHD has also been investigated. Bupropion, an aminoketone, is not chemically related to other antidepressants. Studies in children and adolescents have shown mixed results (see table VI). Overall, results from open and controlled trials suggest that bupropion may be helpful in the treatment of ADHD in both children and teenagers. Dosing parameters for bupropion in treatment of ADHD in juveniles have not been determined. Doses in these studies ranged from 50 milligrams a day to 300 milligrams a day, or .7 mg/kgm/day to 6 mg/kgm/day.

Table VI. Selected Bupropion Studies in Children and Adolescents with Attention-Deficit/Hyperactivity Disorder (ADHD)

First Author /Year	Study Type	Number of Subjects	Outcome
Simeon 1986	Open	17 males w/ ADHD and/or conduct disorder	Marked or moderate improvement in 70%. Two weeks after discontinuation, 41% relapsed.
Clay 1988	Double-blind placebo controlled	30 pre-pubertal children	Statistically significant improvement on CGI. No significant change on Parent and Teacher Questionnaires.
Casat 1989	Double-blind, placebo controlled	30 children and adolescents	Overall clinical improvement in physician ratings.
Spencer 1993	Retrospective	4 with co-morbid Tourette's disorder.	Tics exacerbated with treatment and decreased after discontinuation.
Barrickman 1995	Double-blind controlled crossover comparison w/ MPH	15 children and adolescents w/ ADHD	MPH> bupropion
Conners 1996	Double-blind placebo controlled	109 children	Improvement for hyperactivity and conduct problems with active treatment
Riggs 1998	Open	13 male adolescents with co-morbid conduct disorder and substance use d/o in residential treatment.	39% decline in mean CGI severity ratings.

CGI = Clinical Global Impressions Scale

It should be noted that a 0.4% risk of drug-induced seizures has been reported with buproprion. Patients with a previous history of seizures, those treated at higher-than-recommended doses, and patients with eating disorders appear to be at particularly high risk for this adverse event. Other side effects that may occur during treatment with bupropion include agitation, dermatitis, insomnia, irritability, and headache, but overall, bupropion appears to be generally well tolerated and does not appear to effect cardiac conduction like the TCAs.

Venlafaxine is a selective inhibitor of norepinephrine and serotonin reuptake. Therapeutic effects in the treatment of ADHD were initially reported in three open series and a case report in adults (Adler et al.1995; Findling et al. 1996; Hedges et al. 1995; Wilens, Biederman, and Spencer 1995). There is also evidence suggesting that venlafaxine may have therapeutic effects in the treatment of children and adolescents with ADHD (Olvera et al. 1996; Pleak and Gormly 1995; Kotler et al. 2000) (see table VII). A retrospective review of venlafaxine in 10 children and adults with ADHD and a co-morbid autism spectrum disorder also suggested that improvement in ADHD symptoms and other behaviors may occur when this drug is prescribed to these patients (Hollander et al. 2000).

An optimal dosing strategy for venlafaxine in children and adolescents with ADHD has yet to be established, however, average final total daily doses typically range between 1 and 2 milligrams per kilogram. Although significant blood pressure increases may occur in adults treated with venlafaxine (particularly at higher doses), the available data suggest that this does not typically occur when youths

Table VII. Venlafaxine Studies in Children and Adolescents with Attention-Deficit/Hyperactivity Disorder

First Author/ Year	Study Type	Number of Subjects	Outcome
Olvera 1996	Open 5 weeks	16 children and adolescents	44% overall improved behaviorally but not cognitively. 19% had worsening of hyperactivity.
Hollander 2000	Open retrospective	10 children, adolescents and young adults w/ ADHD and Autism spectrum d/o	6/10 were very much or much improved on CGI improvement scale. Improved inattention, hyperactivity, repetitive behaviors, restricted interest, social deficits, communication and language.
Kotler 2000	Open, 2 weeks	30 children and adolescents	Significant reductions in ADHD symptoms noted.

are treated at a dosage level less than 2 milligrams per kilogram per day. Other side effects that may occur during treatment with venlafaxine include nausea, drowsiness, disinhibition, and insomnia.

At present, it appears that buproprion may be a potentially safe and effective alternative medication for the treatment of ADHD. Venlafaxine also seems to hold promise as a viable treatment option for patients with ADHD. However, there is a significantly larger empiric research base to support the use of buproprion. More research is needed to either confirm or refute the role of venlafaxine for children and adolescents with ADHD.

An experimental compound, GW320659, may also have promise as a treatment for ADHD. GW320659 is a reuptake inhibitor of norepinephrine and dopamine. Its chemical structure is similar to the major active metabolite of buproprion. In a multi-center, open-label, flexible dose study in which 51 youths with a mean age of 9 years were enrolled, treatment with GW320659 was well-tolerated, and associated with ADHD symptom reductions (DeVeaugh-Geiss et al. 2000). Whether or not this compound truly has efficacy for patients with ADHD remains a topic for future placebo-controlled trials.

Tomoxetine, another experimental compound that is a selective noradrenergic re-uptake inhibitor, has recently been investigated as a possible treatment for ADHD in children and teenagers. In an open-label study of 10 males between the ages of 9 and 14 years, atomoxetine therapy was an effective and well-tolerated treatment for ADHD (Kratochvil et al. 2000). Results from larger double-blind studies, which compared the safety and efficacy of atomoxetine to placebo, found that atomoxetine was generally well-tolerated and superior to placebo in its ability to reduce ADHD symptoms (Heiligenstein et al. 2000). In short, atomoxetine appears to be a potentially useful non-stimulant alternative for the treatment of children and adolescents with ADHD.

Selective Serotonin Reuptake Inhibitors (SSRIs)

There are no controlled studies of ADHD treatment with SSRIs. A small open trial suggested fluoxetine (Prozac®) might be helpful for young people with ADHD (Barrickman et al. 1991). There is one open study of paroxetine (Paxil®) in patients with ADHD. In 45 children with Tourette's syndrome with episodic rages who had high rates of co-morbidity for ADHD and OCD, paroxetine was found to improve rage outbursts for most patients (Bruun and Budman 1998).

Clinical evidence suggests that SSRI monotherapy does not appear to be an effective treatment for most children and adolescents with ADHD. Selective serotonin reuptake inhibitors may be used together with psychostimulants for patients with co-morbid mood disorders (Findling 1996), but combination pharmacotherapy with psychostimulants and SSRIs has not been extensively studied. The possibility of an SSRI (sertraline) interacting with stimulants resulting in atrioventricular nodal re-entrant tachycardia in a predisposed patient has been reported (Gracious 1999). This combination treatment should be carefully considered before being initiated, because of such possible complications.

Alpha—2 Noradrenergic Agonists

Clonidine hydrochloride (Catapress®) and guanfacine hydrochloride (Tenex®) are centrally acting antihypertensive agents with alpha—2 adrenoreceptor agonist properties. Clonidine acts preferentially on presynaptic alpha—2 neurons to inhibit the endogenous release of norepinephrine in the brain. Guanfacine is a longer-acting analog that appears to be less sedating than clonidine. Due to its longer plasma half-life, guanfacine is also less likely to cause rebound adrenergic symptoms (such as hypertension) if treatment is abruptly discontinued. Whereas guanfacine is only available as oral tablets, clonidine is available in both oral tablets and as a transdermal patch.

There are numerous reports that have described the utility of clonidine for children with ADHD. It appears that clonidine has greater beneficial effects for symptoms of hyperarousal and aggression than for symptoms of inattention (see table VIII). Studies of guanfacine for the treatment of children and adolescents with ADHD are limited to open trials (see table IX). When compared to clonidine, it appears that symptoms associated with inattention are more robustly improved with guanfacine therapy.

As both clonidine and guanfacine are antihypertensive agents, treatment with either drug can lead to reductions in blood pressure. Therefore, a careful cardiovascular assessment prior to and during treatment with either guanfacine or clonidine is advised (Gutgesell et al. 1999). A common side effect with both these agents is sedation. It appears that clonidine is more likely to induce this adverse event. In order to minimize the risk of medication-induced sedation and cardiovascular changes, gradual initiation of pharmacotherapy with either drug is recommended. Side effects due to hypotension, such as headache and dizziness, may occur during clonidine or guanfacine therapy.

Adverse behavioral effects that can occur during alpha—2 noradrenergic agonist therapy include irritability, depression, or dysphoria (Hunt, Capper, and O'Connell 1990). It is particularly important for clinicians to be aware of this side effect because these low, dysphoric moods can be associated with noticeable increases in disruptive behaviors. In hopes of treating these dysfunctional behaviors, a

Table VIII. Selected Clonidine Studies in Children and Adolescents with Attention-Deficit/Hyperactivity Disorder

First Author/ Year	Study Type	Number of Subjects	Outcome
Hunt et al 1982	Open	4 children and adolescents	Improvement noted by parents and teachers. Distractibility often persisted but more able to return to task and complete
Hunt et al. 1985	Double-blind placebo controlled crossover	12 children	Statistically significant improvement was noted. Best responders were overactive, uninhibited, and impulsive at baseline. Deterioration seen within 2-4 days of discontinuation of clonidine.
Hunt 1987	Open randomized comparison of MPH, oral and trans-dermal clonidine and placebo	10 children	MPH and clonidine both superior to placebo. Effect of both forms of clonidine = MPH. Clonidine increased frustration tolerance but did not decrease distractibility.
Jaselskis et al. 1992	Double-blind placebo controlled crossover	8 boys with autistic disorder and ADHD.	Improvements on a variety of different measures noted during clonidine treatment.
Kemph et al. 1993	Open	17 aggressive children with OPDD or conduct disorder.	88% had a decrease in aggression.
Steingard et al. 1993	Retrospective	54 children and adolescents; 24 with co-morbid tic disorder	Improvement in ADHD and tic symptoms. Patients with co-morbid tic disorder improved more frequently than patients without a tic disorder.
Schvehla et al. 1994	Retrospective	18 prepubertal boys with co-morbid conduct disorder.	61% had marked improvement by clinical impression.
Lichter et al. 1996	Retrospective	53 children and adolescents with Tourette's disorder often with ADHD	Improvement ADHD symptoms was associated with a longer duration of vocal tics before treatment.

First Author/ Year	Study Type	Number of Subjects	Outcome
Prince et al. 1996	Retrospective	62 children and adolescents with associated sleep disturbances	85% had much to very much improvement in sleep. Effective whether or not sleep disturbances were induced by medication treatment.
Van der Meere et al. 1999	Double-blind crossover placebo controlled comparison with MPH	53 children.	Improvement in hyperactivity, impulsivity, aggression and insomnia
Conner et al. 2000	Randomized controlled blinded comparison of clonidine, MPH and the combination of both.	24 children and adolescents w/ ADHD and aggressive ODD or conduct disorder.	Significant improvement in all 3 groups. Clonidine monotherapy was associated with a decrease in fine motor speed.

Table IX. Selected Guanfacine Studies in Children and Adolescents with Attention-Deficit Hyperactivity Disorder (ADHD)

Group/Year	Study Type	Number of Subjects	Outcome
Chappell et al. 1995	Open	10 children with co-morbid Tourette's disorder	40% had moderate to marked improvement. Significant decrease in motor and vocal tics.
Horrigan and Barnhill 1995	Open	15 children and adolescents with treatment resistant ADHD	Significant clinical benefits noted. Improvement in inattention and hyperactivity reported.
Hunt et al. 1995	Open	13 children, adolescents, and young adults	Improvement in hyperactivity and inattention noted.

physician might erroneously increase the dose of either clonidine or guanfacine. It has also been suggested that guanfacine treatment may have precipitated secondary hypomania or mania in a case series of 5 children (Horrigan and Barnhill 1999). Insomnia and nightmares are also potential side effects with these drugs. If the decision is made to discontinue an alpha 2-adrenergic agent, it should be done slowly in order to avoid elevations in blood pressure and pulse.

Clonidine is often combined with stimulants in the treatment of ADHD, with benefits supported by anecdotal clinical experience as well as a controlled study (Connor, Barkley, and Davis 2000). There have been four reported deaths of children who at one time had taken a combination of clonidine and methylphenidate. Although concerns about combining these agents were raised, pre-existing and concurrent medical conditions preclude directly linking these medications with these deaths (Popper 2000).

To summarize, it appears that alpha 2-adrenergic agonists are relatively safe and effective treatments for children and adolescents with ADHD. Symptoms of hyperactivity appear to be more responsive to these agents than symptoms of inattention. As these are antihypertensive agents, cardiovascular monitoring prior to and during treatment is indicated.

ß-ADRENERGIC BLOCKERS AND ANXIOLYTICS

One study has examined the effects of ß-adrenergic blockers in the treatment of ADHD in children. In that study, the salutary effects of pindolol were found to be more modest than that of methylphenidate. Moreover, significant pindolol-related side effects (e.g. parathesias, hallucinations, and nightmares) were found to limit the utility of this drug (Buitelaar et al. 1996). Based on the lack of positive controlled studies in pediatric patients, the use of ß-adrenergic blockers is not generally recommended for the treatment of children and adolescents with ADHD.

Buspirone (Buspar®) is a nonbenzodiazepine anxiolytic with a high affinity to serotonin receptors and a modest effect on the dopaminergic system and alpha-adrenergic activity. Potential beneficial effects of buspirone were reported in an open study of 12 children with ADHD. These youths were treated with buspirone at a dose of 0.5 milligrams per kilogram per day. They showed improvement in disruptive behavior and psychosocial functioning (Malhotra and Santosh 1998). Although buspirone appears to be potentially helpful for ADHD symptoms in pediatric patients, further data are needed before definitive conclusions can be made.

OTHER AGENTS

Older controlled studies with antipsychotics suggest that treatment with these agents can lead to reductions in disruptive behaviors. However, most studies suggest that stimulants are generally more effective than antipsychotics for the treatment of ADHD (Spencer et al. 1996). Due to their suboptimal side effect profile, it has been recommended that the use of antipsychotics generally be limited to complicated or treatment-resistant cases of ADHD (AACAP Practice Parameters 1997).

Caffeine is another compound that is not recommended for use in children with ADHD. Although caffeine may slightly improve vigilance performance and decrease reaction time in healthy children, it does not generally appear to provide significant salutary effects to children in with ADHD (Hughes and Hale 1998).

Presently, two cholinergic agonists appear to show promise as potential treatments for ADHD. Donepezil (Aricept®) is currently marketed as a treatment for Alzheimer's dementia. ABT-418 is an experimental compound (Wilens et al. 1999; Hoopes 1999; Wilens et al. 2000). However, at the present time, there are no data from controlled clinical trials in children and adolescents to definitively support the use of such compounds.

CONCLUSIONS

Based on available safety, effectiveness, and efficacy data, short-acting psychostimulants remain the medication treatment of choice for most school-aged children with ADHD. With limited data, the same appears to hold true for preschool-aged children and adolescents. There is a growing body of literature suggesting that non-stimulant medications may have a role in the treatment of some pediatric patients with ADHD.

The TCAs are the most extensively studied of the non-stimulant drugs. Although they have demonstrated efficacy in the treatment of ADHD, their utility is limited by their side effect profile. Although the irreversible MAOIs seem to be quite effective, the dietary restrictions that accompany their use do not make them practical treatment options. Moclobemide and selegiline are two MAOIs that do not appear to require dietary precautions during their use in young people. Whether or not these agents are truly safe or effective in the treatment of children and teenagers with ADHD remains to be seen.

Bupropion and alpha 2-adrenergic agonists appear to be generally safe and effective alternative treatments for ADHD. Venlafaxine and buspirone appear to ameliorate symptoms of ADHD in anecdotal reports and open studies; however, controlled studies are lacking and warranted. Other promising stimulant alternatives include tomoxetine, GW 320659, donepezil, and ABT-418. More research into the non-stimulant pharmacological treatment of ADHD is needed.

REFERENCES

AACAP 1997. Practice parameters for the assessment and treatment of children, adolescents, and adults with attention-deficit/hyperactivity disorder.

Journal of the American Academy of Child and Adolescent Psychiatry 36:(suppl 10):85–121.

Adler, L. A., Resnick, S., Kunz, M., and Devinsky, O. 1995. Open-label trial of venlafaxine (Effexor) in attention deficit disorder. *Psychopharmacology* Bulletin 31:544.

Antkowiak, R., and Rajewski, A. 1998. Administration of moclobemide in children with attention deficit hyperactivity disorder. *Psychiatria Polska* 32(6):751–7.

Barrickman, L., Noyes, R., Kuperman, S., Schumacher, E., and Verda, M. 1991. Treatment of ADHD with fluoxetine: A preliminary trial. *Journal of the American Academy of Child and Adolescent Psychiatry* 30:762–7.

Barrickman, L. L., Perry, P. J., Allen, A. J., Kuperman, S., Arndt, S. V., Herrmann, K. J., and Schumacher, E. 1995. Bupropion versus methylphenidate in the treatment of attention-deficit hyperactivity disorder. *Journal of the American Academy of Child and Adolescent Psychiatry* 34(5):649–57.

Biederman, J., Baldessarini, R. J., Wright, V., Knee, D., and Harmatz, J. S. 1989. A double-blind placebo controlled study of desipramine in the treatment of ADD: I Efficacy. *Journal of the American Academy of Child and Adolescent Psychiatry*. 28(5):777–84.

Biederman, J., Gastfriend, D. R., and Jellinek, M. S. 1986. Desipramine in the treatment of children with attention deficit disorder. *Journal of Clinical Psychopharmacology* 6(6):359–63.

Bruun, R. D., and Budman, C. L. 1998. Paroxetine treatment of episodic rages associated with Tourette's disorder. *Journal of Clinical Psychiatry* 59(11): 581–4.

Buitelaar, J. K., van der Gaag, R. J., Swaab-Barneveld, H., and Kuiper, M. 1996. Pindolol and methylphenidate in children with attention-deficit hyperactivity disorder. Clinical efficacy and side effects. *Journal of Child Psychology and Psychiatry* 37(5):587–595.

Casat, C. D., Pleasants, D. Z., Schroeder, D. H., and Parler, D. W. 1989. Bupropion in children with attention deficit disorder. *Psychopharmacology Bulletin* 25 (2):198–201.

Chappell, P. B., Riddle, M. A., Scahill, L., Lynch, K. A., Schultz, R., Arnsten A., Leckman J. F., and Cohen D. J. 1995. Guanfacine treatment of co-morbid attention-deficit hyperactivity disorder and Tourette's syndrome: Preliminary clinical experience. *Journal of the American Academy of Child and Adolescent Psychiatry* 34(9):1140–6.

Clay, T. H., Gualtieri, C. T., Evans, R. W., and Guillion, C. M. 1988. Clinical and neuropsychological effects of the novel antidepressant bupropion. *Psychopharmacology Bulletin* 24:143–8.

Conners, C. K., Casat, C. D., Gualtieri, C. T., Weller, E., Reader, M., Reiss, A., Weller, R. A., Khayrallah, M., and Ascher, J. 1996. Bupropion hydrochloride in attention deficit disorder with hyperactivity. *Journal of the American Academy of Child and Adolescent Psychiatry*. 35(10):1314–21.

Connor, D. F., Barkley, R. A., and Davis, H. T. 2000. A pilot study of methylphenidate, clonidine, or the combination in ADHD comorbid with aggressive oppositional defiant or conduct disorder. *Clinical Pediatrics* (Philadelphia) 39(1):15–25.

Cox, W. H., Jr. 1982. An indication for use of imipramine in attention deficit disorder. *American Journal of Psychiatry* 139(8):1059–60.

DeVeaugh-Geiss, J., Conners, C. K., Sarkis, E. H., Winner, P. K., Ginsberg, L. D., Hemphill, J. M., Laurenza, A., Asgharnejad, M., and Webster, C. J. 2000. Efficacy of GW320659 in children with attention-deficit/hyperactivity disorder. Presented at the American Academy of Child and Adolescent Psychiatry, New York, October.

Donnelly, M., Zametkin, A. J., Rapoport, J. L., Ismond, D. R., Weingartner, H., Lane, E., Oliver, J., Linnoila, M., and Potter, W. Z.. 1986. Treatment of childhood hyperactivity with desipramine: Plasma drug concentration, cardiovascular effects, plasma and urinary catecholamine levels, and clinical response. *Clinical Pharmacology Therapy* 39(1):72-81.

Feigin, A., Kurlan, R., McDermott, M. P., Beach, J., Dimitsopulos, T., Brower, C. A., Chapieski, L., Trinidad, K., Como, P., and Jankovic, J. 1996. A controlled trial of deprenyl in children with Tourette's syndrome and attention deficit hyperactivity disorder. *Neurology* 46(4):965–8.

Findling, R. L. 1996. Open-label treatment of co-morbid depression and attentional disorders with co-administration of serotonin reuptake inhibitors and psychostimulants in children, adolescents, and adults: A case series. *Journal of Child and Adolescent Psychopharmacology* 6(3):165–75.

Findling, R. L., Schwartz, M. A., Flannery, D. J., and Manos, M. J. 1996. Venlafaxine in adults with attention-deficit/hyperactivity disorder: An open clinical trial. *Journal of Clinical Psychiatry* 57(5):184–9.

Garfinkel, B. D., Wender, P. H., Sloman, L., and O'Neill, I. 1983. Tricyclic antidepressant and methylphenidate treatment of attention deficit disorder in children. *Journal of the American Academy of Child Psychiatry* 22(4):343–8.

Gastfriend, D. R., Biederman, J., and Jellinek, M. S. 1984. Desipramine in the treatment of adolescents with attention deficit disorder. *American Journal of Psychiatry* 141(7):906–8.

Gracious, B. L. 1999. Atrioventricular nodal re-entrant tachycardia associated with stimulant treatment. *Journal of Child and Adolescent Psychopharmacology* 9(2):125–8.

Gualtieri, C. T., and Evans, R.W. 1988. Motor performance in hyperactive children treated with imipramine. *Perceptual and Motor Skills* 66(3):763–9.

Gualtieri, C. T., Keenan, P. A., and Chandler, M. 1991. Clinical and neuropsychological effects of desipramine in children with attention deficit hyperactivity disorder. *Journal of Clinical Psychopharmacology* 11(3):155–9.

Gutgesell, H., Atkins, D., Barst, R., Buck, M., Franklin, W., Humes, R., Ringel, R., Shaddy, R., and Taubert, K. A. 1999. AHA: Scientific statement: Cardiovascular monitoring of children and adolescents receiving psychotropic drugs. *Journal of the American Academy of Child and Adolescent Psychiatry* 38:1047–50.

Hedges, D., Reimherr, F. W., Rogers, A., Strong, R., and Wender, P. H. 1995. An open trial of venlafaxine in adult patients with attention deficit hyperactivity disorder. *Psychopharmacology Bulletin* 31:779–83.

Heiligenstein, J. H., Spencer, T. J., Faries, D. E., Biederman, J., Kratochvil, C., and Conners, C. K. 2000. Tomoxetine, methylphenidate, placebo: Comparison of treatment effects in children with ADHD. Poster presented at the annual meeting of the American Academy of Child and Adolescent Psychiatry, New York, October.

Hilton, D. K., Martin, C. A., Heffron, W. M., Hall, B. D., and Johnson, G. L. 1991. Imipramine treatment of ADHD in a fragile X child. *Journal of the American Academy of Child and Adolescent Psychiatry* 30(5):831–4.

Hollander, E., Kaplan, A., Cartwright, C., and Reichman, D. 2000. Venlafaxine in children, adolescents, and young adults with autism spectrum disorders: An open retrospective clinical report. *Journal of Child Neurology* 15(2):132–5.

Hoopes, S. P. 1999. Donepezil for Tourette's disorder and ADHD. *Journal of Clinical Psychopharmacology* 19(4):381–2.

Horrigan, J. P., and Barnhill, L. J. 1995. Guanfacine and treatment-resistant attention deficit hyperactivity disorder in boys. *Journal of Child and Adolescent Psychopharmacology* 5:215–23.

Horrigan, J. P., and Barnhill, L. J. 1999. Guanfacine and secondary mania in children. *Journal of Affective Disorders* 54(3):309–14.

Hughes J. R., and Hale K. L. 1998. Behavioral effects of caffeine and other methylxanthines on children. *Experimental and Clinical Psychopharmacology* 6(1):87–95.

Hunt, R. D. 1987. Treatment effects of oral and transdermal clonidine in relation to methylphenidate: An open pilot study in ADD-H. *Psychopharmacology Bulletin* 23(1):111–4.

Hunt, R. D., Arnsten, A. F., and Asbell, M. D. 1995. An open trial of guanfacine in the treatment of attention-deficit hyperactivity disorder. *Journal of the American Academy of Child and Adolescent Psychiatry* 34(1):50–4.

Hunt, R. D., Capper, S., and O'Connell, P. 1990. Clonidine in child and adolescent psychiatry. *Journal of Child and Adolescent Psychophamacology* 1:87–102.

Hunt, R. D., Cohen, D. J., Shaywitz, S. E., and Shaywitz, B. A. 1982. Strategies for study of the neurochemistry of attention deficit disorder in children. *Schizophrenia Bulletin* 8(2):236–52.

Hunt, R. D., Minderaa, R. B., and Cohen, D. J. 1985. Clonidine benefits children with attention deficit disorder and hyperactivity: Report of a double-blind placebo-crossover therapeutic trial. *Journal of the American Academy of Child Psychiatry* 24(5):617–29.

Jankovic, J. 1993. Deprenyl in attention deficit associated with Tourette's syndrome. *Archives of Neurology* 50(3):286–8.

Jaselskis, C. A., Cook, E. H. Jr., Fletcher, K. E., and Leventhal, B. L. 1992. Clonidine treatment of hyperactive and impulsive children with autistic disorder. *Journal of Clinical Psychopharmacology* 12(5):322–7.

Kemph, J. P., DeVane, C. L., Levin, G. M., Jarecke, R., and Miller, R. L. 1993. Treatment of aggressive children with clonidine: Results of an open pilot study. *Journal of the American Academy of Child and Adolescent Psychiatry* 32(3):577–81.

Kotler, L., Findling, R. L., Fried, J., Chuang, S., Lemon, E., Branicky, M. A., Tosyali, C., and Greenhill, L. 2000. An open label study of venlafaxine in children and adolescents with ADHD. Presented at the American Academy of Child and Adolescent Psychiatry Annual Meeting, New York City, October.

Kratochvil, C., Harrington, M., Baker, N., Bohac, D., May, D., and Burke, W. J. 2000. An open-label trial of tomoxetine in pediatric ADHD. Presented at the American Academy of Child and Adolescent Psychiatry Annual Meeting, New York City, October.

Kupietz, S. S., and Balka, E. B. 1976. Alterations in the vigilance performance of children receiving amitriptyline and methylphenidate pharmacotherapy. *Psychopharmacology* (Berlin) 50(1):29–33.

Leonard, H. L., Meyer, M. C., and Swedo, S. E. 1995. Electrocardiographic changes during desipramine and clomipramine treatment in children and adolescents. *Journal of the American Academy of Child and Adolescent Psychiatry* 34:1460–68.

Lichter, D. G., and Jackson, L. A. 1996. Predictors of clonidine response in Tourette syndrome: Implications and inferences. *Journal of Child Neurology* 11(2):93–7.

Malhotra, S., and Santosh, P. J. 1998. An open clinical trial of buspirone in children with attention-deficit/hyperactivity disorder. *Journal of the American Academy of Child and Adolescent Psychiatry* 37(4):364–71.

The MTA Cooperative Group 1999. A 14-month randomized clinical trial of treatment strategies for attention-deficit/hyperactivity disorder. *Archives of General Psychiatry* 56(12):1073–1086.

Olvera, R. L., Pliszka, S. R., Luh, J., and Tatum, R. 1996. An open trial of venlafaxine in the treatment of attention-deficit/hyperactivity disorder in children and adolescents. *Journal of Child and Adolescent Psychopharmacology* 6(4):241–50.

Pleak, R. R., and Gormly, L. J. 1995. Effects of venlafaxine treatment for ADHD in a child. *American Journal of Psychiatry* 152(7):1099.

Popper, C. W. 2000. Pharmacologic alternatives to psychostimulants for the treatment of attention deficit/hyperactivity disorder. *Child and Adolescent Psychiatric Clinics of North America* 9(3):605–646.

Pozzi, M., and Hartley, L. 1984. Hyperactivity, drugs, and attention deficit. *British Journal of Clinical Psychology* 23(3):217–23.

Prince, J. B., Wilens, T. E., Biederman, J., Spencer, T. J., and Wozniak, J. R. 1996. Clonidine for sleep disturbances associated with attention-deficit hyperactivity disorder: A systematic chart review of 62 cases. *Journal of the American Academy of Child and Adolescent Psychiatry* 35(5):599–605.

Prince, J. B., Wilens, T. E., Biederman, J., Spencer, T. J., Millstein, R., Polisner, D. A., and Bostic, J. Q. 2000. A controlled study of nortriptyline in children and adolescents with attention deficit hyperactivity disorder. *Journal of Child and Adolescent Psychopharmacology* 10(3):193–204.

Quinn, P. O., and Rapoport, J. L. 1975. One-year follow-up of hyperactive boys treated with imipramine or methylphenidate. *American Journal of Psychiatry* 132:241–45.

Rapoport, J. L., Quinn, P. O., Bradbard, G., Riddle, K. D., and Brooks, E. 1974. Imipramine and methylphenidate treatments of hyperactive boys: A double-blind Comparison. *Archives of General Psychiatry* 30(6):789–93.

Rapport, M. D., Carlson, G. A., Kelly, K. L., and Pataki, C. 1993. Methylphenidate and desipramine in hospitalized children: I. Separate and combined effects on cognitive function. *Journal of the American Academy of Child and Adolescent Psychiatry* 32(2):333–42.

Riddle, M. A., Hardin, M. T., Cho, S. C., Woolston, J. L., and Leckman, J. F. 1988. Desipramine treatment of boys with attention-deficit hyperactivity disorder and tics: Preliminary clinical experience. *Journal of the American Academy of Child and Adolescent Psychiatry* 27(6):811–4.

Riggs, P. D., Leon, S. L., Mikulich, S. K., and Pottle, L. C. 1998. An open trial of bupropion for ADHD in adolescents with substance use disorders and conduct disorder. *Journal of the American Academy of Child Adolescent Psychiatry* 37(12):1271–8.

Sangal, J. M., Sangal, R. B., and Persky, B. 1996. Prolonged P300 latency in attention deficit hyperactivity disorder predicts poor response to imipramine. *Clinical Electroencephalography* 27(4):191–201.

Saul, R. C. 1985. Nortriptyline in attention deficit disorder. *Clinical Neuropharmacology* 8(4):382–3.

Schvehla, T. J., Mandoki, M. W., and Sumner, G. S. 1994. Clonidine therapy for co-morbid attention deficit hyperactivity disorder and conduct disorder: preliminary findings in a children's inpatient unit. *Southern Medical Journal* 87(7):692–5.

Simeon, J. G., Ferguson, H. B., and Van Wyck Fleet, J. 1986. Bupropion effects in attention deficit and conduct disorders. *Canadian Journal of Psychiatry* 31(6):581–5.

Singer, H. S., Brown, J., Quaskey, S., Rosenberg, L. A., Mellits, E. D., and Denckla, M. B. 1995. The treatment of attention-deficit hyperactivity disorder in Tourette's syndrome: A double-blind placebo-controlled study with clonidine and desipramine. *Pediatrics* 95(1):74–81.

Spencer, T., Biederman, J., and Wilens, T. 2000. Pharmacotherapy of attention deficit hyperactivity disorder. *Child and Adolescent Psychiatric Clinics of North America* 1(9):77–97.

Spencer, T., Biederman, J., Kerman, K., Steingard, R., and Wilens, T. 1993. Desipramine treatment of children with attention-deficit hyperactivity disorder and tic disorder or Tourette's syndrome. *Journal of the American Academy of Child and Adolescent Psychiatry* 32(2):354–60.

Spencer, T., Biederman, J., Steingard, R., and Wilens, T. 1993. Bupropion exacerbates tics in children with attention-deficit hyperactivity disorder and Tourette's syndrome. *Journal of the American Academy of Child and Adolescent Psychiatry* 32(1):211–4.

Spencer, T., Biederman, J., Wilens, T., Steingard, R., and Geist, D. 1993. Nortriptyline treatment of children with attention-deficit hyperactivity disorder and tic disorder or Tourette's disorder. *Journal of the American Academy of Child and Adolescent Psychiatry* 32:205–210.

Spencer, T. J., Biederman, J., Wilens, T., Harding, M., O'Donnell, D., and Griffin, S. 1996. Pharmacotherapy of attention-deficit hyperactivity disorder across the life cycle. *Journal of the American Academy of Child and Adolescent Psychiatry* 35:409–32.

Steingard, R., Biederman, J., Spencer, T., Wilens, T., and Gonzalez, A. 1993. Comparison of clonidine response in the treatment of attention-deficit hyperactivity disorder with and without comorbid tic disorders. *Journal of the American Academy of Child Adolescent Psychiatry* 32(2):350–3.

Trott, G. E., Friese, H. J., Menzel, M., and Nissen, G. 1992. Use of moclobemide in children with attention deficit hyperactivity disorder. *Psychopharmacology* (Berlin) 106 (Suppl):S134–6.

Van der Meere, J., Gunning, B., and Stemerdink, N. 1999. The effect of methylphenidate and clonidine on response inhibition and state regulation in children with ADHD. *Journal of Child Psychology and Psychiatry* 40(2):291–8.

Werry, J. 1980. Imipramine and methylphenidate in hyperactive children. *Journal of Child Psychology and Psychiatry* 21:27–35.

Werry, J., Aman, M. J., and Diamond, E. 1980. Imipramine and methylphenidate in hyperactive children. *Journal of Child Psychology and Psychiatry* 21:27–35.

Wilens, T., Biederman, J., Spencer, T., Bostic, J., Prince, J., Monuteaux, M., Soriano, J., Fine, C., Abrams, A., Rater, M., and Polisner, D. 1999. A pilot controlled clinical trial of ABT-418, a cholinergic agonist, in the treatment of adults with attention deficit hyperactivity disorder. *American Journal of Psychiatry* 156:1931–7.

Wilens, T. E., Biederman, J., Abrantes, A. M., and Spencer T. J. 1996. A naturalistic assessment of protriptyline for attention-deficit hyperactivity disorder. *Journal of the American Academy of Child and Adolescent Psychiatry* 35:1485–90.

Wilens, T. E., Biederman, J., and Spencer, T. J. 1995. Venlafaxine for adult ADHD. *American Journal of Psychiatry* 152:1099–1100.

Wilens, T. E., Biederman, J., Geist, D. E., Steingard, R., and Spencer, T. 1993. Nortriptyline in the treatment of attention deficit hyperactivity disorder: A chart review of 58 cases. *Journal of the American Academy of Child and Adolescent Psychiatry* 32:343–9.

Wilens, T. E., Biederman, J., Wong, J., Spencer, T .J., and Prince, J. B. 2000. Adjunctive donepezil in attention deficit hyperactivity disorder youth: Case series. *Journal of Child and Adolescent Psychopharmacology* 10(3): 217–222.

Winsberg, B. G., Kupietz, S. S., Yepes, L. E., and Goldstein, S. 1980. Ineffectiveness of imipramine in children who fail to respond to methylphenidate. *Journal of Autism and Developmental Disorders* 10(2):129–37.

Yepes, L. E., Balka, E. B., Winsberg, B. G., and Bialer, I. 1977. Amitriptyline and methylphenidate treatment of behaviorally disordered children. *Journal of Child Psychology and Psychiatry* 18(1):39–52.

Zametkin, A., Rapoport, J. L., Murphy, D. L., Linnoila, M., and Ismond, D. 1985. Treatment of hyperactive children with monoamine oxidase inhibitors. I. Clinical efficacy. *Archives of General Psychiatry* 42(10):962–6.

Chapter • 11

Alternative/Complementary Treatments for Attention Deficit Hyperactivity Disorder

L. Eugene Arnold

DEFINITIONS AND BACKGROUND

The terms "alternative," "complementary," "unconventional," and "nontraditional" are often used to refer to the same general group of non-established or nonstandard treatments, depending on the perspective of the speaker and the type of treatment. The nuances differ, varying from pejorative to appreciative and from exclusionary to synthetic. "Alternative" implies substitution for more standard treatments (perhaps even rejection of standard treatments), while "complementary" implies adjunctive use without rejecting standard treatments. "Nontraditional" can be confusing, depending on whose tradition is referenced: "traditional Chinese medicine" is often considered one of the alternative approaches in contrast to modern medicine. Most advocates of nonstandard treatments prefer the term "complementary" in recognition that no single treatment is completely satisfactory. (For further background on evaluating such treatments, see Arnold 1994, 1995).

This chapter and its tables were adapted, condensed, and updated with permission from: Arnold, L. E. 1999. Treatment Alternatives for ADHD. *Journal of Attention Disorders* 3:30-48, and from a chapter of the same name in Jensen, P. S., and Cooper, J. eds. 2001. *Diagnosis and Treatment of ADHD: An Evidenced-Based Approach.* APA Press, in press.

In this report, we are, for convenience, defining alternative/complementary treatments of attention-deficit/hyperactivity disorder (ADHD, DSM-IV 1994) as those other than psychoactive medication and behavioral/psychosocial treatments. Both of the latter have ample documentation of efficacy in the professional peer-reviewed literature and are generally accepted as having statistically and clinically significant effects (e.g., Richters et al. 1995).

The literature was searched on Medline and PsychInfo for ADHD, hyperactivity, hyperkinesis, and minimal brain dysfunction, crossed with alternative treatment and names of specific treatments. Investigators known to be interested in alternative treatments were contacted for unpublished data. The original search was done in 1998 on literature up to that point, and it has been updated since then by casually accrued information and one additional search.

TREATMENTS

Two dozen alternative treatments were identified, ranging in scientific documentation from discrediting controlled studies through mere hypotheses to positive controlled double-blind clinical trials (table I). One of the problems in studying and evaluating alternative treatments is that they often benefit only a small etiologically defined subgroup (if they indeed have benefit), so that if the sample is not selected correctly, the benefit for the small subgroup is lost in the group means by dilution with the unresponsive majority. Therefore sample selection is even more important than for more generic treatments.

Table I. Scientific Status of Treatment (Tx) Alternatives for Attention-Deficit/Hyperactivity Disorder (ADHD).

Treatment	Etiology or Mechanism	Type of data	E.S. or p	Rating* (0–6); recommendation	Risks
Sympathomimetic Stimulants	catecholamine, esp. dopamine	> 100 placebo XOs & RCTs in 1000s	ES 0.7–1.8 p.01–.0001	6; Use if no cause found	side effects; doubt neurotoxic
Anti-depressants, other psych med	catecholamine, serotonin	Multiple placebo-controlled RCTs	ES 0.5–1.5, p .05–.005	6; When stimulants fail	cardiotoxicity, other side effects
Behavioral Tx: BM, contingency	Social learning theory, shaping	ABAB, random wait list controls	ES 0.5–1.2 p .05–.005	5–6; Selective use (severe, comorbid anxiety)	Nuisance, time
Few foods diet (Oligo-antigenic)	Food or additive sensitivity	controlled trial; placebo challenges	ES ≥ 0.5 p .05–.001	5; Define subgroup (profile; % of ADHD)	Nuisance, expense, nutrition

Treatment	Etiology or Mechanism	Type of data	E.S. or p	Rating* (0–6); recommendation	Risks
Enzyme-potentiated desensitization	Food or additive sensitivity	controlled comparison to placebo injections	p .001	4; Replication Define subgroup	injection
Elimination of sugar alone	sugar malaise	placebo-controlled challenges	p >.1	0; Take FH of Diabetes	Delay std Tx
Amino acid supplementation	Precursors of catecholamines	placebo-controlled comparisons	ES up to 0.6, p .01	0 despite short-lived effect	eosinophilia, neurotoxicity
Essential fatty acid supplement	prostaglandins neural membrane	serum level cf cntrl; plac-contr. trials	ES 0.5 $.1 > p > .05$	3; trials of n-3	upsetting balance
glyco-nutritional supplement	Need for glycoconjugates	3 open trials,	2 positive, 1 negative	0	upsetting balance
Dimethyl-amino-ethanol (DMAE)	Acetylcholine precursor	Many open & DB trials, most poor	ES 0.1–0.6; $0.1 > p > 0.05$	3; rigorous placebo trial in ADHD	SE, Expense
Vitamins	deficiency vs. idiopathic need for higher dose	Placebo-controlled trials megavitamin combo, not RDA	Megadose combo no benefit	0 for megacombo; 1 for RDA, specific megavit; Pilot trials	hepatotoxicity, neuropathy in megadose
Iron supplementation	Co-factor to make catecholamines	Open trial supplementation	ES 1.0 $p < .05$	3**; controlled trials	hemochromatosis from excess
Zinc supplementation	Co-factor for many enzymes	Comparison Zn level of ADHD to controls	ES 2.4 $p < .001$	2**; controlled trials	WBC aplasia from excess
Magnesium supplementation	Deficiency cf. to controls	Open trial with control group	ES 1.2–1.4 p. < .05	3**; placebo trials	Aggression from excess
Chinese herbals	clinical exper.	Open trials, one with MPH control	$p < .05$; no diff. from MPH	3; placebo trials	delay of other Tx
Other herbals	clinical exper.	no data	N.A.	1; pilot trials	delay Tx
Homeopathic preparations	clinical exper.	no data	N.A.	1; pilot trials	delay Tx
Laser Acupuncture	stimulate foci for calming	open trial	ES 1.0	2; controlled trial	delay other Tx, burn
EEG Biofeedback	suppress theta, increase beta waves	open & randomized wait list control trials	$p < 0.05$	3; sham-controlled trial	expense, time

Treatment	Etiology or Mechanism	Type of data	E.S. or p	Rating* (0–6); recommendation	Risks
EMG biofeedback, relaxation, hypnosis	lower arousal, muscle tone	Randomized trials with controls	ES 1.0–1.3 p < 0.01	0 for hypnosis; 4 for EMG/relaxn; cf. to med	delay other Tx
Meditation	autonomic effect; focused attn	cf. relaxation, wait list ctrl, med	p < .05	3; Rigorous replication, sham ctrl	Delay other Tx
Mirror feedback	improve deficient self-focus	Randmzd Xover w. and w/o; controls	E.S. 0.5 p < .05	3; replication, instruction to look	May impair non-ADHD children
Channel-specific perceptual training	basic readiness skills, focus	Randomized prevention trial with 2 control groups	ES 0.9 p < 0.01	3; controlled Tx trials	delay other Tx
Vestibular stimulation	modulate behavior, attention, perception	open and single-blind trials	ES 0.4–1.2 p ns–0.001	3; randomized sham-controlled trials	nausea, accident
Massage	Vagal tone, 5HT, soothing	Single-blind comp. to relaxation	ES med-lg p < 0.05	3; replication, better assessments	negligible. bruise if too hard.
Antifungal Tx	GI yeast toxin; breach mucosa	no data in ADHD; other placebo trials	(ES 1.1-3; p<0.003)	1; trials in ADHD	med risk
Thyroid Tx	Thyroid Fx affects AD Sx	placebo trial: 5/8 GRTH, 1/9 other	n.s. if thyroid not abnormal	0 if thyroid nl; 6 if thyroid abnormal	thyroid toxicity
Deleading	lead toxicity causes ADHD Sx.	placebo-ctrl trial of chelation	ES 0.7–1.6 p.05–.001 (= MPH)	4 if blood Pb > 20; 2 if Pb < 20; ctrl trial	toxicity of chelator

*Ratings: 0 = not worth considering further (despite, in the case of amino acids, some evidence of short-lived effect); 1 = credible hypothesis or collateral support or wide clinical experience, needs pilot data; 2 = promising systematic data, but not prospective trial; 3 = promising prospective data (perhaps with random assignment to control or objective/blind measures) lacking some important control -OR- controlled trial(s) with trends suggesting further exploration; 4 = one significant double-blind controlled trial needing replication -OR- multiple positive controlled trials in a treatment not easily blinded; 5 = convincing double-blind controlled evidence but needs further refinement (e.g., define target subgroup) for clinical application ; 6 = should be considered established Tx for the appropriate subgroup.

**The rating would be 6 for patients showing frank deficiency of vitamins, iron, zinc, or other nutrients.

ES = effect size, Cohen's d (number of standard deviations difference between means): small ES < 0.3; moderate ES = 0.5; large ES = 1.0;

p = probability. Table rev. 3/27/01

Adapted with permission from: Arnold, L.E., 1999 Treatment Alternatives for ADHD. *Journal of Attention Disorders* 3:30–48, and from chapter in: Jensen, PS, and Cooper, J., eds, *Diagnosis and Treatment of ADHD: An Evidenced-Based Approach.* In press, 2001.

See also: Arnold L.E., 2000. Methylphenidate vs. Amphetamine: Comparative Review. *Journal of Attention Disorders* 3(4):200–211.

Elimination Diets

Oligoantigenic or few-foods diets now have convincing double-blind evidence of efficacy in multiple trials for a properly selected subgroup (table II). Prior to the 1982 NIH Consensus Development conference on Defined Diets and Hyperactivity, the literature was equivocal. However, since then there have been at least eight controlled studies (either with sham control diets or placebo challenges of problem foods) demonstrating significant effect with moderate to large effect size (ES, Cohen's d, difference from control condition divided by standard deviation). The positive results likely were facilitated by more "enriched" sample selection and by more restrictive diets. An example of a typical few foods diet is in table III. It is not intended for indefinite consumption, but a two-week test; if improvement occurs, then other foods are added back one at a time to find the "culprits," which are different from one patient to another. The most likely responder is a preschooler with a history of allergies or food intolerance, irritability, sleep disturbance, and somatic complaints (Arnold 1999, 2001). This profile has some importance in view of the current national concern over medicating preschoolers; they may be the very group most likely to respond to such an alternative treatment. In fact, a well-controlled study (Bateman et al., 2001) in 3-year olds found a 30% favorable response (ES = 0.5) regardless of diagnostic status. Enzyme-potentiated desensitization to allergenic foods has one placebo-controlled positive study. Simple sugar restriction has little support despite many published controlled studies (Arnold 1999, 2001).

Table II. Some controlled Studies of Few-Food (Oligoantigenic) Diets. (E.S. = effect size, Cohen's d). Reproduced with permission from: Arnold, L. E. Treatment Alternatives for ADHD. *Journal of Attention Disorders* 3:30-48, 1999 and from chapter in: Jensen, P. S., and Cooper, J., eds, *Diagnosis and Treatment of ADHD: An Evidenced-Based Approach.* In press, 2001.

Reference	Subjects	Design	Results	E.S., p
Egger et al, 1985	special Diet clinic, HK, Conners>14	76 Ss open trial few foods; 28 Ss placebo crossover challenge	62/76 improved in trial 23/28 better on placebo, worse on challenge.	p .001
Kaplan et al, 1989	Ads, DSM-3, Conners 1sd, physical Sx	24 preschoolers placebo diet cross-over (3+4wk) with all food provided; multiple elimination	Over half had reliable behavior improvement, no placebo effect	ES 0.5 p. 01
Pollock & Warner, 1990	Ped. allergy clinic, survey; selected by parent observ behavior	39 Ss placebo-controlled dye challenge while on elimination diet; only 19 completed	Food colors small adverse effect on Conners rating, not globally detected by parent	ES small p. < .01

Reference	Subjects	Design	Results	E.S., p
Egger et al, 1992	special Diet clinic, HK criteria, Conners Index>15	185 Ss 4-wk open few foods; 40 Ss parallel random assignm to Plac or enzyme-potentiated desensitization (EPD)	116/185 responded openly with reintroduction 16/20 with EPD, only 4 with placebo became tolerant	p.001
Carter et al, 1993	special Diet clinic, HK criteria, Conners Index>15	78 Ss open trial few foods; 23 placebo crossover challenge with provoking foods; 19 compl.	59/78 improved openly. 14/19 placebo better behavior and Psy test	p .05–.01 ES 0.6
Rowe & Rowe, 1994	hyperactivity referrals hospital ped. clinic	200 Ss 6-wk open dye-free diet 34 Ss (23 reactors, 11 uncertain) & 20 controls 3-wk daily repeat Plac cf. to 6 doses tartrazine	150/200 improved, relapsed on open chall. 19/23, 3/11, and 2/20 were clear reactors: irritable, restless, sleep disturb.	ES 0.8 p .05
Boris & Mandel, 1994	DSMIII-R Criteria for ADHD	26 Ss open multiple elimination 19 responders placebo -controlled DB challenge; 16 completed	19/26 openly responded Placebo days significantly better than challenge days	p. 001 p. 003 ES 1.5
Schmidt et al, 1997	hyperactive, disruptive inpatients	49 Ss in DB placebo crossover of oligoantigenic & control diet; 36 also compared to MPH	12/49 signif. behavioral improvement cf. control diet. 16/36 resp. MPH	

Boris, M., and Mandel, F.S. 1994. Foods and additives are common causes of the attention deficit hyperactive disorder in children. *Annals of Allergy* 72:462–468.

Carter, C.M., Urbanowicz, M., Hemsley, R., Mantilla, L., Strobel, S., Graham, P.J., and Taylor, E. 1993. Effects of a few food diet in attention deficit disorder. *Archives of Disease in Childhood* 69: 564–568.

Egger, J., Carter, C.M., Graham, P.J., Gumley, D., and Soothill, J.F. 1985. Controlled Trial of Oligoantigenic Treatment in the hyperkinetic syndrome. *Lancet,* 540–545.

Egger, J., Stolla, A., and McEwen, L.M. 1992. Controlled trial of hyposensitization in children with food-induced hyperkinetic syndrome. *Lancet,* 339.

Kaplan, B.J., McNicol, J., Conte, R.A., and Moghadam, H.K. 1989b. Overall nutrient intake of preschool hyperactive and normal boys. *Journal of Abnormal Child Psychology* 17:127.

Rowe, K.S. 1988. Synthetic food colorings and hyperactivity: A double-blind crossover study. *Australian Pediatric Journal* 24:143–147.

Rowe, K.S., and Rowe, K.J. 1994. Synthetic food coloring and behavior: a dose-response effect in a double-blind, placebo-controlled, repeated-measures study. *Journal of Pediatrics* 125:691–698.

Schmidt, M.H., Mocks, P., Lay, B., Eisert, H.G., Fojkar, R., Fritz-Sigmund, D., Marcus, A., and Musaeus, B. 1997. Does oligoantigenic diet influence hyperactive/conduct-disordered children —a controlled trial. *European Child & Adolescent Psychiatry* 6:88–95.

Table III. Example of oligo-antigenic or few-foods diet. "Few foods" implies that it's easier to list what is allowed than what is eliminated. The following are allowed in this example:

Lamb
Chicken
Potatoes
Rice
Banana
Apple
Cucumber
Brassica (cabbage, cauliflower, broccoli, brussel sprouts)
Celery
Carrots
Parsnip
Salt, pepper
Calcium
Vitamins

Nutritional Supplementation

The evidence is less compelling for supplementation than for dietary elimination. Iron supplementation, magnesium supplementation, and dimethylaminoethanol have promising pilot data. Glyconutritional supplementation had two promising open trials and one negative one, and does not seem well-supported at this time. Amino acid supplementation, though mildly effective in the short term, is not effective beyond a few weeks. Iron is a co-enzyme for production of catecholamines, believed important in pathogenesis of ADHD. It may be especially relevant for menstruating girls with ADHD, but an open trial in nonanemic boys also suggested a small effect on parent ratings (but not teacher ratings). Magnesium (if it works) has a U-shaped response curve. Dimethylaminoethanol (DMAE, deanol) was formerly marketed as the drug Deaner, but FDA approval was withdrawn when evidence of efficacy was required under new FDA rules, and it is now marketed as a nutritional supplement. Dosage may be critical to determining whether it acts in a cholinergic or anticholinergic fashion. It has some promising pilot data suggesting a possible small to moderate effect (Arnold 2001).

Comparisons of essential fatty acid (EFA) levels between ADHD and control subjects show significantly lower levels in ADHD, but clinical trials of EFAs, both of the n-3 series and the n-6 series, have yielded equivocal results (Arnold 1994, 1999, 2000a, 2001; Arnold, Pinkham, and Votolato 2000). The failure to find significant effects might result from failure to select subjects deficient in the particular EFA series ($n-3$ or $n-6$) being tested; because the two series compete for desaturase enzymes, an excess of the wrong series could make some subjects worse, neutralizing the responders' data in group means. Alternatively, there may be an unaddressed complicating deficiency of l-carnitine, which is necessary for EFA elongation.

Zinc (and other mineral levels) have been reported significantly lower in ADHD, and deficiencies of zinc (and other minerals) can cause symptoms reminiscent of ADHD (jitters, decreased concentration), but there has been no controlled trial of simple zinc supplementation (Arnold 2001).

Naturally, any patient with a demonstrated nutritional deficiency should have it treated, but for those without such deficiency, there is currently little to no evidence of benefit for supplementation. Nevertheless, mild nutritional deficiencies may be more prevalent than suspected, in view of the "junky" diets many children eat. A controlled trial of RDA multivitamins/minerals showed increased concentration and less fidgeting in lower-socioeconomic 6-yr olds with a poor diet who were not diagnosed with ADHD (Benton and Cook 1991). Unfortunately, there has been no controlled trial of simple RDA supplementation for diagnosed ADHD, but conservative medical practice would suggest a dietary history and, if the diet is suspect, a trial of RDA vitamin/mineral supplementation,

There have been three controlled trials of megadose multivitamin supplementation, none of which demonstrated a significant effect. There may also be dangers of such megadosage, which may well act more like a drug, interfering with metabolism, than like a vitamin, supporting normal metabolism. Single-vitamin megadosage has some intriguing pilot trial data, and may deserve further study as a means of altering metabolism in a specific direction.

Herbal Treatment

Herbs are essentially primitive drugs and need to be distinguished from nutrients. This is an important distinction because many people think of them as "nutritional" just because they come from plants, and assume they are safe. However, many modern drugs, including some psychoactive ones, originated with plants. The refinement and standardization of such plant chemicals was a great advance in safety and efficacy. The unrefined drugs in herbs may interact with prescription medicine, so physicians need to ask about herb use before prescribing. There are at least three large open trials of Chinese herbal treatment, one with randomized comparison to methylphenidate. All showed promising results deserving further study. No published controlled (or open) trial of Western herbals for ADHD could be found.

Psychological and Physical Treatments

Electromyographic (EMG) biofeedback with relaxation training has convincing controlled evidence of efficacy, but with a somewhat weaker effect than methylphenidate. Electroencephalographic (EEG) biofeedback, meditation, mirror feedback, channel-specific perceptual training, massage, and vestibular stimulation all have promising prospective pilot data, much of it controlled (wait list, sham treatment, random assignment), but for various reasons cannot be considered established at this time. Home-administered meditation, massage, and vestibular stimulation are so easy, cheap, and safe (and have some documented benefit in other applications) that they might be used clinically until better data are obtained. In one report, vestibular stimulation seemed most effective in younger children, making it relevant to those who seek alternatives to psychoactive medication of preschoolers. Laser acupuncture has promising unpublished pilot data. Hypnosis seems ineffective in ADHD, largely because of the difficulty children with moderate and severe ADHD have attaining a hypnotic trance, in contrast to the ease with which most children can do it.

Standard Medical Treatments in Alternative Mode

Several mainstream medical treatments from other specialty areas have been proposed for ADHD. Thyroid treatment is effective in the presence of documented thyroid abnormality, but not otherwise. In the presence of lead levels of >20 mcg/dL, chelation is reported at least as effective as methylphenidate and better than placebo; presumably the same would apply to other heavy metals. Antifungal therapy is based on a hypothesis supported by animal data and some human data, but has no systematic clinical trial data in ADHD.

SUMMARY/CONCLUSION

Most alternative/complementary treatments for ADHD need research to determine whether they are effective and/or to define the applicable subgroup. Some are effective or probably effective. In some cases they are the treatment of choice for an etiologic subgroup, and initial evaluation should consider the relevant etiologies that they might address. A few have failed to prove effective in controlled trials. Some seem most useful or appropriate for younger children, making them relevant to the national concern about psychoactive medication of preschoolers and the desire to find alternative treatments for them.

The following have convincing controlled data: elimination diets, EMG biofeedback with relaxation training, deleading if serum lead is > 20, thyroid treatment if thyroid level is abnormal. The following have enough data and appear cheap and safe enough to use clinically until definitively studied, though the data are not compelling:

massage, meditation, vestibular stimulation, mirror feedback, desensitization, RDA multivitamins/minerals in the presence of a "junky" diet, and channel-specific perceptual training as substitute for individual tutoring. The following seem ineffective: multivitamin megadosage, simple sugar restriction, amino acids (beyond a few weeks), glyconutritional supplements. The following have promising pilot data requiring further research: EEG biofeedback, minerals (iron, zinc, magnesium), DMAE, EFAs, Chinese herbals, single-vitamin megadosage, laser acupuncture, and immunologic treatment. The following do not have enough data to make a judgment: Western herbals, antifungal therapy, and homeopathic remedies.

REFERENCES

Arnold, L. E. 1994. Screening and evaluating alternative and innovative psychiatric treatments: A contextual framework. *Psychopharmacology Bulletin* 30(1):61–67.

Arnold, L. E. 1995. Some nontraditional (unconventional and/or innovative) psychosocial treatments for children and adolescents: Critique and proposed screening principles. *Journal of Abnormal Child Psychology* 23(1):125–40.

Arnold, L. E. 1999.Treatment alternatives for ADHD. *Journal of Attention Disorders* 3:30–48.

Arnold, L. E. 2000a. *Contemporary Diagnosis and Management of ADHD.* Newtown, PA: Handbooks in Health Care Co.

Arnold, L. E. 2000b. Methylphenidate vs. Amphetamine: Comparative Review. *Journal of Attention Disorders* 3(4):200–211.

Arnold, L. E. 2001. Treatment alternatives for ADHD. In *Diagnosis and Treatment of ADHD: An Evidenced-Based Approach,* eds. P. S. Jensen, and J. Cooper. In press.

Arnold, L. E., Pinkham, S. M., and Votolato, N. 2000. Does zinc moderate essential fatty acid and amphetamine treatment of attention-deficit/hyperactivity disorder? *Journal of Child & Adolescent Psychopharmacology* 10(2):111–17.

Arnold, L. E., Kleykamp, D., Votolato, N., Gibson, R. A., and Horrocks, L. 1994. Potential link between dietary intake of fatty acids and behavior: Pilot exploration of serum lipids in ADHD. *Journal of Child & Adolescent Psychopharmacology* 4(3):171–80.

Bateman, B., Hutchinson, E., Warner, J., Dean, T., Rowlandson, P., Gant, C., Grundy, J., Fitzgerald, C., and Stevenson, J. 2001. The effects of a double-blind controlled artificial food coloring and benzoate preservatives challenge on hyperactivity in a general population sample of pre-school children. Posted at 10th meeting of the International Society for Research on Child and Adolescent Psychopathology, Vancouver.

Benton, D., and Cook, R. 1991. Vitamin and mineral supplements improve the intelligence scores and concentration of six-year-old children. *Personality and Individual Differences* 12:1151–8.

Boris, M., and Mandel, F. S. 1994. Foods and additives are common causes of the attention deficit hyperactive disorder in children. *Annals of Allergy* 72:462–68.

Carter, C. M., Urbanowicz, M., Hemsley, R., Mantilla, L., Strobel, S., Graham, P. J., and Taylor, E. 1993. Effects of a few food diet in attention deficit disorder. *Archives of Disease in Childhood* 69:564–68.

Egger, J., Stolla, A., and McEwen, L. M. 1992. Controlled trial of hyposensitization in children with food-induced hyperkinetic syndrome. *Lancet* 339.

Egger, J., Carter, C. M., Graham, P. J., Gumley, D., and Soothill, J. F. 1985. Controlled trial of ligoantigenic treatment in the hyperkinetic syndrome. *Lancet* 540–45.

Kaplan, B. J., McNicol, J., Conte, R. A., and Moghadam, H. K. 1989. Overall nutrient intake of preschool hyperactive and normal boys. *Journal of Abnormal Child Psychology*:17:127.

Richters, J. E., Arnold, L. E., Jensen, P. S., Abikoff, H. B., Conners, C. K., Greenhill, L. L., Hechtman, L., Hinshaw, S. P., Pelham, W. E., and Swanson, J. M. 1995. The NIMH collaborative multisite multimodal treatment study of children with ADHD (MTA): I. Background & rationale. *Journal of The American Academy of Child and Adolescent Psychiatry* 34(8):987–1000.

Rowe, K. S. 1988. Synthetic food colorings and hyperactivity: A double-blind crossover study. *Australian Pediatric Journal* 24: 143–47.

Rowe, K. S., and Rowe, K. J. 1994. Synthetic food coloring and behavior: A dose-response effect in a double-blind, placebo-controlled, repeated-measures study. *Journal of Pediatrics* 125:691–98.

Schmidt, M. H., Mocks, P., Lay, B., Eisert, H. G., Fojkar, R., Fritz-Sigmund, D., Marcus, A., and Musaeus, B. 1997. Does oligoantigenic diet influence hyperactive/conduct-disordered children—a controlled trial. *European Child and Adolescent Psychiatry* 6:88–95.

Chapter • 12

Long-Term Outcome and its Predictors in Children with Attention Deficit Hyperactive Disorder (ADHD)

Lily Hechtman

There is increasing clinical (Feifel 1996; Murphy 1996; Roy-Byrne et al.) and scientific (Hechtman 1992b; Weiss and Hechtman 1993; Seidman et al. 1998; Katz et al. 1998; Spencer et al. 1998) evidence that ADHD continues into adolescence (Weiss et al. 1971; Gittelman et al. 1985; Barkley et al.; 1990, Biederman et al. 1996b) and adulthood (Weiss and Hechtman 1993; Weiss et al. 1985; Mannuzza et al. 1998). However, examining the clinical picture of ADHD in adolescents and adults provides only a partial view of outcome because it does not include those individuals who are not seeking treatment, either because they are functioning very well or very poorly. In addition, results of studies on long-term outcome of ADHD provide diverse outcome pictures because of marked methodological differences (Hechtman 1992b).

METHODOLOGICAL DIFFERENCES

Prospective versus Retrospective Studies

Prospective studies are clearly superior to retrospective studies that need to rely on sketchy old chart records or skewed parental and patient memories. For these reasons, only prospective studies are discussed here.

Attrition Rate and Sample Size

There is great variation between different studies in the proportion of the original sample that is lost to follow up. Generally, the longer the follow-up period, the greater the loss; significant loss of the original sample makes the findings questionable. Cox et al. (1977) clearly showed that subjects lost to follow up often make up a more pathological group. Small sample size, even without attrition, makes it difficult to assess statistical significance of the data obtained and raises concerns about the generalizability of the findings and validity of the conclusions.

Diagnostic Criteria and Subject Characteristics

Diagnostic criteria, methods, and instruments differ greatly in different studies. Studies also vary in whether or not and how they address comorbidity. It has been shown that the presence of certain comorbid conditions (e.g., conduct disorder) can significantly affect the picture at follow up (August et al. 1983; Barkley et al.; 1990, 1991, Gittelman et al. 1985; Mannuzza et al. 1989; Biederman et al. 1998; Moffitt 1990).

Control Comparison Groups

Many follow-up studies do not have appropriate, matched control or comparison groups who grew up at the same time and places as the study group. This shortcoming prevents us from determining if the findings in the experiment group are significantly different from those in a matched control or comparison group. This limits the utility of follow-up findings.

Assessment Procedures

Assessments at the follow up have been very different in different studies. Some studies (Laufer et al. 1971) used mailed questionnaires, others (Weiss and Hechtman 1993) directly interviewed subjects and their families and obtained school, employers, and police and court records. The breadth of assessments also varies with some studies looking only at one dimension, e.g., arrest records (Satterfield et al. 1982), while others have comprehensive assessments of psychiatric, academic, and social functioning (Weiss and Hechtman 1993). Assessments also vary as to the use of standardized evaluations and forms and whether these are completed by the subjects, parents, or professionals.

Age and Length of Follow Up

Outcome studies also differ in how old subjects are at follow up and how long a follow-up period is involved. Thus studies range from a two year follow up of pre-adolescents (Riddle et al. 1976) to a 25 year follow up of adults 30 years of age (Borland et al. 1976).

The methodological differences and problems described above require that we evaluate studies critically and draw conclusions with full awareness of the strength and weakness of the studies involved. These differences may account for the diverse findings and theories regarding long-term outcome of ADHD.

Cantwell (1985) clearly summarized the differing theoretical views of ADHD outcome. Early theories suggested a developmental lag that children outgrew in adolescence. A second theory postulated continuing symptoms into adulthood. A third theory advocated that ADHD may be a precursor to serious adult pathology. The critical review of recent studies of adolescent and adult outcome illustrates which theory or combination of theories has the greatest empirical support and what factors influence different outcomes.

There have been a number of review articles on adolescent and adult outcome in ADHD (Hechtman 1985, 1989; Hechtman and Weiss 1983; Hechtman 1992b; Hechtman and Offord 1994; Klein and Mannuzza 1991; Thorley 1984, 1988; Weiss 1985). The various outcomes are illustrated by key prospective studies.

ADOLESCENT OUTCOME

One of the first controlled prospective (5 year) follow-up studies of children with ADHD was carried out by Weiss et al. (1971). Ninety-one of 103 subjects, age 10-18 (mean age 13.3), were compared with a control group matched for age, sex, I.Q., and social class. Most ADHD adolescents continued to be distractible, inattentive, impulsive, and emotionally immature but less hyperactive. Compared to the control group, the ADHD group had poor self-esteem, more academic problems, and 25% had significant antisocial behavior.

In another early controlled prospective study, Satterfield et al.(1982) compared 110 hyperactive adolescents and 88 matched control subjects. At follow up (mean age 17.3 years), compared to matched control subjects, hyperactive adolescents had more felony arrests for burglary, grand theft, or assault with a weapon (50% versus less than 10%); and more institutionalizations (19% versus 0%). Neither social class nor stimulant treatment in childhood influenced these results.

Satterfield et al. (1981) conducted a subsequent 3-year prospective uncontrolled study of 100 hyperactive children who received multimodal treatment. Treatment programs were individualized to the needs of each child and family and included stimulant medication, academic tutoring, and individual and/or group therapy for both the child and parents. The group that stayed in treatment longer seemed to have better academic and social outcome.

Lambert, Hartsaugh, and Sassone (1987) re-assessed 59 pervasively hyperactive subjects and matched controls at age 12. They found only 20% of the hyperactives were relatively problem free. Eighty percent had persistent learning, behavioral, and emotional problems. Initially, stimulant medication, academic, and psychosocial interventions were provided to all hyperactives. The group with persistent problems required more treatment.

The findings of Satterfield's (1981) study and those of Lambert (1987) are somewhat contradictory. One found the longer treatment was associated with better outcome, although the other found that continued treatment was reflective of greater problems and worse outcome. Factors such as family functioning may be a mitigating element that can explain this discrepancy. In Satterfield's study, better functioning families may have persisted with treatment while less motivated and less well functioning families may have dropped out. Severity of initial symptomatology and various comorbidities may also play a role in explaining these diverse results.

Hart et al. (1995), in a 4 year follow-up study of 106 clinic referred boys with ADHD found that hyperactive impulsive symptoms declined with increasing age but inattention symptoms did not. The rate of decline in the hyperactive impulsive symptoms was independent of the amount of treatment received. Boys who still met criteria for ADHD were younger, had more hyperactive impulsive symptoms and were more likely to have conduct disorder in year one. Thus symptom severity and comorbidity versus treatment appear important in this outcome study.

Several authors have documented the persistence of ADHD from childhood to adolescence. Gittelman-Klein (1987) found that 68% of her long-term follow-up subjects continued to meet criteria for ADHD in adolescence. Cantwell and Baker (1989), in a 4 year follow-up study of 151 subjects referred to a speech/language clinic, 80% of the those originally diagnosed with ADHD still had the diagnosis 4 years later.

Barkley and colleagues (Barkley et al. 1990, 1991; Fischer et al.1990) conducted an 8-year prospective study of 100 ADHD subjects and 60 community control subjects. At follow up, the mean age of the two groups was 15 and 14 years respectively. The authors found that 71.5% of the ADHD group and 3% of the community control group met DSM-III-R criteria for ADHD, whereas 60% of the ADHD subjects and 11% of the controls also received a diagnosis of oppositional defiance disorder (ODD). Oppositional defiant disorder was associated with more negative mother-child interactions, greater ratings of home conflict, and maternal psychological distress. Furthermore, about 40%

of the ADHD subjects and 1.6% of the controls met criteria for conduct disorder. Conduct disorder (CD) was associated with greater use of cigarettes and marijuana (though not alcohol) and more school expulsions and suspensions.

There was also a tendency for families of the ADHD children to be less stable with higher divorce rates, more frequent moves, and more frequent job changes. Fathers of ADHD children also had more antisocial behavior. Despite the availability and use of special education and mental health services (including medication), most ADHD children continued to have significant academic, social, and emotional problems as adolescents.

In a recent 4 year prospective follow-up study of 128 ADHD children and 109 non ADHD comparison boys, Biederman and his group (Biederman et al. 1996a, 1996b) reported that in mid adolescence 85% of the ADHD group continued to have the disorder. Familiarity of ADHD, psychosocial adversity and comorbidity with conduct, mood and anxiety disorders predicted persistence of ADHD.

Children with ADHD also had significantly more impaired cognitive, family, school, and psychosocial functioning than the controls. The ADHD adolescents were also more likely to begin smoking cigarettes early (Milberger et al. 1997), and there was a significant positive association between cigarette smoking and conduct, major depressive, and anxiety disorders.

Summary of Adolescent Outcome

The studies described, all show that 70% to 85% of adolescents who had ADHD in childhood continue to meet diagnostic criteria for ADHD. They frequently have educational problems with poor academic performance. Immaturity and impulsivity give rise to social problems with parents, teachers, and peers. Many have very poor self-esteem. Antisocial behavior is frequently seen, particularly in children who had unsocialized aggression, oppositional defiant disorder or conduct disorder when first seen. There is an increased risk of early cigarette smoking (Millberger et al. 1997) as well as non-medical drug and alcohol use. Motor vehicle driving competence is also impaired in adolescents with ADHD (Barkley, Murphy, and Kwasnik 1996), and they have more car accidents and traffic offenses (Nada-Rja et al. 1997).

ADULT OUTCOME

A picture of adult outcome of ADHD can be obtained from controlled prospective follow-up studies, retrospective studies, evidence of similar adult disorder, and family studies of parents and relatives with

ADHD. Of these, controlled prospective follow-up studies provide the most reliable picture.

Controlled Prospective Studies of Adult Outcome

Weiss and Hechtman (1993) carried out one of the first long-term (15 years) controlled prospective follow-up studies of ADHD children. The 103 ADHD children had a mean age of 8 years when first seen, 13 years at 5 year follow-up (n = 91), 19 years at 10 year follow-up (n = 75), and 26 years at 15 year follow-up (n = 64). The control group (n = 45) matched the ADHD group in age, sex, and I.Q. and socioeconomic status (SES). Half the subjects lost to follow up could not be traced and probably represented a more negative outcome group. The other half, when contacted by telephone, described in detail that they were doing well but refused to be evaluated because they did not wish to be reminded of past difficulties. They reflect a more positive outcome group. The comprehensive assessments included demographic, academic, work, psychiatric, social (including antisocial behavior, driving history, non-medical drug and alcohol use), as well as physiological and psychological domains. Information was obtained via direct structured interviews and testing of subjects and parents and reports from schools, employers, and the court system.

The adult outcome of ADHD subjects was worse than normal controls. Demographically, they moved more often and few were living at home. Academically, ADHD subjects received lower marks, failed more grades, and completed fewer grades (Weiss et al. 1979). They continued to perform more poorly on cognitive tests (Hopkins et al. 1979). Although most hyperactives were employed, their work status was generally inferior to controls, and they changed jobs much more frequently (Weiss et al. 1978). Hyperactive adults reported more non-medical drug use and had more court referrals. Twenty-three percent of the hyperactives and only 2.4% of the controls met DSM-III criteria for antisocial personality disorder (mild) (Hechtman and Weiss1988; Hechtman et al. 1984a).

Furthermore, two thirds of the ADHD adults continued to have at least one disabling core symptom of the syndrome, e.g., restlessness, impulsivity, or inattention. Hyperactive adults also had poorer social skills, lower self-esteem, and more suicide attempts (Weiss et al. 1985). Overall, hyperactive subjects had more symptoms and received more psychiatric diagnoses.

Physiologically, there were no significant differences in adult measures of height, weight, blood pressure, and pulse (Hechtman, Weiss, and Perlman 1978) or on electroencephalogram (EEG) (Hechtman, Weiss, and Metrakos 1978). A comparison of EEG's of hyperactive subjects over time (i.e., initially and 5 and 10 year follow up), suggested that EEG's of hyperactives tended to normalize over time, particularly in late adolescence.

In a similar controlled, comprehensive, prospective follow-up study, Gittelman and colleagues (1985) initially evaluated 101 hyperactive children and 100 matched normal controls. At 5 to 11 year follow up (mean 9 years), ninety-eight percent of the sample were assessed. The age range was 16 to 23 (mean age 18 years). Compared with matched controls, more hyperactives met DSM-III criteria for full ADHD syndrome (31% vs. 3%) for CD or antisocial personality disorder (23% vs. 8%), or for drug use disorder (16% vs. 3%). Affective and anxiety disorders did not differ significantly between the two groups. There were also no significant differences in height between hyperactives who received an average daily dose of 45 mg of Methylphenidate for 6 months to 5 years during childhood ($n = 66$), and controls ($n = 99$). Thus methylphenidate treatment did not compromise final growth (Klein and Mannuzza 1988).

Details of antisocial behavior in this group was documented by Mannuzza et al. (1989). Judicial records of hyperactives and controls revealed that hyperactives were arrested almost twice as often as controls (39% vs. 20%, $p < .01$). More of the hyperactives were charged with aggression or felonies. More hyperactive subjects were convicted and incarcerated (9% vs. 1%, $p < 0.02$), and more had multiple arrests (23% vs. 8%, $p < .001$).

A diagnosis of antisocial personality disorder at follow up was a strong predictor of arrests, but the presence of ADHD (without antisocial disorder) was not. The findings thus do not support a direct link between ADHD and criminality or arrests but suggest the necessary presence of an antisocial personality disorder diagnosis. However, it is uncertain if childhood ADHD increases the risk of developing antisocial personality disorder and criminality without the presence of childhood conduct disorder.

Mannuzza et al.(1988) also showed that those follow-up subjects who did not meet criteria for any DSM-III diagnosis did worse than controls in school adjustment but no differences were seen in occupational adjustment, temperament, alcohol use, or antisocial behavior. Thus some hyperactives have more positive outcome than others. The continuation of ADHD symptoms and the development of antisocial personality disorder appear to be significant in influencing more negative outcome.

A 17-year follow up of the same subjects (Mannuzza et al. 1993), 24 to 33 years of age, showed that the pattern of outcome at age 26 is similar to that seen at 18, although, there is an overall decrease of dysfunction in adulthood. When compared to controls, hyperactives still had more ADHD (11% vs. 1%, $p < .06$), antisocial personality disorder (18% vs. 2%, $p < .001$), and substance abuse disorder (16% vs. 4%, $p < .02$). There was not a significant difference between the two groups in affective or anxiety disorders. The hyperactives also completed less formal schooling when compared to controls (2 years less on average) and had lower ranking occupational positions (Mannuzza et al. 1997).

Similar adult outcomes for ADHD subjects were described by Loney et al. (1983). She compared 22 pairs of adult hyperactives, age 21 to 23, with their brothers. Hyperactives received an antisocial personality diagnoses more frequently than their brothers (45% vs. 18%). However, they did not have increased drug or alcohol use. The hyperactives reported no increased police contact, but they were incarcerated more frequently than their brothers (41% vs. 5%, $p < .02$) suggesting that their offenses were more serious, particularly against other persons.

Barkley et al. (1998) recently completed a 15-year prospective follow-up study of 148 hyperactive subjects and 76 matched controls. Ninety four percent of the original sample was followed and the mean age at follow up was 21.1 years for the hyperactives and 20.6 years for the controls. The number of hyperactives still meeting DSM criteria for ADHD depended largely on the informant. Thus 3% of the hyperactives met DSM criteria for ADHD by self-report. However, this increased to 42% when parent reports were used. Educational status was significantly worse in the hyperactive subjects when compared to the control group. The hyperactives had lower grades in high school. Fewer hyperactives than controls completed high school (67% vs. 100%, $p < .001$) and fewer were currently students (22% vs. 74%, $p < .001$). More of the hyperactives than controls were suspended (60% vs. 18%, $p < .001$) or expelled (14% vs. 5%, $p < .06$).

The work histories of the hyperactive group were also more problematic. Even though there was no difference between the hyperactives and controls with respect to subjects who were currently working (73% vs. 68%), more hyperactives had had periods where they were neither working nor at school (23% vs. 6%, $p < .01$). Supervisors also rated more of the hyperactives than controls as having ADHD (51% vs. 37%, $p < .001$), ODD symptoms (25% vs. 19%, $p < .001$), and poorer work performance ($p < .001$). The hyperactives had also been fired more often (81% vs. 19%, $p < .001$). The two groups did not differ significantly in the mean hours per week that they worked or in their annual income. However, the hyperactives had had more full time jobs (2.7% vs. 1.3%, $p < .001$).

In exploring comorbid psychiatric disorders, the hyperactive subjects were more likely than controls to have major depression (27.5% vs. 11.8%, $p < .007$). No differences were found in the two groups with regard to dysthymia, manic depression disorder, anxiety disorder, or obsessive compulsive disorder. However, the control group had more bulimic disorders (3.9% vs. 0%, $p < .02$). The hyperactive group, however, had significantly more personality disorders when compared to the control group, e.g., passive (18.8% vs. 7.9%, $p < .03$), histrionic (11.4% vs. 0%, $p < .002$), narcissistic (5.4% vs. 0%, $p < .04$), borderline (14.1% vs. 2.6%, $p < .007$), and antisocial (21.5% vs. 3.9%, $p < .001$) personality disorders. No differences were seen in avoidant, dependent, aggressive, or paranoid personality disorders in the two groups.

The two groups also differed significantly in the type of antisocial behavior they exhibited. Hyperactives were more likely than controls to steal property (85% vs. 66%, $p < .008$), break and enter (20% vs. 8%, $p < .02$), have disorderly conduct (68% vs. 54%, $p < .03$), and commit physical assaults (74% vs. 53%, $p < .001$) and assaults with a weapon (22% vs. 7%, $p < .003$). They were also more likely to set fires intentionally (16% vs. 5%, $p < .02$), carry a weapon (39% vs. 11%, $p < .001$), and run away from home (31% vs. 16%, $p <.01$). It is therefore not surprising that compared to the controls, more hyperactive subjects had more felony arrests (22% vs. 3%, $p < .03$), were more often on probation (38% vs. 12%, $p < .001$), and/or were sent to jail (20% vs. 4%, $p < .001$). It is important to note that the two groups did not differ significantly with regard to possession of drugs (51% vs. 43%), or selling drugs (24% vs. 20%).

Hyperactives, however, used more non-medical drugs when compared to controls. Specifically more hyperactives than controls had used cocaine (37% vs. 18%, $p < .02$), amphetamines (29% vs. 8%, $p < .004$), and tranquilizers (17% vs. 4%, $p < .02$). There was no difference in the two groups with respect to the use of alcohol (97% vs. 99%), marijuana (100% vs. 100%), LSD (52% vs. 49%), or narcotics (4% vs. 4%). The hyperactive group also had significantly more drug treatment than the control group (12% vs. 4%, $p < .04$).

It is interesting to note that sexual activity was different in the two groups. Compared to controls, hyperactives had intercourse earlier (15.4 years vs. 16.5 years, $p < .002$), had more sexual partners (18.5 vs. 6.5, $p < .008$), were less likely to use birth control (76% vs. 91%, $p < .02$), and more likely to have a pregnancy (38% vs. 4%, $p < .001$), sexually transmitted diseases (17% vs. 4%, $p < .005$), and be tested for HIV (54% vs. 21%, $p < .001$). There was no difference in the two groups with regard to the frequency of sexual intercourse or homosexual or bi-sexual orientation.

Generally, Barkley's et al.(1998) findings suggest that in young adulthood, hyperactives have significantly more impairment than a matched control group. The hyperactives have completed less education, have a poor work record, and have more depression and personality disorders. They have more antisocial behavior resulting in more felony arrests, probation and incarceration. They have more non-medical drug use. In addition, hyperactives become sexually active earlier, have more sexual partners, are less likely to use birth control, and so are more likely to become pregnant, have children, and have sexually transmitted diseases. These findings on the whole resemble those of other controlled prospective studies. It is interesting to note that a recent study on adult outcome of hyperactive children from the Shanghai Mental Health Center by Yan (1996) showed results that were similar to those described above involving Canadian and U.S. populations.

In the 15 year follow-up study, Yan (1996) compared 197 subjects diagnosed in childhood with minimal brain dysfunction (MBD) or ADHD and 103 normal controls. Subjects averaged 25 years of age at follow up. The author found that 70% of the MBD (ADHD) subjects still had symptoms of the disorder in adulthood. The hyperactive group compared to the control group had completed less formal schooling and had lower status jobs, but did not have more conduct problems. The authors noted that about 30% of the sample of hyperactive subjects was functioning not too badly.

RETROSPECTIVE STUDIES

Previous reviews (Hechtman 1985, 1989, 1992b; Thorley 1984, 1988; Weiss 1985) provided detailed descriptions of retrospective studies of adolescent and adult outcomes of ADHD. To illustrate the general nature of such studies and the type of outcomes they report, two studies are briefly described.

Borland and Heckman (1976) compared 20 men (mean age 30), whose childhood medical records met criteria for ADHD, with their brothers (mean age 26). The hyperactive men had completed high school, were consistently employed and self-supporting. However, they had more work and emotional problems when compared to their brothers.

In another retrospective study, Feldman, Denhoff, and Denhoff (1979) found that 48 young adults who were previously diagnosed as hyperactive, at age 21 were generally working or at school. However, compared to their siblings, the hyperactives had lower educational achievement, poorer self-esteem, and more drug and alcohol use.

Evidence of Similar Adult Syndromes

Another view of adult outcome of ADHD is derived from adult patients whose current symptoms resemble those found in ADHD. In recent years, there has been growing clinical awareness (Craig 1996; Feifel 1996; Fargason 1994; Bellak and Black 1992; Roy-Byrne et al. 1997; Murphy 1996) and scientific exploration, (Seidman et al. 1998; Katz et al. 1998; Downey et al. 1997; Shekim et al. 1990; Murphy and Barkley 1996) of adults who present with ADHD type symptoms in adulthood. Many clinicians and researchers (Barkley and Biederman 1997; Applegate et al. 1997) have raised questions about the appropriateness of DSM-IV criteria for adults. Specifically, requiring an age of onset before age 7 and the types and number of symptoms required were all derived from field trials on children and are not appropriate for adults.

Despite this limitation, it is striking that the picture of newly diagnosed ADHD adults is very similar to the view provided of hyperactive adults seen in long-term prospective follow-up studies. Thus Murphy and Barkley (1996) described 172 adults diagnosed with ADHD and 30 adults referred to the same ADHD clinic who were not so diagnosed. The ADHD subjects had greater prevalence of oppositional, conduct, and substance abuse disorders than the control adults. Moreover, adults with ADHD displayed greater self reported psychological maladjustment, more violations for speeding, and more suspensions of their driving license. The ADHD group had a history of poorer educational performance, more frequent school disciplinary actions against them than adults without ADHD. The ADHD adults had more frequent changes in employment, had performed poorly, quit and been fired from their job more often than controls. Multiple marriages were also more likely in the ADHD group. However, anxiety and depression were *not* found to be more prevalent in the ADHD group.

Shekim et al. (1990) presented the clinical and demographic profile of 56 adults (48 men, 8 women) age 19 to 65 who met DSM-III-R criteria for ADHD. Twelve and a half percent had only ADHD. Others were comorbid for a variety of conditions, e.g., generalized anxiety disorder 53%, alcohol abuse or dependence 34%, drug abuse 30%, dysthymic disorder 25%, and cyclothymic disorder 25%. Similarly, Downey et al. (1997) found that adults with ADHD were comorbid for depressive disorder, antisocial personality disorder, and alcohol and drug abuse/dependence.

Seidman et al. (1998) studied 64 adults with ADHD age 19 to 57 and 73 non-ADHD controls. Adults with ADHD performed significantly worse than controls on various neuropsychological tests. Despite comparable educational level and I.Q., ADHD adults had a trend toward lower occupational attainment and had significantly more academic problems in school.

We thus see that adults seeking treatment for ADHD in adulthood, present a picture similar to a subgroup ADHD subjects followed prospectively into adulthood. This subgroup had continuing symptoms, was comorbid for antisocial personality disorder, and tended to have more drug and alcohol abuse. They had more difficulties in school, at work, and with interpersonal relationships. It is important to note that the subgroup of ADHD subjects who were doing well at follow up would be quite different from the adult ADHD clinical group.

FAMILY STUDIES

Data suggesting a strong genetic component in ADHD has led to the assumption that by examining the adult relatives of ADHD children, one would have some view of adult outcome of this condition. Details of some of the early family studies of ADHD children are presented in the chapter "Families of Hyperactive Children" in Weiss and Hechtman (1993). A comprehensive discussion of issues related to families of children with ADHD was presented by Hechtman (1996).

There are higher rates (20-50%) of childhood ADHD in family members, siblings (Safer 1973; Welner et al. 1977; Faraone et al. 1993); parents (Morrison and Stewart 1971; Morrison 1980; Cantwell, 1972; Frick et al. 1991); and other biological relatives (Biederman et al. 1990, 1992; Faraone 1994) of children with ADHD when compared to families of a normal control or a psychiatric comparison group.

In addition to increased rates of ADHD in families of hyperactive children, other conditions are also found with some frequency in these families. Thus Morrison and Stewart (1971) and Cantwell (1972) found that biological parents of hyperactive children had higher rates of "sociopathy, hysteria, and alcoholism" compared to parents of normal controls. Morrison (1980) also found a higher incidence of unipolar but not bipolar affective disorder in the combined second degree blood relatives of hyperactive children. McCormick (1995) found that mothers of children with ADHD had higher rates of major (17.9%) and minor (20.5%) depression when compared to a group of women in a primary care outpatient clinic (4-6% and 6-14% respectively).

The most extensive family studies to date have been carried out by Biederman and his colleagues (Biederman et al. 1990, 1992). In the first of these studies (Biederman et al. 1990), they compared 73 male ADHD probands and 264 of their first-degree relatives to 26 psychiatrically referred, but not ADHD children, 101 of their first-degree relatives, 26 normal pediatric clinic controls, and 92 of their first-degree relatives. The authors used blinded interviews, structured psychiatric interviews, and controlled for gender, generation of relative, age of proband, social status, and intactness of the family. Relatives of ADHD probands had higher morbidity risks for ADHD (25.1% vs. 5%

vs. 4.6%, $p < 0.00001$), antisocial disorders (24.3% vs. 6.9% vs. 4.2%, $p <$ 0. 00001), and mood disorders (27.1% vs. 13.9% vs. 3.6%) than did relatives of psychiatric and normal controls. In a more recent similar expanded study (Biederman, Faraone, and Lapey 1992) of 140 probands, 120 normal controls, and 822 of their first-degree relatives, relatives of ADHD probands had a higher risk for ADHD (25% vs. 8%) antisocial disorders, major depressive disorders (26% vs. 9%), substance dependence, and anxiety disorders.

It has been argued that families with chronically ill and disabled children are at greater risk for parental pathology because of the stress of caring for and living with the chronically ill child. To explore this issue, Roizen et al. (1996) compared families of 140 children with ADHD and 163 children with Down syndrome (DS). The families were comparable on socioeconomic status. From parental reports, the ADHD children, compared to the DS children, were more likely to have a parent affected by alcoholism ($p < .007$), other drug abuse ($p < .001$), learning disabilities ($p < .001$), and ADHD ($p < .001$). Similar patterns were evident in other first and second degree relatives.

In summary, these studies show that adult relatives of ADHD children have higher prevalence of ADHD, antisocial disorders, mood disorders, and substance dependence. This picture is not unlike that seen in some subgroups of ADHD subjects followed prospectively into adulthood.

Family Studies and Comorbidity

Comorbidity was generally not addressed by early family studies. More recent family studies suggest that children with ADHD and conduct disorder (CD) have different family patterns than children who have ADHD alone.

Biederman, Munik, and Knee (1987) compared the families of children with ADHD only, ADHD with CD or ODD, and normal controls. Relatives of children with ADHD and CD/ODD had more antisocial, oppositional, depression, and overanxious personality disorders compared to relatives of the other two groups of children. Relatives of both ADHD groups had high rates of ADHD (34%). However, the three groups of relatives did not differ significantly in drug and alcohol abuse or depression.

In Biederman's et al. (1987) study, all clinical groups had ADHD, some with and some without CD/ODD. It was therefore unclear if the CD/ODD was associated with the negative family picture or if the combination of CD/ODD and ADHD was the key element. Lahey et al. (1988) shed some light on this issue when he compared parental pathology in three groups of children (age 6 to 13). One group had only CD ($n = 37$), one group only ADHD ($n = 18$), and one group had both disorders. Parents of conduct disordered children had more substance abuse, and mothers of such children were more frequently depressed and more often had the combination of antisocial personality disorder, substance abuse and somatization disorder. Fathers of children with both ADHD and CD were more likely to have a history of aggression, arrests, and incarceration. Significantly, parents of children with only ADHD did not have any significant disorders. Lahey's study suggests that CD and the combination of CD with ADHD is associated with a negative family picture whereas ADHD alone is not.

However, Barkley et al. (1991) suggested that ADHD alone may be associated with significant parental pathology. In his study, Barkley et al. (1991) compared fathers of hyperactive children, fathers of hyperactive and conduct disordered children, and normal control children. The authors found that fathers of hyperactive children, compared to fathers of normal control subjects, had more antisocial acts, alcohol abuse, police contacts, and arrests. Their job histories were less stable, and they were less financially responsible. Fathers of hyperactive children, compared to fathers of normal controls, were more likely to meet criteria for DSM-III-R diagnosis of antisocial personality disorder (11% vs. 1.6%, $p < .5$). Fathers of children who were hyperactive and conduct disordered had more antisocial acts than fathers of children who were hyperactive only. Fathers of hyperactive only children, however, still had more antisocial acts than fathers of normal controls. This study suggests that *both* ADHD and CD independently are associated with negative family pictures with the combined CD/ADHD group having the most problematic families. Generally, family studies clearly show that the combination of ADHD and CD is associated with significant parental pathology.

Cadoret and Stewart (1991) examined the complex relationship between parental pathology and childhood ADHD and its adult outcome. The authors divided 283 adoptees, age 18 to 40, into two groups based on whether or not biological parents showed evidence (from adoption agency records) of psychiatric or behavioral problems. The authors then evaluated adoptees and their adoptive parents. The study showed that criminality and delinquency of the biological parent predicted increased antisocial personality disorder in adult adoptees *only* when the adoptees were placed in lower SES homes. The lower SES homes had no effect on developing antisocial personality disorder when there was no criminality in the biologic background. The important role of environmental factors was seen in that psychiatric problems in the adoptive parents were associated with aggressivity in the adoptees, and lower SES of the adoptive home increased the incidence of ADHD. Aggressivity but *not* ADHD predicted antisocial personality in adult adoptees. This study shows the important interaction of genetic (biologic parental pathology) *and* environmental (SES and pathology of adoptive family) factors in the development of adult antisocial personality disorder.

Summary of Adult Outcome

As seen in this review of various types of follow-up studies, the adult outcome of children with ADHD can vary significantly (Hechtman et al. 1981). Three different outcome groups can generally be detected. The first group is composed of ADHD subjects who in adulthood function fairly well and not significantly different from a matched normal control group. A second group is composed of adults who continue to have significant concentration, social, emotional, and impulsive problems. These symptoms often result in difficulties with work, interpersonal relations, poor self-esteem, impulsivity, irritability, anxiety, and emotional liability. Most hyperactive young adults fall into this group. Finally, a third group includes hyperactive subjects who in adulthood have significant psychiatric and antisocial problems or both. These hyperactive adults may be severely depressed—even suicidal—heavily involved in drug-alcohol abuse, or may exhibit significant antisocial behavior, which includes assault, armed robbery, breaking and entering, or drug dealing. Fortunately, only a small proportion of hyperactive children have this negative outcome. We are left with the challenge of identifying factors that may influence positive versus negative outcome.

Predictors of Outcome

It is clear that the adolescent and adult outcomes of children with ADHD can be very different. It thus becomes important to try to identify factors that may influence positive or negative outcomes. Such factors can be grouped into three distinct categories: (1) Individual characteristics of the child, e.g., I.Q., type and severity of symptoms and comorbidity; (2) Family parameters such as socioeconomic status, parental pathology, and child rearing practices, and (3) treatment (types, duration, etc.).

Studies that focused on predictors of outcome (Hechtman et al. 1984b; Hechtman 1992a and b; Loney et al. 1983; Mannuzza et al. 1990; Mannuzza and Klein 1992) have all indicated that outcome is not associated with any particular initial variable, but with the additive interaction of characteristics of the child, the family, the environmental parameters, and treatment, all acting together and cumulatively. In the interest of clarity, each of these areas and parameters within these areas will be discussed separately, but their interaction and cumulative effect should always be kept in mind.

CHARACTERISTICS OF THE CHILD

Intelligence Quotient (I.Q.).

A number of authors (Handen, Janosky, and McAuliffe 1997; Lie 1992) have shown that children who have ADHD and low I.Q. (e.g., mental retardation) have poorer prognosis than those with ADHD alone. In addition, Handen, Janosky, and McAuliffe (1997) suggested that children with ADHD and less mental retardation showed greater clinical improvement on stimulant medication than those with ADHD and greater degrees of mental retardation. However, even in children with ADHD and I.Q. in normal range, I.Q. levels were important predictors of outcome. Weiss et al. (1971) and Minde, Weiss, and Mendelson (1972) showed that initial I.Q. level predicted adolescent academic performance as well as overall outcome. Fischer et al. (1993) showed that childhood cognitive and academic competence was related to adolescent academic skills, and special education enrollment was associated with more emotional problems in adolescents.

The importance of I.Q. in predicting outcome was also seen in Hechtman's et al. (1984b) follow-up study of children with ADHD into young adulthood. Intelligence Quotient was involved with almost every outcome measure but was particularly important in outcome of academic achievement and non-medical drug use. Loney, Kramer, and Milich (1981) also showed that ADHD children with lower I.Q. at referral reported more alcoholic symptoms as young adults (age 21) and were more likely to be diagnosed as alcoholics, although not drug abusers. Low I.Q. in childhood was also related to more antisocial acts and more diagnosis of antisocial personality disorders. Menkes, Rowe, and Menkes (1967) showed that I.Q. was the only variable from the diagnostic work-up that predicted self-support status in adulthood.

In summary, one can see that I.Q. seems to be a specific predictor for academic achievement and in conjunction with other factors (e.g., family parameters, SES, comorbidity), a more general predictor of adolescent and adult outcome.

Symptoms

A number of key initial ADHD symptoms have been linked to adolescent and adult outcome. Specifically Loney, Kramer, and Milich (1981) found that initial measures on the hyperactivity factor, which included hyperactivity, inattention, impulsivity, and immaturity, predicted adolescent academic achievement. Similarly, Weiss et al. (1971) found that adolescents who were succeeding in school had lower initial measures of hyperactivity and distractibility. Fergusson, Lynskey, and Horwood (1997) also showed that early attentional difficulties were associated with later academic problems and this relationship was linear with greater initial inattention resulting in greater later academic impairment.

Hechtman et al. (1984b) showed that initial hyperactivity in conjunction with other factors (social and family parameters) predicted adult emotional adjustment, school performance, work record, police involvement, and car accidents. Gittelman et al. (1985) showed that persistence of ADHD symptoms was associated with a greater likelihood of developing antisocial personality disorder and substance abuse in adulthood. Loeber et al. (1995) also showed that ADHD predicted early onset of conduct disorder in children, and Fischer et al. (1993) pointed out that childhood impulsivity, hyperactivity, and potential antisocial acts were associated with later oppositional defiant disorder. Taylor et al. (1966), in the follow up of their community sample, found that at age 16 to 18, children who were pervasively hyperactive at age 6 to 7 were more likely to have impaired social adjustment, including the development of psychiatric disorders, independently of the existence of conduct problems.

We thus see that ADHD symptoms in childhood can significantly influence adult and adolescent outcome, either directly (inattention predicting academic performance) or indirectly through the development of ODD, CD, or antisocial personality disorder. Greene et al. (1997) showed that children with ADHD and social disability were at greater risk for later conduct disorder and substance abuse disorder compared to ADHD children who were socially competent. Feehan et al. (1995) in their large epidemiological sample followed from age 3 to 18 also stressed that poor social competence was an important predictor of later disorders. It may thus be the social disability that many children with ADHD have that influences outcome rather than ADHD alone.

Comorbidity

In recent years, the importance of the presence of various comorbid conditions in the outcome of children with ADHD has been recognized. Barkley et al. (1990) and Biederman et al. (1992, 1996a) have suggested that children with ADHD generally have higher rates of comorbidity than normal controls and clinical comparison groups. Furthermore, several authors (Barkley et al. 1990; Biederman, Mick, and Faraone 1998; August, Steward, and Holmes 1983; Lie 1992) have shown that children with ADHD who have comorbid conditions have more negative outcome compared to children who have ADHD alone. It is therefore important to explore the impact of comorbidity on outcome.

Specific Learning Disability

In an early study, Akerman, Dykman, and Peters (1977) compared the outcome at age 14 of a normal control group (n = 31), a learning-disabled group (n = 39), and a group that was both learning disabled and hyperactive (n = 23). All subjects had an I.Q. of at least 80. The group that was comorbid for hyperactivity and learning disability had significantly more oppositional or delinquent behavior, lower self-esteem, more impulsivity, fidgetiness, immaturity, and inattentiveness. Their academic performance was worse than the control group but not worse than the other learning-disabled group.

Aggression

Aggression in children with ADHD has been shown to predict negative long-term outcome. Weiss et al. (1971) showed that overt antisocial behavior in adolescents with ADHD was associated with higher initial aggression scores in childhood. Similarly, Loney et al. (1981, 1983) found that childhood aggression in children with ADHD was predictive of adolescent aggression and antisocial behavior (offenses against persons and property, and illegal drug use) and adult violence (carrying a weapon and fighting with a weapon). Loeber et al. (1995) also stressed the importance of physical fighting in predicting the onset of conduct disorder. Thus we see that aggression in itself and as a precursor for conduct disorder and later antisocial behavior is an important predictor of outcome.

Oppositional Defiant Disorder (ODD)

It has been estimated (Biederman et al. 1992) that 40% to 60% of children with ADHD are comorbid for oppositional defiant disorder. Barkley et al. (1990, 1991) showed that the ADHD subjects who were also comorbid for ODD had more negative mother-child interactions, more home conflicts, and greater maternal psychological distress. Sixty percent of the ADHD subjects and 11% of the controls met criteria for comorbid oppositional disorder in adolescence. Studying the same population, Fischer et al. (1993) pointed out that child defiance in ADHD subjects predicted later arrests. Satterfield et al. (1994) also showed that ADHD boys with high childhood defiance ratings had significantly higher felony offenses than ADHD boys with low ratings. However, the ADHD boys with low defiance ratings still had more felony offenses than matched controls.

The most important predictive aspects of comorbid oppositional defiant disorder is that it often is a precursor for conduct disorder (Loeber, 1995), which has serious long-term consequences.

Conduct Disorder (CD)

In an early study, August, Steward, and Holmes (1983) followed a group of hyperactives with and without CD and reassessed them at age 14 years. The group with both hyperactivity and CD continued to have ADHD symptoms, aggressivity, non-compliance, antisocial behavior, and alcohol use at follow up. The group with hyperactivity only at initial assessment had few conduct problems at age 14. Thus the children with ADHD and comorbid CD had worse outcome when compared with those who had ADHD only.

Barkley et al. (1990) showed that in adolescent ADHD subjects who were comorbid for conduct disorder (40% of the ADHD subjects and only 1.6% of the controls) had more cigarette and marijuana use (but not alcohol) and more school expulsions and suspensions.

Satterfield and Schell (1997) in their prospective study of 89 subjects with ADHD and 87 normal controls had adolescent follow-up intervals that ranged from 13 to 21 years and adult follow up ranged from 18 to 23 years. Official arrest records were obtained on all subjects. Hyperactive subjects had significantly higher juvenile (46% vs. 11%) and adult (21% vs. 7%) arrest rates. The risk of becoming an adult offender was associated with conduct problems in childhood and serious antisocial behavior in adolescence. The authors concluded that hyperactive children who do not have conduct problems are not at increased risk for later criminality. Similar conclusions were reached by Lie (1992) who indicated that ADHD subjects with CD had high rates of subsequent law breaking and more alcohol and illicit drug use. Attention deficit hyperactivity disorder subjects without CD did not have any increased frequency of delinquency.

The importance of the combination of attention deficit disorder (ADD) and delinquency on long-term outcome was also stressed by Moffit (1990). The author followed a large (n = 435) birth cohort from age 5 to 15 years. At age 13, they divided the sample into four groups: a non-disordered group, a group with only ADD, a group with only delinquency, and a group with both ADD and delinquency. Measures involving antisocial behavior, verbal intelligence, reading difficulty, and family adversity were obtained every 2 years from age 3 to 15.

The group comorbid for ADD and delinquency had scored consistently worse on measures of family adversity, verbal intelligence, and reading. Their antisocial behavior generally started before they were school aged, increased when they entered school, and continued into adolescence. In contrast, the ADD-only children had normal family, intelligence, and reading scores, and showed only mild antisocial behavior in middle childhood. Unexpectedly, the delinquent-only boys showed no early problems with family ratings, intelligence, or reading and were relatively free of conduct problems until they initiated delinquent behavior at age 13. The authors predicted persistence of criminal offending beyond adolescence for the ADD and delinquent boys.

Thus many authors (August, Steward, and Holmes 1983; Barkley et al. 1990, 1991; Gittelman et al. 1985; Mannuzza et al. 1989; Satterfield and Schell 1997; Moffitt 1990) have stressed the important of the coexistence of hyperactivity or ADHD and conduct or antisocial personality disorder on poor adolescent or adult outcome as opposed to hyperactivity alone. Farrington (1990), however, followed 411 inner city London boys from age 8 to age 32. In childhood, subjects were classified as to whether or not they had hyperactivity, impulsivity, and attentional (HIA) problems as well as CD or ODD. Subjects were thus divided into four groups: those with HIA and conduct problems ($n = 59$), those with HIA only and no conduct problems ($n = 34$), those with no HIA and only conduct problems ($n = 40$), and those with neither HIA nor conduct problems ($n = 278$). The group with both HIA and conduct problems had the worst prognosis with chronic criminal behavior. The group with only HIA and no conduct problems in childhood, however, also had some later criminal behavior. This result is somewhat surprising because it suggests that hyperactivity alone may have increased risks for later criminality. This finding also differs from that of other studies outlined previously, which suggested the importance of the coexistence of ADHD and CD in negative adult outcome and not hyperactivity alone. Cadoret and Stewart (1991) showed the importance of environmental factors such as SES and psychopathology in adoptive families in influencing outcome. It may well be that the lower SES of these subjects in inner-city London, coupled with the ADHD, combined to increase the risk of more negative outcome, whereas hyperactivity alone may not have. This area clearly requires further research.

Substance Use and Abuse

Comorbid conduct disorder is often associated with later antisocial behavior and arrests. It has also been linked to later substance abuse. Gittelman et al. (1985) showed a 12% increased prevalence of substance abuse disorder (but not alcohol) in their young adult ADHD group compared to normal controls. The substance abuse was linked to conduct disorder or antisocial life-style and continuation of ADHD symptoms.

There is considerable controversy regarding the link between childhood ADHD and adolescent and adult substance abuse. Generally, studies that examine adults with alcoholism or psychoactive substance use disorder (PSUD) find high rates of retrospectively reported childhood ADHD symptoms in these adults (Horner and Scheibe 1997; Carroll and Rounsaville 1993; Levin, Evans, and Kleber 1998). Similarly, when examining clinically referred adults with ADHD and comparing them to non-ADHD referred adults, Biederman et al. (1995) found that ADHD adults had a higher lifetime risk for PSUD (though not alcoholism) than the comparison group (52% vs. 27%).

However, prospective follow-up studies of ADHD subjects into adolescence and adulthood provide conflicting pictures. Biederman et al. (1997) in their 4-year prospective study of 140 ADHD subjects and 120 matched controls showed a 15% rate of PSUD in both groups. Conduct and bipolar disorders predicted PSUD independent of ADHD status. In an early study, Loney, Kramer, and Milich (1981) showed that drug and alcohol use in ADHD subjects followed into adolescence was not significantly different than these reported in the Iowa or National Surveys. In a later study (Loney et al. 1983) of these subjects as adults, increased drug and alcohol use was observed. Henker et al. (1981) also showed no greater drug or alcohol use in adolescence with ADHD compared to a community control group. Stimulant treatment of the ADHD subjects did not affect these results. Likewise, Hechtman et al. (1984a; Hechtman and Weiss 1988) in their prospective follow up of children with ADHD into adulthood, did not find significantly increased drug and alcohol abuse in their young adult hyperactive subjects compared to matched controls. However, recently, Barkley et al. (1998) did show increased substance abuse in his prospectively followed ADHD subjects, now age 21, compared to matched controls.

Thus we see that some studies support the link between childhood ADHD and later substance use and abuse although others do not. Comorbid conduct disorder is certainly an important mitigating factor. However, exploring other variables, such as other comorbid conditions, SES, and parental pathology, may shed light on these divergent findings.

Mood Disorder (Depression and Anxiety)

It has been reported (Biederman et al. 1992; Bird, Gould, and Staghezza 1993) that the rate of comorbid depression and/or anxiety and ADHD ranges from 20% to 40%, depending on the sample and how it is diagnosed. However, there is relatively little data on how these comorbid conditions affect long-term outcome. Evidence from a follow-up study of the Mandsley Hospital Child Psychiatric Clinic attendees suggested that whereas child CD was associated with significant increased risk for adult criminality, the risk was completely unaffected by the presence or absence of depression during childhood (Harrington et al. 1991). Thus comorbidity of depression and anxiety with ADHD may have a less negative effect than the combination of ADHD and CD.

FAMILY PARAMETERS

The importance of family parameters in contributing to the positive or negative outcome of a child's condition has long been recognized. The family parameters that will be explored include parental psychopathology, child rearing practices or parent-child relationship, overall family functioning, and socioeconomic status. It should be stressed that there is a great deal of overlap and interrelationship in these different family factors. Thus an emotionally disturbed parent is likely to have a poor parent-child relationship and a stressed marital relationship, and the family functioning as a whole may be impaired. In addition, these family factors act together and cumulatively with the parameters pertaining to the child and to treatment in predicting outcome. However, for the sake of clarity, each aspect will be dealt with separately while keeping in mind their interrelationship and cumulative effects.

Parental Pathology

In an early 5 year prospective study of ADHD children into adolescence, Weiss et al. (1971) showed that poor mental health of parents coupled with a poor mother-child relationship and punitive child-rearing practices predicted overt antisocial behavior at adolescence, particularly in ADHD children who were initially aggressive. We thus see the interrelationship between parental pathology, child-rearing practices, and characteristics of the child.

Loney, Kramer, and Milich (1981) in their follow up of 65 hyperactives into young adulthood, age 21 to 23, also found that parental pathology was associated with frequent job changes, unemployment, violence, and traffic offenses in the young adults. Hechtman et al. (1984b) in exploring initial predictors of adult outcome of hyperactive subjects showed that mental health of family members was important in influencing the emotional adjustment, police involvement, car accidents, and non-medical drug and alcohol use of the young adults followed. However, these studies did not specify what type of parental pathology is associated with what type of negative outcome. Recent studies have pinpointed more specific associations.

Fischer et al. (1993) in their 8-year prospective follow up of hyperactive subjects into adolescence showed that paternal antisocial acts were associated with later oppositional defiant behaviors which, in turn, predicted later arrests. School conduct was predicted by other variables, including early family stress. In addition, positive parental functioning, e.g., parental personal competence, was associated with adolescent social competence. Biederman et al. (1997) in his 4 year prospective follow up of 140 ADHD subjects and 120 controls showed that a family history of substance dependence and antisocial disorders was associated with adolescent Psychoactive Substance Use Disorder (PSUD) in controls but less clearly so in the hyperactive subjects. Loeber et al. (1995) too found that parental substance abuse, as well as low socioeconomic status and oppositional behavior, were all key factors in boys developing conduct disorder.

We thus see that parental pathology has a negative impact on long-term adolescent and adult outcomes of children with ADHD. Specifically parental substance abuse and antisocial behavior seems to predict later drug and alcohol abuse and antisocial behavior and arrests in the hyperactive adolescent and adult. Parental pathology may exert its effect by its impact on parent-child relationships and child-rearing practices.

Child-Rearing Practices

Several studies have redefined aspects of the parent-child interaction into specific types of child-rearing practices and looked at the predictive influence of these practices on adolescent and adult outcomes. Weiss et al. (1971) showed that punitive child-rearing practices at initial referral were a factor which, in association with other factors, predicted overall antisocial behavior in the hyperactive adolescents.

In a later follow up of the same subjects, Hechtman et al. (1984b) showed that child-rearing practices were associated with several adult outcome measures. Specifically academic outcome was negatively influenced by inconsistent, authoritarian, and overprotective child rearing. No control and overprotective child-rearing practices were linked to adult police involvement. Loney, Kramer, and Milich (1981) found that parental control and hostility generally had a negative outcome in adolescents with regard to adolescent offenses and academic achievement. In adulthood, the picture was less clear with some outcome measures being positively affected, e.g., less unemployment and job changes, with others being negatively affected, e.g., more drunkenness and antisocial behavior. Werner and Smith (1977) also showed the importance of parenting variables in long-term outcome. The authors followed a group of learning-disabled hyperactive children from age 10 and assessed their outcome on achievement, interpersonal, and self-esteem measures at age 18. Three-fourths of the group were found to have poor outcome, and one-fourth were thought to have improved. Parenting variables such as consistency, firmness, and respect for the child, differentiated the improved and unimproved groups. These findings are also supported by Feehan et al. (1991) in their study of a large community sample followed from childhood, ages 7 to 9, to adolescence, age 15. The authors found that inconsistency and low levels of strictness was associated with externalizing disorder.

The suggestion that parenting variables may be influenced by other factors (e.g., socioeconomic status) was made by Paternite, Loney, and Langhorne (1976). They showed that low-socioeconomic-status parents of hyperactive children were more lax, easygoing, and inconsistent when compared to their high-socioeconomic-status counterparts. In addition, parenting style was associated with secondary symptoms such as aggressive behavior and low self-esteem. Thus parent-child relationship and/or child-rearing practices can have an important effect on long-term outcome. Generally, inconsistency, excessively punitive, uncontrolling, or restrictive child-rearing practices influence negative outcome. However, factors such as parental pathology, child characteristics, and socioeconomic class interact with child-rearing practices to exert the influence.

SOCIOECONOMIC STATUS

A family's socioeconomic status may be an important predictive factor. Socioeconomic status can influence parental psychopathology, the parent-child relationship, and the availability of appropriate treatment resources (e.g., special education, counseling, tutoring). However, when this measure is looked at in terms of whether or not it predicts good or poor outcome, findings are contradictory.

Weiss et al. (1971) in the 5 year prospective study of 91 adolescent hyperactives, found that socioeconomic status was not a predictive variable for succeeding in school, overt antisocial behavior, or emotional adjustment at adolescence. Similarly, Loney, Kramer, and Milich (1981) found that socioeconomic class per se was not a strong predictor of adolescent outcome, although factors related to socioeconomic class, such as urban versus rural residence and number of children in the family, predicted adolescent offenses against property, involvement with illegal drugs, and WIAT achievement scores. In each case, urban residence and a larger number of children in the family were associated with negative outcome. In Loney's follow up of hyperactive adults (Loney et al., 1983), socioeconomic class was not a strong predictor of adult outcome. Huessy, Meloyer, and Townsend (1974) compared their 15 best and worse outcome subjects in their 8 to 10 year follow up of 83 subjects seen in childhood for behavior problems and placed on medication. They found no significant difference in income distribution in the three groups. Satterfield, Hoppe, and Schell (1982) in comparing arrest records in their 110 hyperactive boys in adolescence (mean age 17) and 88 matched control subjects, found that offender rates did not vary significantly as a function of socioeconomic status in either group.

The lack of impact of SES on outcome, outlined above, is counterbalanced by a number of studies which suggest SES may be an important factor in outcome. Millman et al. (1979) in an early study, involving a prospective follow up of 73 hyperactive subjects to age 19 years, found that lower socioeconomic status was associated with poorer global outcome as measured by psychiatric diagnosis and academic, work and social functioning. Hechtman et al. (1984b) in examining initial predictors of adult outcome in ADHD subjects, found that SES was an important predictor in educational and work outcome and police involvement. It had less impact in adult emotional adjustment, or drug and alcohol use. Biederman et al. (1996a) in his 4 year perspective study of ADHD subjects into adolescence, found that one of the factors that predicted persistence of symptoms into adolescence was psychosocial adversity which included poverty or low SES. Feehan et al. (1995) in their community sample of 890 subjects followed from age 3 to age 18, boys from socially disadvantaged backgrounds in early childhood had an elevated risk of disorder at age 18. Finally, Loeber et al. (1995) in their 6 year longitudinal study of 177 pre-adolescent boys, showed that low socioeconomic status of the parent, ODD in the child, and parental substance abuse, best-predicted onset of conduct disorder.

We thus see that the contradictory picture of how much SES contributes to long-term outcome may be explained by the fact that SES often acts in concert with parental and child pathology to exert its influence on outcome. It should therefore be explored as a factor in its own right but also in conjunction with other important child and family parameters.

TREATMENT

Generally, it is difficult to evaluate the impact of treatment on long-term outcome of ADHD. The difficulty involves some the following reasons.

Few Randomized Trials

There are relatively few controlled randomized trials of any treatment interventions. The absence of such randomization results in a self selection bias with possibly the most severely affected and disabled children receiving treatment and the less disabled children not receiving it or staying in treatment for shorter period of time. Families may also contribute to the bias with poorly functioning families often dropping out of or not completing treatment trials. Thus treated and not treated children may differ in symptom severity, comorbidity and family parameter.

Duration of Treatment and Maintenance of Treatment Effects

Most treatment studies are relatively short. One or two years are the longest reported studies to date (Hechtman and Abikoff 1995; Arnold et al. 1997a and b; MTA Cooperative Group; 1999). Thus evaluating impact of treatment, which at best has lasted a few months, on outcome 5, 10, 15, or 20 years later, does not seem reasonable. Many treatments (e.g., stimulant medication, behavioral therapy) seem to have an important impact on functioning when they are being used, and this impact decreases when the interventions stop. So maintaining treatment effects after treatment has discontinued is often difficult. Expecting this treatment to have an impact on functioning 20 years later is possibly unrealistic.

Keeping these serious limitations in mind, a brief summary of some long-term impacts of various treatments is presented.

Remedial Education and Tutoring

In an early study, Minde, Weiss, and Mendelson (1972) assessed the effectiveness of remedial educational help on adolescent outcome of hyperactive children. Two thirds of the hyperactive subjects were considered to have learning problems sufficient to benefit from individual or small-group remediation. People carrying out this treatment were interested, but not specifically trained in remediation of perceptual problems. At follow up, authors did not see improvement on any of the psychological tests in the children who received remedial therapy. Akerman, Dykman, and Peters (1977) too looked at educational intervention and its effect on academic progress at age 14 in three groups (hyperactive, hypoactive, and normoactive) of learning-disabled boys. Educational intervention ranged from intermittent private tutoring to resource rooms to full-time programs. Moderate to intense educational interventions produced no dramatic long-term results. In fact, boys who received the more intense programs were further behind academically at age 14 than those in the less intense programs.

However, it must be stressed that the treatment assignment was not random, and boys in the more intense programs had more initial deficits. One again sees the difficulty in assessing the long-term efficacy of a particular treatment when the level of initial deficit is not controlled. However, in an extensive review on the efficacy of remedial programs in learning-disabled children on longer-term academic outcome, Helper (1980) showed that few studies had found long-term benefits from such programs. Recently, Tannock R. (personal communication) reported that a specific 8 week reading remediation program which is combined with medication, is showing promising (1 year) follow-up results.

Behavior Modification

It is clear from the comprehensive review of behavior modification treatment approaches (Pelham and Sams 1992) that this intervention, which includes clinical behavior therapy wherein parents and teachers are trained to provide the behavioral management as well as direct contingency management when professionals carry out the interventions, is effective in short-term studies (8 to 20 weeks). However, the impact of the treatments often decrease after they stop. Furthermore, there are no long-term follow-up studies available on the duration of treatment effects. Frequently, behavioral treatments are compared to and combined with stimulant medication. In these studies, stimulants prove better than behavioral treatments, and there is little benefit from the combined approach. There is, however, some suggestion that the combined approach may decrease the required stimulant dose in ADHD children. Again, there are no long-term outcome studies of this combined approach.

Stimulant Treatment

The short-term efficacy of stimulant medication for children with ADHD has been well documented by many studies and reviewed comprehensively by Greenhill (1992). However, again, there are few long-term medication outcome studies. Studies that exist, basically report on children who were given medication during childhood for varying lengths of time (1 month to 7 years) at varying dosages and reporting their adolescent and adult outcome.

In an early study, Weiss et al. (1975) compared three groups of hyperactive children; the first received 3 to 5 years of methylphenidate (20–50 mg/day), the second received chlorpromazine for 18 months to 5 years (mean dose 75 mg/day), while the third group received no medication treatment. The three groups were matched for age, I.Q., sex, and SES. At adolescence, no significant differences in emotional adjustment, delinquency, or academic performance was seen in the three groups.

It was surprising to see that children who received stimulants for 3 to 5 years in childhood did not have better long-term outcome than those who did not receive this treatment. However, it should be pointed out that in those subjects who were on stimulant medication, having a good family situation was significantly correlated with good outcome as defined by academic achievement, absence of delinquency, and emotional adjustment. Thus the interaction of medication and other factors (e.g., family functioning) appears more important in predicting outcome than medication in and of itself. Similar findings were reported by Conrad and Insel (1967) and Loney, Kramer, and Milich (1981). Loney, Kramer, and Milich (1981) in their study of adolescent outcome, explored stimulant treatment as a predictor. Average duration of treatment in childhood was 29 months and the average dose was 34 mg/day. In summary, response to medication was a factor in only three of the many outcome measures in adolescence. Subjects who responded well to medication in childhood had a less negative affect at follow up, were less involved in non-medical drug use, and scored better on the Wide Range Achievement Test in reading and arithmetic. Duration of stimulant treatment did not predict any outcome measure. Charles and Stein (1981) also explored duration (6 months to 4 years) of stimulant treatment as a predictor of outcome and found no differences in behavioral, social, or academic outcome measures that were related to treatment duration. In contrast, Satterfield, Satterfield, and Cantwell (1981) found that ADHD children who received longer multimodal treatment which included stimulants, academic remediation, as well as group and individual parent and child counseling, had better outcomes than children who discontinued treatment earlier. However, family functioning may have been a factor in the group that dropped out of treatment.

Satterfield's findings are different from those of Fischer et al. (1993) and Lambert, Hartsaugh, and Sassone (1987) who found that ADHD children who had longer treatment, had more negative outcome. In fact, these authors felt that the increased length of required treatment may be a marker for greater severity of the condition.

Many of the more recent prospective, longitudinal studies, (Gittelman et al. 1985; Mannuzza et al. 1993; Barkley et al. 1990, 1998; Biederman et al. 1996b) have involved ADHD children who received stimulant treatment in childhood. Thus they present an outcome picture of a childhood medicated population.

There has been a great deal of concern about the possibility that stimulant treatment in childhood would predispose ADHD children to substance abuse in adolescence and adulthood. Generally, the longitudinal studies (outlined above) of children with ADHD who have received stimulant treatment in childhood do not show increased drug or alcohol abuse in adulthood. The substance abuse is most often linked to comorbid conduct disorder and antisocial personality disorder and not stimulant treatment. In fact, in a recent review, Loney (1998) indicated that stimulant treatment in childhood decreases the likelihood of substance abuse in adulthood.

The early Weiss et al. (1971) studies involved children who were not medicated because stimulants were generally not used in Canada at the time. Subsequently, Hechtman et al. (1984c) compared the young adult outcome of ADHD children who were medicated during childhood with those who were not because they were seen before medication was widely used. These two groups were compared with each other and a matched normal control group. The authors found that as young adults, stimulant treated and untreated hyperactive subjects were fairly similar to each other and significantly different from a matched normal control group. Hyperactive subjects continued to have more educational and work difficulties. They had more emotional problems and more problems with aggression. Drug and alcohol abuse was generally not significantly different in the three groups. However, the stimulant treated group seemed to have better social skills and self esteem when compared to the untreated hyperactive group. Thus with few exceptions, the two hyperactive groups had similar outcomes. Medication in childhood generally did not affect adult outcome.

Multimodal Treatment

Satterfield, Satterfield, and Cantwell (1981) suggested that the outcome of ADHD children receiving multimodal treatment was superior to the outcome seen in studies where ADHD children received only stimulants (Satterfield, 1982). However, his multimodal treatment was not randomized and not well controlled. More recently, Hechtman (1993), Hechtman and Abikoff (1995), conducted a randomized control trial of children receiving multimodal treatment, attentional control treatment, and conventional medication treatment. All three groups received well-titrated stimulant medication. The treatments were intense for 1 year with booster sessions (monthly in each intervention) in the second year. Generally, there was no significant difference in many domains of functioning in the three groups at the end of two years. However, a follow-up study is under way to determine possible long-term outcome differences.

The superiority of stimulant treatment to psychosocial treatment and the lack of advantage of combining both treatments was also seen in a 6-site multimodal treatment study of 576 ADHD children, age 7 to 9 (MTA Cooperative Group 1999). Follow up of these children is also ongoing to determine long-term treatment effects (Richter et al. 1995; Greenhill et al. 1996; Arnold et al. 1997a, 1997b; Hinshaw et al. 1997).

SUMMARY

In determining the influence of various factors on outcome, one must keep in mind that these parameters do not act alone but probably exert their influence in a cumulative and interactive manner. Thus characteristics of the child, such as severity of symptoms, comorbidity, I.Q., interaction with family parameters, such as parental pathology, socioeconomic status, family adversity, and treatment, influence long-term outcome. Some of these variables (e.g., comorbid conduct disorder, low I.Q., parental pathology) have been important in influencing negative outcome. Treatment, particularly stimulant treatment, has been shown to be effective in many short-term studies, but the long-term impact of treatment remains uncertain. The continuation of treatment may be crucial in influencing positive long-term outcome. Research in the area continues to evolve. New findings will, we hope, continue to improve both the quality of life for patients and families, and positive influence of long-term outcome.

REFERENCES

Akerman, P., Dykman, R., and Peters, J. 1977. Teenage status of hyperactive and non-hyperactive learning disabled boys. *American Journal of Orthopsychiatry* 47:577–96.

Applegate, B., Lahey, B. B., Hart, E. L., et al. 1997. Validity of the age-of-onset criterion for ADHD: A report from the DSM-IV field trials. *Journal of the American Academy of Child and Adolescent Psychiatry* 36(9):1211–21.

Arnold, E., Abikoff, H., Cantwell, D., et al. 1997a. NIMH Collaborative multimodal treatment study of children with ADHD (MTA) I: Design, methodology, and protocol evaluation. *Journal of Attention Disorders* 2(3):141–59.

Arnold, E., Abikoff, H., Cantwell, D., et al.1997b. Multimodal treatment study of children with ADHD (MTA) II. Design, methodology, and evolution. *Archives of General Psychiatry* 54:865–70.

August, G. J., Steward, M. A., and Holmes, C. S. 1983. A four-year follow-up of hyperactive boys with and without conduct disorder. *British Journal of Psychiatry* 143:192–98.

Barkley, R. A., and Biederman, J. 1997. Toward a broader definition of the age-of-onset criterion for attention-deficit hyperactivity disorder. *Journal of the American Academy of Child and Adolescent Psychiatry* 36(9):1204–10.

Barkley, R. A., Fischer, M., Fletcher, K., et al.1998. Young Adult Outcome of Hyperactive Children: A 15 year follow-up study. Presented at NIMH Consensus Conference Washington, November.

Barkley, R. A., Fischer, M., Edelbrock, C. S., et al 1990. The adolescent outcome of hyperactive children diagnosed by research criteria: An 8 year prospective follow-up study. *Journal of the American Academy of Child and Adolescent Psychiatry* 29:546–57.

Barkley, R. A., Fischer, M., Edelbrock, C. S., et al 1991. The adolescent outcome of hyperactive children diagnosed by research criteria III: Mother-child interactions, family conflicts and maternal psychopathology. *Journal of Child Psychology and Psychiatry* 32:2:233–55.

Barkley, R. A., Murphy, K. R., and Kwasnik, D. 1996. Motor vehicle driving competencies and risks in teen and young adults with attention deficit hyperactivity disorder. *Pediatrics* 6 Pt1:1089–95.

Bellak, L., and Black, R. B. 992. Attention-deficit hyperactivity disorder in adults. *Clinical Therapy* 14(2):138–47.

Biederman, J., Faraone, S., Keinan, K. et al. 1990. Family-genetic and psychosocial risk factors in DSM-III attention deficit disorder. *Journal of the American Academy of Child and Adolescent Psychiatry* 29:526–33.

Biederman, J., Faraone, S., Keinan, K., et al.1992. Further evidence for family-genetic risk factors in attention deficit hyperactivity disorder patterns of comorbidity in probands and relatives in psychiatrically and pediatrically referred samples. *Archives of General Psychiatry* 49:728–38.

Biederman, J., Faraone, S., and Lapey, K. 1992. Comorbidity of diagnosis in attention deficit hyperactive disorder. *Child Adolescent Psychiatry Clinics of North America* 1:335–60.

Biederman, J., Faraone, S., Milberger, S., et al.1996a. Predictors of persistence and remission of ADHD into adolescence: Results from a four-year prospective follow-up study. *Journal of the American Academy of Child and Adolescent Psychiatry* 35(3):343–51.

Biederman, J., Faraone, S., Milberger, S., et al.1996b. A prospective 4-year follow-up study of attention-deficit hyperactivity and related disorders. *Archives of General Psychiatry* 53(5):437–46.

Biederman, J., Mick, E., and Faraone, S. 1998. Normalized functioning in youths with persistent attention-deficit/hyperactivity disorder. *Journal of Pediatrics* 133(4):544–51.

Biederman, J., Munik, K., and Knee, D. 1987. Conduct and oppositional disorders in clinically referred children with attention deficit disorder: A controlled family study. *Journal of the American Academy of Child and Adolescent Psychiatry* 26:724–27.

Biederman, J., Wilens, T., Mick, E., et al.1995. Psychoactive substance use disorders in adults with attention deficit hyperactivity disorder (ADHD): Effects of ADHD and psychiatric comorbidity. *American Journal of Psychiatry* 152(11):1652–8.

Biederman, J., Wilens, T., Mick, E., et al.1997. Is ADHD a risk factor for psychoactive substance use disorders? Findings from a four-year prospective follow-up study. *Journal of the American Academy of Child and Adolescent Psychiatry* 36(1):21–29.

Bird, H. R., Gould, M. S., and Staghezza, B. M. 1993. Patterns of diagnostic comorbidity in a community sample of children aged 9 through 16 years. *Journal of the American Academy of Adolescent Psychiatry* 32:361–68.

Borland, B., and Heckman, H. 1976. Hyperactive boys and their brothers: A 25-year follow-up study. *Archives of General Psychiatry* 33:669–76.

Cadoret, J. R., and Stewart, M. A.1991. An adoption study of attention deficit hyperactivity/aggression and their relationship to adult antisocial personality. *Compr Psychiatry* 32:73–82.

Cantwell, D. 1972. Psychiatric illness in families of hyperactive children. *Archives of General Psychiatry* 27:414–23.

Cantwell, D. 1995. Hyperactive children have grown up: What have we been learning about what happens to them. *Archives of General Psychiatry* 42:102–108.

Cantwell, D., and Baker, L. 1989. Stability and natural history of DSM-III childhood diagnoses. *Journal of the American Academy of Child and Adolescent Psychiatry* 28:691–700.

Carroll, K. M., and Rounsaville, B. J. 1993. History and significance of childhood attention deficit disorder in treatment-seeking cocaine abusers. *Compr Psychiatry* 34(2):75–82.

Charles, L., and Stein, R. A. 1981. A four year follow-up study of the effects of Methylphenidate on the behavior and academic achievement of hyperactive children. *Journal of Abnormal Child Psychiatry* 9:495–505.

Conrad, W. G., and Insel, J. 1967. Anticipating the response to Amphetamine therapy in the treatment of hyperkinetic children. *Pediatrics* 40:96–98.

Cox, A., Rutter, M., and Yule, B. 1977. Bias resulting from missing information: Some epidemiological findings. *British Journal of Preventive and Social Medicine* 31:131–36.

Craig, C. 1996. Clinical recognition and management of adult attention deficit hyperactivity disorder. *Nurse Practitioner* 21(11):101–106, 108.

Downey, K. K., Stelson, F. W., Pomerleau, O. F., et al. 1997. Adult attention deficit hyperactivity disorder: Psychological test profiles in a clinical population. *Journal of Nervous Mental Disorders* 185(1):32–38.

Faraone, S. V., Biederman, J., and Lehman, B. K., et al.1993. Intellectual performance and school failure in children with attention deficit hyperactivity disorder and in their siblings. *Journal of Abnormal Psychology* 102:616–23.

Faraone, S. V., Biederman, J., and Milberger, S. 1994. An exploratory study of ADHD among second-degree relatives of ADHD children. *Biological Psychiatry* 35:398–402.

Fargason, R. E., and Ford, C. V. 1994. Attention deficit hyperactivity disorder in adults: diagnosis, treatment, and prognosis. *Southern Medical Journal* 87(3):302–309.

Farrington, D. P. 1990. Long-term criminal outcomes of hyperactivity-impulsivity-attention deficit (HIA) and conduct problems in childhood. In *Straight and Devious Pathways from Childhood to Adulthood*, eds. L.N Robins and M. Rutter. New York: Cambridge University Press.

Feehan, M., McGee, R., Stanton, W. R., et al. 1991. Strict and inconsistent discipline in childhood: consequences for adolescent mental health. *British Journal of Clinical Psychology* 30:325–31.

Feehan, M., McGee, R., Williams, S. M., et al. 1995. Models of adolescent psychopathology: childhood risk and the transition to adulthood. *Journal of the American Academy of Child and Adolescent Psychiatry* 34(5):670–79.

Feifel, D. 1996. Attention-deficit hyperactivity disorder in adults. *Postgraduate Medicine* 100(3):207–11, 215–18.

Feldman, S., Denhoff, B., and Denhoff, E. 1979. The attention disorders and related syndromes: Outcome in adolescence and young adult life. In *Minimal Brain Dysfunction: A Developmental Approach*, eds. E. Denhoff and L. Stern. New York, NY: Musson Publishers.

Fergusson, D. M., Lynskey, M. T., and Horwood, L. J. 1997. Attentional difficulties in middle childhood and psychosocial outcomes in young adulthood. *Journal of Child Psychology and Psychiatry* 38(6):633–44.

Fischer, M., Barkley, R. A., Edelbrock, C. S., et al. 1990. The adolescent outcome of hyperactive children diagnosed by research criteria II: Academic, attentional and neuropsychological states. *Journal of Consulting and Clinical Psychology* 58(5):580–88.

Fischer, M., Barkley, R. A., Fletcher, K. E., et al.1993. The adolescent outcome of hyperactive children: predictors of psychiatric, academic, social, and emotional adjustment. *Journal of the American Academy of Child and Adolescent Psychiatry* 32(2):324–32.

Frick, P. J., Lahey, B., Benjamin, B., et al.1991. History of childhood behavior problems in biological relatives of boys with attention-deficit disorder and conduct disorder. *Journal of Clinical Child Psychology and Psychiatry* 20:445–51.

Gittelman-Klein, R. 1987. Prognosis of attention deficit disorder and its management. *Adolescence Pediatrics in Review* 8:216–23.

Gittelman, R., Mannuzza, S., Shenker, R., et al.1985. Hyperactive boys almost grown-up. *Archives of General Psychiatry* 42:937–47.

Greene, R. W., Biederman, J., Faraone, S. et al.1997. Adolescent outcome of boys with attention-deficit/hyperactivity disorder and social disability: Results from a 4-year longitudinal follow-up study. *Journal of Consulting Clinical Psychology* 65(5):758–67.

Greenhill, L. 1992. *Pharmacotherapy: Stimulants in Child Psychiatric Clinics of North America*. Ed. G. Weiss G. Vol 1, No 2:411–49.

Greenhill, L., Abikoff, H., Arnold, E., et al.1996. Medication treatment strategies in MTA study: Relevance to clinicians and researchers. *Journal of the American Academy of Child and Adolescent Psychiatry* 35:1304–14.

Handen, B. L., Janosky, J., and McAuliffe, S. 1997. Long-term follow-up of children with mental retardation/borderline intellectual functioning and ADHD. *Journal of Abnormal Child Psychology* 25(4):287–95.

Harrington, R., Fudge, H., Rutter, M., et al 1991. Adult outcome of childhood and adolescent depression. II. Links with antisocial disorder. *Journal of the American Academy of Child and Adolescent Psychiatry* 30:434–39.

Hart, E. L., Lahey, B. B., Loeber, R., et al.1995. Developmental change in attention-deficit hyperactivity disorder in boys; A four-year longitudinal study. *Journal of Abnormal Child Psychology* 23(6):729–49.

Hechtman, L. 1985. Adolescent outcome of hyperactive children treated with stimulants in childhood: A review. *Psychopharmacology Bulletin* 21:178–91.

Hechtman, L. 1989. Attention deficit hyperactivity disorder in adolescence and adulthood: An updated follow-up. *Psychiatric Annals* 19:11:597–603.

Hechtman, L. 1992a. Resilience and vulnerabiltiy in long-term outcome of attention deficit hyperactive disorder. *Canadian Journal of Psychiatry* 37(2):148–49.

Hechtman, L. 1992b. Long-term outcome in attention deficit hyperactivity disorder. In *Child and Adolescent Clinics of North America*, Guest ed. G. Weiss. Philadelphia: WB Saunders Inc. 1(2):553–63.

Hechtman, L. 1993. Aims and methodological problems in multimodal treatment studies. *Canadian Journal of Psychiatry* 38:458–64.

Hechtman, L. 1996. Families of children with attention deficit hyperactivity disorder: A review. *Canadian Journal of Psychiatry* 41:350–60.

Hechtman, L., Abikoff, H. 1995. Multimodal treatment plus stimulants vs. stimulant treatment in ADHD children: Results from a two year comparative treatment study. Paper presented at the Annual Meeting of the American Academy of Child and Adolescent Psychiatry, New Orleans.

Hechtman, L., and Offord, D. R. 1994. Long-term outcome of disruptive disorders. In *Child and Adolescent Clinics of North America.* Guest ed. L. Greenhill. Philadelphia:WB Sanders Inc. 3(2):379–403.

Hechtman, L., and Weiss, G. 1983. Long-term outcome of hyperactive children. *American Journal of Orthopsychiatry* 53:532–41.

Hechtman, L., and Weiss, G. 1988. Controlled prospective 15-year follow-up of hyperactives as adults: On-medical drug and alcohol use and antisocial behaviour. *Canadian Journal of Psychiatry* 31:557–67.

Hechtman, L., Weiss, G., and Metrakos, K. 1978. Hyperactives as young adults: Current and longitudinal electroencephalographic evaluation and its relation to outcome. *Canadian Medical Association Journal* 118:912–23.

Hechtman, L., Weiss, G., and Perlman, T. 1978. Growth and cardiovascular measures in hyperactive individuals as young adults and in matched normal controls. *Canadian Medical Association Journal* 118:1247–50.

Hechtman, L., Weiss, G., Perlman, T., et al. 1981. Hyperactives as young adults: Various clinical outcomes. *Adolescent Psychiatry* 9:295–306.

Hechtman, L., Weiss, G., Perlman, T., et al. 1984 a. Hyperactives as young adults: Past and current antisocial behavior (stealing, drug abuse) and moral development. *American Journal of Orthopsychiatry* 54:415–25.

Hechtman, L., Weiss, G., Perlman, T., et al. 1984b. Hyperactives as young adults: Initial predictors of adult outcome. *Journal of the American Academy of Child Psychiatry* 25:250–60.

Hechtman, L., Weiss, G., Perlman, T., et al. 1984c. Young adult outcome of hyperactive children who received long-term stimulant treatment. *Journal of the American Academy of Child and Adolescent Psychiatry* 23(3):261–69.

Helper, M. M. 1980. Follow-up of children with minimal brain dysfunction: Outcomes and Predictors. In *Handbook of Minimal Brain Dysfunction: A Critical Review*, eds. H. W. Rie and E. D. Rie. New York:Wiley.

Henker, B., Whalen, C., Bugental, D. B., et al. 1981. Licit and illicit substance use patterns in stimulant-treated children and their peers. In *Psychosocial Aspects of Drug Treatment for Hyperactivity*, eds. K. Gadow and J. Loney. Boulder, CO: Westview Press.

Hinshaw, S., Arnold, E., Abikoff, H., et al. 1997. Comprehensive assessment of childhood attention-deficit hyperactivity disorder in the context of a multisite multimodal treatment trial. *Journal of Attention Disorders* 1(4):217–35.

Hopkins, J., Perlham, T., Hechtman, L., et al.1979. Cognitive style in adults originally diagnosed as hyperactives. *Journal of Child Psychology and Psychiatry* 20:209–16.

Horner, B. R., and Scheibe, K. E. 1997. Prevalence and implications of attention-deficit hyperactivity disorder among adolescents in treatment for substance abuse. *Journal of the American Academy of Child and Adolescent Psychiatry* 36(1):30–36.

Huessy, H. R., Meloyer, M., and Townsend, M. 1974. 8–10 year follow-up of 84 children treated for behavioral disorder in rural Vermont. *Acta Pedopsychiatrica* 40:230–35.

Katz, L. J., Wood, D. S., Goldstein, G., et al.1998. The utility of neuropsychological tests in evaluation of Attention-Deficit/Hyperactivity Disorder (ADHD) versus depression in adults. *Assessment* 5(1):45–52.

Klein, R. G., and Mannuzza, S. 1988. Hyperactive boys almost grown up. III. Methylphenidate effects on ultimate height. *Archives of General Psychiatry* 45(12):1131–34.

Klein, R. G., and Mannuzza, S. 1991. Long-term outcome of hyperactive children: A review. *Journal of American Academy of Child and Adolescent Psychiatry* 30(3):383–87.

Lahey, B., Piacentini, J., McBurnett, M., et al. 1988. Psychopathology in the parents of children with conduct disorder and hyperactivity. *Journal American Academy of Child and Adolescent Psychiatry* 27:163–70.

Lambert, N., Hartsaugh, C., and Sassone, D. 1987. Persistence of hyperactivity symptoms from childhood to adolescence. *American Journal of Orthopsychiatry* 57:22–31.

Laufer, M. 1971. Long-term management and some follow-up finding on the use of drugs with minimal cerebral syndromes. *Journal of Learning Disabilities* 4:55–58.

Levin, F. R., Evans, S. M., and Kleber, H. D. 1998. Prevalence of adult attention-deficit hyperactivity disorder among cocaine abusers seeking treatment. *Drug and Alcohol Dependency* 52(1):15–25.

Lie, N. 1992. Follow-ups of children with attention deficit hyperactivity disorder (ADHD). Review of literature. *Acta Psychiatr Scand Suppl* 368:1–40.

Loeber, R., Green, S. M., Keenan, K., et al. 1995. Which boys will fare worse? Early predictors of the onset of conduct disorder in a six-year longitudinal study. *Journal of the American Academy of Child and Adolescent Psychiatry* 34(4):499–509.

Loney, J. 1998. Risk of treatment versus non-treatment. Presented at NIMH ADHD Consensus Development Conference, Washington, abstract:175–79.

Loney, J., Kramer, J., and Milich, R. 1981. The hyperkinetic child grows up: Predictors of Symptoms, Delinquency, and Achievement at Follow-Up. In *Psychosocial Aspects of Drug Treatment for Hyperactivity*, eds. K. D. Gadow and J. Loney. Boulder, CO: Westview Press.

Loney, J., Whaley–Klahn, M. A., Kosier, T., et al. 1983. Hyperactive boys and their brothers at 21: Predictors of aggressive and antisocial outcomes. In *Prospective Studies of Crime and Delinquency*, eds. K. T. Van Dusen and S. A. Mednick. Boston: Kluwer-Nijhoff.

Mannuzza, S., Gittelman-Klein, R., and Bonagura, N. 1988. Hyperactive boys almost grown up: II. Status of subjects without a mental disorder. *Archives of General Psychiatry* 45:13–18.

Mannuzza, S., Gittelman-Klein, R., Horowitz-Konig, P., et al. 1989. Hyperactive boys almost grown-up. IV: Criminality and its relationship to psychiatric status. *Archives of General Psychiatry* 46:1073–79.

Mannuzza, S., and Klein, R. G. 1992. Predictors of outcome of children with attention-deficit hyperactivity disorder. *Child and Adolescent Psychiatric Clinics of North* 1:569–78.

Mannuzza, S., Klein, R. G., Bessler, A., et al. 1993. Adult outcome of hyperactive boys. *Archives of General Psychiatry* 50:565–76.

Mannuzza, S., Klein, R. G., Bessler, A., et al. 1997. Educational and occupational outcome of hyperactive boys grown up. *Journal of American Academy of Child Adolescent Psychiatry* 36(9):1222–27.

Mannuzza, S., Klein, R. G., Bessler, A., et al. 1998. Adult psychiatric status of hyperactive boys grown up. *American Journal of Psychiatry* 155(4):493–98.

Mannuzza, S., Klein, R. G., Konig, P. H., et al. 1990. Childhood predictors of psychiatric status in the young adulthood of hyperactive boys: A study controlling for chance associations. In *Straight and Devious Pathways from Childhood to Adulthood*, eds. L. Robins and M. Rutter. New York: Cambridge University Press.

McCormick, L. H. 1995. Depression in mothers of children with attention deficit hyperactivity disorder. *Family Medicine* 26:724–27.

Menkes, M. M., Rowe, J. S.,and Menkes, J. H. 1967. A Twenty-Five-Year Follow-Up Study on the Hyperkinetic Child with Minimal Brain Dysfunction. *Pediatrics* 39:393–99.

Milberger, S., Biederman, J., Faraone, S.V., et al. 1997. ADHD is associated with early initiation of cigarette smoking in children and adolescents. *Journal of the American Academy of Child and Adolescent Psychiatry* 36(1):37–44.

Millman, D. H. 1979. Minimal Brain Dysfunction in Childhood: Outcome in late adolescence and early adult years. *Journal of Clinical Psychiatry* 40:371–80.

Minde, K., Weiss, G., and Mendelson, N. 1972. A five-year follow-up of 91 hyperactive school children. *Journal of the American Academy of Child and Adolescent Psychiatry* 11:595–610.

Moffitt, T. E. 1990. Juvenile delinquency and attention deficit disorder: Boys' developmental trajectories from age 3 to age 15. *Child Development* 61:893–910.

Morrison, J. 1980. Adult psychiatric disorders in parents of hyperactive children. *American Journal of Psychiatry* 137:825–27.

Morrison, J., and Stewart, M. 1971. A family study of the hyperactive child syndrome. *Biological Psychiatry* 3:189–95.

MTA Cooperative Group. 1999. A 14 month randomized clinical trial of treatment strategies for Attention-Deficit Hyperactive Disorder. *Archives of General Psychiatry* 56:1073–86.

Murphy, K. 1996. Adults with attention deficit hyperactivity disorder: Assessment and treatment considerations. *Seminars in Speech and Language* 17(3):245–53; quiz 254.

Murphy, K., and Barkley, R. A. 1996. Attention deficit hyperactivity disorder adults: comorbidities and adaptive impairments. *Comprehensive Psychiatry* 37(6):393–401.

Nada-Raja, S., Langley, J. D., McGee, R., et al. 1997. Inattentive and hyperactive behaviors and driving offences in adolescence. *Journal of the American Academy of Child and Adolescent Psychiatry* 36(4):515–22.

Paternite, C. E., Loney, J., and Langhorne, J. E. 1976. Relationships between symptomatology and SES-related factors in hyperkinetic/MBD boys. *American Journal of Orthopsychiatry* 46:291–301.

Pelham, W. E., and Sams, S. E. 1992. *Behavior Modification in Child Psychiatric Clinics of North America,* ed. G. Weiss, Vol.1, No.2:505–19.

Richter, J., Arnold, E., Jensen, P., et al. 1995. National Institute of Mental Health collaborative multisite multimodal treatment study of children with attention deficit hyperactivity disorder (MTA).I Background and rationale. *Journal of the American Academy of Child and Adolescent Psychiatry* 34(8):987–1000.

Riddle, K., and Rapoport, J. 1976. A two-year follow-up of 72 hyperactive boys. *Journal of Nervous Mental Disorders* 162:126–34.

Roizen, N. J., Blondis, T. A., Irwin, M., et al.1996. Psychiatric and developmental disorders in families of children with attention-deficit hyperactivity disorder. *Archives of Pediatric Adolescent Medicine* 150(2):203–208.

Roy-Byrne, P., Scheele, L., Brinkley, J., et al. 1997. Adult attention-deficit hyperactivity disorder: Assessment guidelines based on clinical presentation to a speciality clinic. *Comprehensive Psychiatry* 38(3):133–40.

Safer, D. J. 1973. A familial factor in minimal brain dysfunction. *Behavioural Genetics* 9:175–86.

Satterfield, J., Hoppe, C., and Schell, A. 1982. Prospective study of delinquency in 110 adolescent boys with attention deficit disorder and 88 normal adolescent boys. *American Journal of Psychiatry* 139:797–98.

Satterfield, J., Satterfield, B., and Cantwell, D. 1981. Three year multimodality treatment study of 100 hyperactive boys. *Journal of Pediatrics* 98:680–88.

Satterfield, J. H., and Schell, A. 1997. A prospective study of hyperactive boys with conduct problems and normal boys: Adolescent and adult criminality. *Journal of the American Academy of Child and Adolescent Psychiatry* 36(12):1726–35.

Satterfield, J., Swanson, J., Schell, A., et al. 1994. Prediction of antisocial behavior in attention-deficit hyperactivity disorder boys from aggression/defiance scores. *Journal of the American Academy of Child and Adolescent Psychiatry* 33(2):185–90.

Seidman, L. J., Biederman, J., Weber, W., et al. 1998. Neuropsychological function in adults with attention-deficit hyperactivity disorder. *Biological Psychiatry* 44(4):260–68.

Shekim, W. O., Asarnow, R. F., Hess, E., et al. 1990. A clinical and demographic profile of a sample of adults with attention deficit hyperactivity disorder, residual state. *Comprehensive Psychiatry* 31(5):416–25.

Spencer, T., Biederman, J., Wilens, T. E., et al. 1998. Adults with attention-deficit/hyperactivity disorder: A controversial diagnosis. *Journal of Clinical Psychiatry* 7:59–68.

Taylor, E., Chadwick, O., Heptinstall, E., et al. 1966. Hyperactivity and conduct problems as risk factors for adolescent development. *Journal of the American Academy of Child and Adolescent Psychiatry* 35(9):1213–26.

Thorley, G. 1984. Review of follow-up and follow-back studies of childhood hyperactivity. *Psychological Bulletin* 96:116–32.

Thorley, G. 1988. Adolescent Outcome for hyperactive children. *Archives of Disorders of Childhood* 63:1181–83.

Weiss, G. 1985. Follow up studies on outcome of hyperactive children. *Psychopharmacological Bulletin* 21:169–77.

Weiss, G., Hechtman, L. 1993. *Hyperactive Children Grown Up*. New York: Guilford Press.

Weiss, G., Hechtman, L., and Perlman, T. 1978. Hyperactives as young adults: School, employers and self-rating scales obtained during 10 year follow-up evaluation. *American Journal of Orthopsychiatry* 48:438–45.

Weiss, G., Hechtman, L., Perlman, T., et al. 1979. Hyperactives in young adulthood: A controlled prospective ten-year follow-up of 75 children. *Archives of General Psychiatry* 36:675–81.

Weiss, G., Hechtman, L., Milroy, T., et al. 1985. Psychiatric status of hyperactives as adults: A Controlled prospective 15-year follow-up of 63 hyperactive children. *Journal of the American Academy of Child Psychiatry* 23:211–20.

Weiss, G., Kruger, E., Danielson, U., et al. 1975. Effects of long-term treatment of hyperactive children with Methylphenidate. *Journal of the Canadian Medical Association* 112:159–65.

Weiss, G., Minde, K., Werry, J., et al. 1971. A five year follow-up study of 91 hyperactive school children. *Archives of General Psychiatry* 24:409–14.

Welner, Z., Weiner, A., Stewart, M.A., et al. 1977. A controlled study of siblings of hyperactive children. *Journal of Nervous Mental Disease* 165:110–17.

Werner, E. E., Smith, R. S. 1977. *Kauai's Children Come of Age*. Honolulu: University of Hawaii Press.
Yan, W. 1996. An investigation of adult outcome of hyperactive children in Shanghai. *Chinese Medical Journal* (Eng) 109:877–80.

Index